STALKERS

Jean Ritchie is a journalist and author of eleven books. She is married with three sons.

STALKERS

HOW HARMLESS DEVOTION
TURNS TO SINISTER OBSESSION

JEAN RITCHIE

HarperCollins*Publishers*

HarperCollins*Publishers*
77–85 Fulham Palace Road
Hammersmith, London W6 8JB

A Paperback Original 1994

1 3 5 7 9 8 6 4 2

Copyright © Jean Ritchie 1994

Jean Ritchie asserts the moral right to
be identified as the author of this work

A catalogue record for this book
is available from the British Library

ISBN 0 00 638338 6

Set in Linotron Sabon by
Rowland Phototypesetting Ltd
Bury St Edmunds, Suffolk

Printed in Great Britain by
HarperCollinsManufacturing Glasgow

CONTENTS

ACKNOWLEDGEMENTS

The author would like to thank all those who helped with this book, especially the many victims of stalking who agreed to share their harrowing experiences. Particular thanks are due to Janey Buchan, who was unfailingly encouraging and helpful with all sections of the book, not just her own story.

The author is also indebted to Chris Mowbray, John Scott, Leon Wagener and, most of all, Mike Atchinson, for their invaluable research.

INTRODUCTION

'IT'S THE NIGHTS that are the worst. I don't know where he is, but my imagination tells me he is close at hand. In daylight I can keep the fears down; at night I am alone with the terror that he has created. If he rings me every ten minutes I think I will go mad with it; if he does not ring I worry that he is outside, watching me.'

The words of one stalking victim are echoed time and time again through the pages of this book. All stalking victims have different stories to tell, but all have one thing in common: fear. Stalking is a modern crime, a growing crime, a crime born out of loneliness and isolation. In America, where stalking has been studied and analysed far more than it has in Britain, there are an estimated 200,000 people who are being stalked, and the country's greatest expert on the subject says that one in five women will at some time in their lives be the victim of unwanted pursuit.

In Hollywood, the most famous celebrities may have as many as five hundred people each writing 'inappropriate' letters to them, any one of whom may tip over the edge and become a dangerous stalker.

Pursuing celebrities is the type of stalking that makes the headlines, and for that reason it has defined the popular image of the problem. Nobody is surprised to find that a sexy young film starlet gets a barrage of kinky letters from lonely men. But stalking is not just about obsessional fans who turn up outside Hollywood mansions with knives or loaded guns in their pockets: stalking exists in all walks of life, it crosses all age and gender barriers, it knows no class distinctions. Even in California, the capital of the film industry, where the problems for celebrities are much greater than they are anywhere else in the world, celebrity stalking accounts for fewer than half of all cases. Elsewhere in America it is less than ten per cent, a figure that is probably consistent with British experience, although no comparable research has been carried out.

The dictionary definition of stalking is 'to pursue prey stealthily', and that is exactly what the human stalker does. His technique may be to make endless phone calls, or to send unwanted taxis and pizza deliveries, or to mail a stream of obscene letters. He may threaten violence, and he may even carry out his threats. Or he may simply, boringly, repetitively, to the point of persecution, try to insinuate himself in someone else's life. However he does it, he is the hunter and his victim is the prey: he is a stalker.

Not all stalkers, of course, are male, there are some female stalkers about. More women become involved in celebrity stalking – pursuing an unattainable figure from a distance – than any other kind. But the majority of stalkers, more than eighty-five per cent, are men, according to American statistics. For them, stalking is connected with control; they want power over their victims and they can achieve this by frightening them, or – more simply – by knowing everything about their lives.

For the purposes of this book, stalking has been broken down into four broad categories: celebrity stalking, stalking by a complete stranger, stalking by an acquaintance and stalking by an ex-partner (boyfriend, girlfriend, husband, wife). This last category is the largest but also the hardest to define: ex-partners often behave with irrational jealousy, and that behaviour alone does not make them into stalkers. They usually have genuine ties with their victims: there may be children in common, property in common, or at least a social life in common, and the break can be emotionally devastating, leading to a certain amount of clinging on, refusing to give up. But there comes a point when this is no longer the acceptable reaction of a grieving ex. Recognizing that point may be hard (it is hard for all stalking victims, whatever category they come into, but especially hard for this group). When there are phone calls coming at all hours day or night, when there is a car parked outside or a figure lurking in the shadows, *that* is stalking. Because of the severed emotional ties it is often more difficult for the victim to deal with it, and more difficult for the stalker to accept that his or her behaviour is objectionable.

Stalking by someone who is known to the victim is the second biggest category. A casual acquaintance suddenly starts to take an overwhelming interest in all the details of their victim's life, they misinterpret small gestures of friendship into large expressions of love, they begin to write, phone, follow the person they are fixated on. As they get no encouragement they feel rejected, and that turns their love into hatred. Threats and obscenities usually follow.

This pattern is repeated by the stalkers who latch on to complete strangers, as well as by those who persecute celebrities. In both these groups, the pursuit is of an unrealistic ideal: the stranger or the celebrity is endowed with all the attributes the stalker is looking for in a partner. Their beliefs about their love-object may go off the sanity scale, but they are deeply held. Gay pop singer Boy George enjoyed the joke immensely when a woman claimed he was the father of her child. He delighted in telling the journalists outside the court in which she sued him for maintenance for the child that it would be a miracle if he was the father as 'I have never penetrated a woman in my life.' Yet there was a part of the woman that believed her own wild claims.

For many of these celebrity or stranger stalkers, with rejection comes anger and feelings of betrayal, which can lead to threats, obscene abuse and in some cases real violence.

Stalkers are all suffering from some degree of mental derangement, ranging from a severe psychotic illness like schizophrenia, in which the sufferer often believes he is responding to voices in his head which dictate his behaviour, to simple obsession, when behaviour can be quite normal in all other respects. This milder form is a version of more readily acceptable obsessions: there are football fanatics who plaster their bedroom walls with pictures of their favourite players and whose whole conversation and social life revolves around their team; there are railway enthusiasts who can crawl out of bed on cold wet mornings to collect train numbers at grimy stations; there are fitness freaks who suffer from withdrawal symptoms if they don't get their daily workout. What starts as an interest and a hobby edges into a position of paramount importance; for the stalker it is the same slow build up. Many adolescents have crushes on music and film stars which are gradually superseded by real-life love affairs. Many people keep their youthful infatuations with them for life – plenty of happily married mothers and grandmothers turn up to have their heartstrings fluttered by Cliff Richard or Tom Jones in concert. But they have a sense of proportion: the rock star is a small and harmless helping of escapism. For a few, though, real life cannot or does not take the place of the fantasy, and the obsession with the star builds up until it dominates life enough to turn the fan into a fanatic, the fanatic into a stalker.

Similarly, a normal part of the business of growing up is to experience a painful love affair, to be rejected, to love unrequited from afar. Anyone who claims never to have been let down in love is probably lying or has a conveniently selective memory. Getting over it can be painful and protracted: adolescents, particularly, are inclined to feel that they will never love again. As Plato said, love is a serious mental condition: love casts out intelligence. The vast majority, of course, do get over it; for one or two, the experience assumes such epic dimensions that it dominates their lives, and the person they love becomes the focus of an obsession.

This is the more rational end of stalking, the tipping of the balance from the normal madness of love to unacceptable behaviour. Many a young person will have dialled the number of the person who is ignoring them, and then hung up. Many will have hung around the college corridors or the pubs and clubs their loved one frequents in the hope of catching a glimpse, even though they know that their affection is not returned. When the dialling of the phone number and the hanging around become a habit, then the delicate balance has shifted.

But there are much wilder shores of stalking, and these are the shores of clinical madness, where the stalker is psychotically ill. Because these stalkers dance to the tunes of their own fractured minds, they will not respond to normal reasoning or pleading, to the law, to physical threats, to anything. Imprisoning the mentally ill does not help, although holding them in secure mental hospitals is sometimes the only consolation that the victims can hope for because, as with so much psychotic illness, containment and not cure is all that can be provided.

David Nias is a clinical psychologist who lectures at London University, and who has worked at Broadmoor Hospital, a secure unit for the criminally insane, and has studied the varying degrees and effects of obsession. Many stalkers, he believes, are suffering from a condition known as De Clerembault's Syndrome, named after the French doctor who discovered it. Sufferers put romantic constructions on to the most innocuous exchanges, eventually losing touch with reality and becoming obsessed with an unobtainable person, believing that this person reciprocates their feelings. They commonly believe that other people or things are thwarting the relationship. In this extreme form the condition is known as erotomania.

'All the old clichés about love are true: life-long passion, madly in love, blinded by love, hopelessly in love. They are all, quite literally, true for some people. The classic symptoms are delusion,' says Dr Nias. 'The person who stalks a stranger, a celebrity or someone they only know slightly is usually a psychotic, carrying delusions about someone who is in a higher position socially and with whom they have very little in common. They become convinced this person is in love with them and plague their lives. They are irrational, and however hard you try to dissuade them they can come up with evidence of their own that their beliefs are true. They are, quite literally, madly in love.

'Some doctors believe that erotomania, the delusion that one is loved by another, is a form of schizophrenia, and treat patients with major tranquillizers (anti-psychotic drugs: the name is misleading because they are not related to normal tranquillizers). If they have come to the attention of the medical profession because their behaviour has been inappropriate, they are often held in secure units until it is judged medically that they are safe to be released. But the trouble is that away from their obsession many of them seem perfectly normal, rational people.

'They try to persuade doctors that they are over their obsession: then you visit their room and the wall is plastered with pictures or references to their victim.

The most worrying aspect is that this sort of personality disorder can lead to suicide and the threat to take other lives, particularly that of their victim. Often the fantasies get sicker, more sordid and more frightening as the condition progresses.

'The people who suffer from obsession are usually rather pathetic, unsuccessful at sexual relations. The obsession feeds their imagination. Anyone in the public eye can be selected as a target, but not only celebrities are at risk. Anyone thought of as a superior could be a victim: women could fall for their GP, priest or bank manager, men with a work colleague, a barmaid or the girl next door. There are quite a few cases in Broadmoor of patients who are dangerously in love with ordinary people.

'Obsession and stalking can be separate, although they are close. Obsession is a very intense feeling of acute need. There is a childish level of demand for another person, a wave of inner desperation and desolation that makes the sufferer want to own the victim. Obsession affects more men than women. It can be biological, or the result of childhood traumas or problems. The difficulty with knowing whether obsessive love is dangerous is that a lot of people have suffered some form of it: the pangs of despised love, as Hamlet called it, are familiar enough. In some ways it is just an extreme of an emotion we all possess: arguably some of the greatest love affairs are obsessive, frantic and jealous. But the need to know everything about a new partner is not normal, not just an extension of passion: it is a mental disorder.

'Stalking is often just seeing someone out of reach. Becoming fixated on a stranger is a useful way of avoiding reality – there is less chance of the fantasy being broken. It is a personality disorder, and you only really hear about it when it comes to court: at the lower levels the stalker is merely infatuated, and unless their behaviour presents a real threat to the person they love it does not come to public notice. Many do not even want to make direct contact with their love object, but some do. The sufferer will build up a fantasy world around the person and follow them to find out every detail of their lives. At first the stalker may send polite notes and flowers to try to attract their victim's attention, but as these are ignored the stalker becomes gradually more angry. The tone of the notes becomes abusive, showing the signs of frustration that lead to aggression.

'If the love is unrequited, the love turns to hate. Two sides of the same coin. Love letters turn into hate mail, often accompanied by horrendous threats, although these are usually only an attempt to gain attention. To many sufferers from obsessional love, the love is the peak experience of their lives. It is the only time they have fallen in love, it comes like a bolt from the blue. Often the sufferer believes obsessive behaviour is simply a way of getting through to someone, with the rationale that anyone can have anything if they try hard enough.

'Harmless fantasy can easily turn into dangerous obsession, especially if the sufferer is a lonely person with a vivid imagination. If a man is strongly attracted to a woman he can become wildly jealous. To him she is coming and going as she pleases and yet he thinks she is his. But she doesn't even know he exists. He feels constantly rejected and you get dysfunctional attempts at taking control of her life.'

Dr Nias confirms that there is no single effective cure. Some sufferers from obsessional love do recover spontaneously, but for many it takes twenty or more years to loosen the grip of an obsession.

'For many it is merely a part of another disorder. The textbooks say there is no known cause and no known cure. There has been little research into this specific area, but there is also no real cure for a lot of mental disorders. Doctors may try a form of therapy which attempts to change the way in which the sufferer thinks, but many sufferers do not accept or admit that there is a problem. To them, it is obvious that the victim loves them. They are confident that in time the object of their desire will come around and accept them.

'The law, police, court, prison have no effect. Love will conquer all. A prison sentence is useless, and a stay in a secure hospital is no better, apart from the fact that we can make the victim feel safer when the persecutor is locked up. Tragically, some victims will know no respite, because the stalker's obsession will be lifelong and unshakeable. Unless he switches his allegiance to a new target, they will remain in the frame. Sometimes a doctor takes the place of the original victim, and they may be able to cope better, but they face the same problems. It is more than an occupational hazard, it is something a doctor dreads. A second obsession is no less binding than a first.'

The life sentence for the victim is a prognosis also given by Professor David Allen, a clinical psychologist based in Paris: 'Being a stalking victim can be a death sentence – it is certainly a life sentence, spent looking over the shoulders. There is no cure. In extreme cases it can lead to murder, although that is very rare. For the sufferer, there is an absolute conviction that they are loved: every word, every gesture, every facial tic is interpreted as evidence of that. A simple "See you tomorrow" takes on huge significance in their minds.'

Professor Allen's wife Michelle is a leading French psychoanalyst who has dealt professionally with stalkers and obsessives: 'I can listen to women and men who are in the grip of an obsession with another person and I can offer them analysis and they can go into therapy, which may contain and control them, but it will not cure them. They may drop their object of desire but latch on to someone else, another victim. Nothing will shake their self-belief. There is no division between fantasy and reality. In extreme cases, life and death become blurred, too, and they become a danger, a walking time bomb.'

More studies of stalking and stalkers have been done in America than anywhere else because stalking has been accepted as a crime in the States since 1990, when California pioneered the first anti-stalking laws through its state legislature (fuelled by the enormous problems the Hollywood stars were experiencing). Since then every other state has followed suit, which makes it possible to determine and examine a specific group of people who have been found guilty of stalking offences. In Britain, some stalkers are pursued under civil law, some under criminal law, and many not at all (see 'A Paper Shield', pp. 319–37).

'Most stalkers are men, and they come in all ages

and from all ethnic backgrounds, and from varied social and family backgrounds,' says Houston forensic psychologist Jerome Brown. 'Many are relatively intelligent men with a history of inept inadequate heterosexual relationships. They are motivated by fantasies of romantic involvement with their victims, but they have no idea what 'love' really means. To many of them, love equals possession. At first, they usually don't want to hurt their victims, just possess them. The thrill of the chase increases the satisfaction they feel upon "obtaining" them. They're not able to see the person of their obsession as a real person. When the "thing" does not respond to them properly, they're likely to get angry at it.'

Stanton Samenow, an American psychologist and author of a book called *Inside the Criminal Mind* says stalkers vacillate between considering themselves 'No. 1' and 'nothing'.

'The stalking is the tip of the iceberg. The stalking props up their self-esteem,' he says. When the stalker is rejected he suffers a huge blow to his feeling of self-worth, and this, coupled with the realization that he is not going to be able to have what he wants, leads to violence.

The predominance of men among stalkers is borne out by British Telecom statistics, which show that twice as many malicious calls are made by men than by women. The only other measure of the gender profile of the British stalker is anecdotal: four out of every five cases that are reported in a newspaper involve a man stalking a woman. It could be that these receive more publicity – women are more likely to look to the police and the courts for help, and the presence of a physically powerful male stalker may actually be more threatening than the continued attentions of a female one. But, even allowing for this distortion, it is likely that we follow the American pattern and have a much higher number of males stalking females than the other way round.

'Women who are rejected may act destructively towards themselves, or turn to others for nurturing to get over the rejection. Men use aggression to restore the equilibrium of their self-esteem,' says New York forensic psychologist Dr James Wulach.

Almost all stalking has an underlying sexual motive, although there are cases where the stalker is simply trying to get into the victim's life for other reasons, usually associated with feelings of prestige and identity: they want the same role as their victim, they want to belong to the same social group/family/ work organization (see the cases of Bob and Kathleen Krueger and Janey Buchan).

Analysis of the backgrounds of stalkers has shown that although they come from across all levels of society (with a slight predominance of better-educated individuals) one common factor appears to be an absence of a father figure in their childhood, plus a hot-and-cold relationship with their mothers, sometimes adored and sometimes ignored. With women stalkers (who generally latch on to celebrities or strangers) there is a general absence of any loving relationship in adult life. Women stalkers are usually more clearly recognizable as social inadequates; men may be holding down good jobs and have an out-wardly successful life.

This book looks at every type of stalking, from the

sort of harassment that is more of a nuisance than anything else, to the most sinister and dangerous stalking of all – that which ends in death.

PART ONE

The Price of Fame

'YOU CAN RUN, BUT YOU CAN'T HIDE'

A COYOTE'S HEAD, some dog's teeth, a bed pan, a syringe of blood, a toy submarine, a half-eaten chocolate bar, eight tubes of red lipstick, a shampoo coupon, a disposable razor, a photograph of the victim's home, a map of the victim's home town and a set of medical photographs of corpses with the victim's face pasted over the head – this is just a small sample of the items sent to Hollywood celebrities in their mail.

The kind of letters they get are just as bizarre:

I am afraid I made a mistake when I told you I was your father. Some guy showed me a picture of you and your father standing together when you got your award. I was so proud when I thought I was your pop. I guess that means that my daughter ain't your sister either . . . I asked your manager to borrow ten thousand dollars, I hope she lets me have it. Before I go I just want to say that the only reason I thought I was your pop was because I used to go with a person that looked like you

wrote a middle-aged man to a young pop singer.

Another man wrote to a female celebrity:

Hello darling this is youre New friend . . . we will soon be together for our love honey. I will write and mail some lovely photo of myself okay. I will write to you Soon, have lovely Easter time hoping to correspond . . . here is a postcard for you . . . honey how are you doing . . . wishing to correspond with you Soon . . . hoping we do some camping and Barbecueing Soon okay.

Yet another fan wrote to a television personality:

I would like to Have lots of pictures of you sex symBol woman like you are all the times if you don't mine at all if you take off your clotHes for me and I can see wHat you Got to the world then ever that love any How I would like to know How LonG is your breast anyHow I would like to know How mucH milk Do your carry in your Breast anyHow I would like to know How far does your Breast stick out on you anyHow I by playBoy Books all the times . . . I would like you to put up your legs and take pictures of you in the nude . . . I would like Have larGe pictures of you in tHe nude lots of them then ever were so I will take with me and have lots of women in tHe nude I like sex symBols womens to look at all the times.

One habitual letter-writer to a Hollywood female celebrity was a mental patient who had been found guilty of committing a murder, and who had also been involved in a gunfight with police after escaping from hospital, stealing a gun and ammunition and attacking the police who he believed were starving the star. He wrote afterwards:

Please disregard the other letter I sent to you. Disregard this letter if your are married or have a boyfriend as I don't want to break up an existing relationship. I would like to be one of the following to me a) a lover, b) a girlfriend or c) a wife. I want it to be a forever thing, if we have faith

in each other and don't cheat. You must fulfil the following:
1) you must be vegetarian 2) you must not have another
boyfriend 3) you must not hold hands or do anything
beyond that point with another unless I give you permission
4) I believe in birth control devices and (foetus removal)
abortion, to take the fear away form women so they can
have a complete orgasm. Men never have to worry because
they don't have the baby. 5) You must not wear pants
unless the temperature drops below 50 degrees F or you
engage in hazardous work (like coal mining) 6) you can
view pornographic movies.

. . . I was in a gunfight with the police because I thought
you didn't have to eat food. I was real sick at the time. I was
arrested but should be getting out soon. I'm in a hospital for
observation. I was wounded as was one policeman. We are
both okay now. A bystander was wounded by another
policeman . . . Let's sit in a little room together. Let's drive
to the end of the world. Let's look in each others eyes. Let's
magnetically attract each other from close up. Let's
talk till we want each other more than anyone else . . .
Please call or write or come here by February 6th or else
I'll have to look for someone else . . .

One famous actor's wife received the following
letter from a woman who claimed the actor was
father of her child:

I know that Jason is my beautiful baby and that [the star]
is the daddy. I never been in love and I always been a queen
. . . I don't know much of anything other than the fact I
love my son and [the star] very much. I don't know very
much about life I was never told about life or how to love
or be loved . . . I know that I don't deserve a man like [the
star]. I know that I hurt him so much by writing to people
all over the world about his son . . . Tell him to come get
Jason and take him Home with you and the boys.

These samples of the sort of letters that pour constantly into the homes and offices of major stars are taken from the archives of Gavin de Becker Inc., a Los Angeles-based security consultation agency – *the* security consultation agency for California's hundreds of celebrities, where the problem of stalking has been known about for over thirty years. It was in the 1980s that the threats to stars – and attacks on some – escalated, and de Becker's business boomed. Unlike so many security firms, de Becker offers far more than just muscle: he collects, files and classifies all the suspicious mail his clients receive; he analyses the content of it through a computer program; he sorts out the really dangerous 'fans' and he goes into reverse-stalking mode – his staff track down and watch the movements of any stalker they regard as likely to carry out threats to attack celebrities. His experience coupled with the help he has had from the leading medical expert in the world on the subject of stalkers, Dr Park Dietz, means that he can frequently anticipate the actions of a deranged fan. He worked hard to get the law changed for the protection of his clients, but even before stalking was criminalized in California, de Becker was able to advise police forces just how they could nail stalkers under obscure and forgotten laws.

When Dr Dietz, who is clinical professor of psychiatry and biobehavioural sciences at the School of Medicine at the University of California, was called in to prepare a 600-page report for the US government on 'Mentally Disordered Offenders in Pursuit of Celebrities and Politicians', it was to de Becker's files that he turned for the raw material he needed for his five years of research. De Becker has more than 200,000 items of correspondence on file, all indexed and cross-indexed to show up which stalkers were pursuing more than one celebrity.

Some of the really big Hollywood names have as many as five hundred individuals writing to them what de Becker classifies as 'inappropriate' letters (a top star will regularly receive as many as 4,000 genuine fan letters per month). All the staff in his clients' offices are primed to send on to him any mail that is sinister, disjointed, bizarre, unreasonable or threatening, and to help them decide what falls into these categories they are specifically asked to be on the lookout for letters containing references to death, suicide, weapons, assassins, obsessive love or special destiny.

Dietz and colleagues analysed a scientifically chosen sample of mail from persistent letter writers in a bid to see if they could draw up a profile of the kind of writer who actually shows up at the celebrity's home or workplace, and the conclusions are fascinating.

Obviously, those who make a direct attempt to speak or make physical contact with the celebrity are potentially far more dangerous than those who merely write letters, however incoherent, threatening and frightening the letters may be.

Letter writers who send mail from different addresses are more likely to be dangerous than those who consistently post their letters in the same place – the ones who are moving around may already be trying to track down the celebrity or, as the survey conclusion puts it, 'travelling in a random pattern as they become increasingly frantic to find the celebrity, to escape their persecutors or for other unexplained reasons'. (Both Mark Chapman and John Hinckley travelled frantically in the days leading up to the assassination of John Lennon and the attempt on President Reagan's life.)

Those who are likely to try to make contact with the star write significantly more letters to their idols, in fact they will usually send twice as many letters as other 'inappropriate' letter writers, although their attempts to get physically close to their victim may start after only one or two letters. Anyone who writes more than ten letters and keeps on writing for more than a year is potentially dangerous. They don't write significantly longer letters though; *most* of these 'inappropriate' letters are long by normal standards, with six and a half pages a typical length (and one, in de Becker's files, running to over two thousand pages).

The writers who want to marry, have sex with or have children with the celebrity turn out to be less potentially dangerous than those who simply expressed a strong desire to meet the star face-to-face, with no sexual propositions. And while almost a quarter of all writers made threats in their letters, this was found not to influence whether they actually turned up outside the celebrity's home or office — perhaps the most important finding of the research.

There were some other interesting conclusions: anyone who writes on regular tablet-sized note paper is less dangerous, anyone who attempts to instil shame into the celebrity is less dangerous and anybody who repeatedly mentions other public figures is not a high level threat.

The research bore out one of Dietz's earlier theories: that stalkers who write hate mail are less dangerous than those who write to stars romantically. 'The person who sends hate mail is achieving their catharsis from putting the note in the mail,' he said. The fan who believes he is destined to have a romance with the celebrity, on the other hand, will experience nothing but disappointment and rejection, and is more liable to have aggression born of frustration. Male stalkers are more likely to 'act it out in a violent way' says Dietz, but adds that this does not mean that women letter writers should be ignored. The same criteria for deciding which ones are likely to attack a celebrity apply to women as well as to men, it is simply that more men match the criteria.

Dr Dietz is accepted as the top world authority on stalking, and works as a consultant to a number of big American companies, helping them identify potentially dangerous employees. He has appeared as an expert witness at numerous trials, including those of John Hinckley and serial killer Jeffrey Dahmer, and is known to some sections of the American press as 'the FBI's premier shrink'. Legend has it that he was the inspiration behind Thomas Harris's book *The Silence of the Lambs*. He became fascinated by the criminal mind as a student after reading a book by Britain's famous forensic pathologist Professor Keith Simpson.

He sees the rise of celebrity stalking as moving in parallel with the growth of television and video, bringing ever more intimate images of stars into the homes of potentially obsessed fans. It is now possible to replay on video, in the privacy of a bedroom, the exact moment in a film or TV programme when the stalker imagines the star is talking directly to him. It is not hard, for the determined stalker, to track down a star. 'There's an entire industry devoted to selling proximity to celebrities. There are books published on how to call and write famous people. In Hollywood there are tours to stars' homes, and magazines often give overly personal information about stars. And stars themselves often reveal overly personal information in publicity interviews such as talk shows,' he says.

In Britain and the rest of Europe, as well as America, a whole new 'profession' has been born from the public's obsession with the famous, and we even have a new word for it: paparazzi. These are photographers who earn their living hanging around stars, always hopeful of a compromising or in some way interesting picture to sell to the ever-hungry newspapers and magazines. Some of them have grown rich from their dedication to hanging around outside nightclubs until the early hours of the morning. While the celebrities claim, perhaps genuinely, to be distressed by this level of media intrusion, there is a peculiarly symbiotic relationship between the two camps. The line between stardom and obscurity is a thin one, easily crossed; celebrities have been known to go back inside a club or hotel when there were no photographers waiting for them, and emerge again at the pop of a flashbulb.

Professor Dietz says that there has been more celebrity stalking in the last ten years than in the whole of previous show business history: 'We have more celebrities at risk than ever before. The reason is . . .

because of how visible and personal they become. We have close-ups of every glamorous performance, or even a personal interview about someone's favourite restaurant or artistic likes. And the more personal and intimate the media portrayal, the more that mentally disordered people will misinterpret this as something personal for them.'

He has known instances where the mentally ill stalker has proved more adept at locating a celebrity than the police or mental health professionals who were trying to warn the star. The stalker, he explained, may have nothing else to do but pursue the career of the star, filing away every kernel of information they can glean. As Gavin de Becker once ruefully observed, the people he monitors may be unbalanced but they are not idiots: at least they CAN write letters.

Dr Dietz understands but does not approve of the feelings of reciprocation celebrities have towards their fans. Just as they court the attentions of the media, many stars accept the 'where would you be without us' attitude of a large number of fans. They may, as the actor Tom Conti puts it, regard obsessional fans as 'a complete pain in the butt', but on another level they feel grateful to their public who have, as they are constantly being reminded, given them the wealth, security and self-esteem that go with fame. What they fail to do, until they have the help of an expert like de Becker, is differentiate between the 'normal' fan and the potential stalker.

Dr Dietz believes the first and foremost rule for any star is not to respond to the stalker, and if he had his way famous people would never send out photographs of themselves, would certainly never sign them 'with love from' and would reduce the frequency with which they answer their fan mail.

'The best thing a celebrity can do is to vanish as far as their private lives are concerned,' he says. He believes court action against a stalker is a last resort, to be taken only when life is in danger.

'The one thing that is certain to guarantee persistence is to respond on the level he seeks.

'I want people to understand that nut mail is not harmless and that waiting for threats is not appropriate. Customarily, people who do not know anything about this will say "Well, we don't have to worry about this person. He's mentally ill, and he hasn't made a direct threat." The truth is that direct threats are not associated with whether or not people make attacks. On the other hand, several kinds of non-threatening but inappropriate communications have a definite relationship to attacks.'

Dr Dietz does not give advice directly to Hollywood stars about how to avoid or deal with stalkers, but to their security consultants, like Gavin de Becker. The stars themselves, he believes, are difficult to advise because they refuse to accept that they cannot act like normal people and stay safe. It is left to de Becker to put Dietz's theories – and his own, because he has been in the business long enough to have drawn some firm conclusions about celebrity stalkers – into a cogent code of practice for stars.

De Becker (who has not co-operated with the writing of this book) has a staff of over thirty people constantly monitoring the letters, phone calls, domestic security arrangements and public appearance plans of more than a hundred of the most famous people in the world. He does not name names, but his clientele – some of whom pay him half a million dollars a year – is believed to include Robert Redford, Michael J. Fox, John Travolta, Elizabeth Taylor, Tina Turner, Jane Fonda, Joan Rivers, Cher, Warren Beatty, Sheena Easton, Dolly Parton, Madonna, Olivia Newton John, Jessica Lange, Shaun Cassidy and Victoria Principal. It is almost easier to name the Hollywood stars who are *not* clients; Frank Sinatra and Sylvester Stallone head that, much shorter, list.

He came into the business after high school, when he got a job helping out with protection for Liz Taylor and Richard Burton. He was young and inexperienced but he learned fast, and he soon learned that what stars need is something much more sophisticated than being ringed by a posse of muscle-bound bodyguards. The enemy was cleverer than that; stalkers have proved they can get over barbed wire or past trained guard dogs, and they have even been prepared to take jobs with telephone companies to get access to unlisted phone numbers. Others have been taken on as security guards for their stars' concerts; when de Becker discovers this he makes sure they are moved to low security areas. At least one stalker has applied for a job directly to the celebrity, using an assumed name.

De Becker sorts the threats delivered to his clients into three categories: harmless ones, serious ones which need to be monitored and urgent ones. About twenty-five per cent of this last group actually show up outside the celebrity's home or office, although very few are able to commit any act that gets them arrested or their names into the newspapers – de Becker's men are there to thwart them. There have been occasions when a stalker has turned up at Los Angeles airport and found himself being driven to his hotel, unknowingly, by one of de Becker's staff. Others have attended concerts without realizing that the 'fans' sitting on either side of them work for de Becker.

Gavin de Becker agrees with Dietz that the rise in the stalking phenomenon is associated with the familiarity that television breeds. 'If you are in the public eye – whether it's the local newscaster or Jackie Onassis, whether your audience is 10,000 or one billion – someone will react in an unpredictable and inappropriate way,' he said. 'Today you have an entire sub-population who relate more to television characters – soap opera stars and such – than they do to real people.'

He works hard at understanding his adversaries, the stalkers. After the murder of actress Rebecca Schaeffer (not one of his clients) he said: 'This killing ... like the attack on Theresa Saldana, involved somewhat obscure and unusual target selection. This was not Victoria Principal or Madonna. This was somebody with a far smaller audience. There is a dynamic which says "Whitney Houston is for everyone, but you're for me."'

He also sees celebrity stalking as a particularly American phenomenon, born not just out of the many stars who are centred on Hollywood but also out of the American ethic. 'We are a nation that gives rise to and authenticates virtually unlimited expectations ... We are taught to feel that if we work hard we can do anything and be anything. And very few people want to be ordinary ... Some people will do anything to be recognized. It's part of the American myth that anybody can be unique and remarkable and important.'

His own observations lead him to assert that stalkers are at their most dangerous between the ages of twenty-eight and thirty-two. As Dietz's research into the de Becker archives shows, only five per cent of all persistent letter writers do so anonymously, so de Becker's staff have few problems tracing the potentially dangerous ones. If they track them down to a psychiatric institution or a prison, the authorities are notified and attempts are made to ensure they are not released.

The most dangerous threats, Dietz found, were the specific ones; those which gave a time and a place for the attack on the celebrity. De Becker always takes those very seriously.

He accepts that the stars he looks after do not want to cut themselves off entirely from their public, and will probably never agree to retiring away from the spotlight as much as, perhaps, Dr Dietz would suggest they do. One part of de Becker's job he sees as counselling them to live with the ever-present stalking threat. He calls it his 'you don't have to change your life when you get a dead chicken in the mail' message.

There are things that should be done, though, and de Becker is not the only security man dispensing advice. Homes and cars should never be bought in the celebrity's own name (stars should set up trust funds to handle impersonally those sort of purchases), phone numbers should never be listed in their names, even as ex-directory numbers, because the leaks from telephone companies are unstoppable. All bills and paperwork should be handled through an agent's office.

The police in Los Angeles are probably better equipped to deal with stalkers than any other force in the world, simply because they have had so much more experience of celebrity stalking than any other city. Since 1991 the Los Angeles Police Department has had a Threat Management Unit which deals exclusively with stalkers, although not all of them are pursuing stars. In the first three years of its operation the unit dealt with 200 cases.

The FBI, too, has had to wake up to the threat caused by stalkers, and has become involved in some investigations which mirror the kind of work de Becker is doing privately. When Stephanie Zimbalist, a Hollywood actress who starred in the TV series *Remington Steele*, received 212 intimidating letters from a stalker, it was FBI agent Karen Gardner who was assigned to the case. FBI interest in stalking dates from 1989 and the death of Rebecca Schaeffer; before that local police departments had handled it. But by the late 1980s the number of stalking cases had escalated so greatly that the national agency realized it would have to get involved, and the Stephanie Zimbalist case was one of their first triumphs. The fact that the letter writer, who always signed himself 'Your Secret Admirer', mentioned the FBI in several of the letters was a spur to them to take on the investigation.

The stalker gave great detail in his letters about Stephanie's movements. He not only knew the dates and times of her visits to other cities, but he could even specify which floor of the hotel she stayed on. His information was so compellingly accurate that Stephanie stopped making any public appearances; her stalker simply sent her more chilling letters: '. . . following you around different cities, waiting for you at the hotel, seeing you at the theatre, looking for you late at night; these have become the most important things in my life . . . My continued patience depends on at least being able to see you on the road.' In another letter he wrote, 'You can run, but you can't hide.'

In Ronald Kessler's book *The FBI*, Karen Gardner reveals how she painstakingly assembled any clues the stalker had given about his whereabouts in any of his letters. She matched flight passenger lists and hotel guest lists until she was able to identify the stalker: a lonely 42-year-old bachelor who lived with his elderly mother. He appeared to be a harmless if disturbed fan, but when his room was searched, amongst the videos of Stephanie and a large collection of magazine articles about her, there was a gun. He pleaded guilty to mailing threatening communications, and was given a two-year sentence and ordered to have psychiatric counselling, as well as being ordered to keep away from Stephanie and her family.

At present in Britain there is no equivalent of a Gavin de Becker, and there has been no funding for research into stalking as there has for Dr Dietz and his colleagues in the States. Show business stars here can get straightforward security advice about their homes and their business premises, and a lot of the 'rules' for dealing with fans come down to common sense. The major television companies, approached for this book, deny that they have encountered the problem on behalf of their stars, and have not issued any guidelines about coping with unwanted attentions, but this defence is probably in itself part of a deliberate strategy. There is no doubt that a television company like Granada, which fields the long-running and phenomenally popular soap *Coronation Street*, has been aware of the danger of stalkers for years now. There may well not have been a policy document enshrining their tactics for dealing with the danger, but there will have been discussion of it. Talking publicly about the problem is seen as counterproductive, both here and in America; publicity about stalking can have a copycat effect.

If the problem continues to grow at its present rate (it's increasing in America, and most British crime patterns follow America with a lag of about ten years), then it would be sensible for the big show business agents and television stations to start thinking about it more constructively. Out there, at any moment, someone, somewhere, is picking up a pen to write what Dr Park Dietz calls, with academic restraint, 'an inappropriate communication'. And if they are writing it on a page of paper torn from an exercise book, and they have been writing to 'their' star for more than a year, and they are posting the letters from different areas of the country, then their 'victim' could be in for a very bumpy time.

'It will only be a matter of time before we have a stalker here in Britain who tips over into extreme violence,' predicts Dr David Nias.

'BANG, BANG, YOU'RE DEAD'

THE EIGHTH OF DECEMBER 1980 was the day that stalking was blasted into public awareness by a snub-nosed five-shot revolver. As John Lennon followed his wife back into the Dakota Building, the famous New York apartment block where they lived, a fat bespectacled youth called Mark Chapman approached him. Chapman had for a few days been one of the regular fans who hung around hoping to glimpse the ex-Beatle, but by 8.30 p.m. on a cold dark night the others had all drifted away. The doorman of the exclusive apartment block had been chatting normally to the young man only minutes before, and said afterwards that Chapman was calm and rational.

As Yoko Ono swept passed him Chapman said 'Hello'. Lennon, who was behind her, stared for a few seconds at his nemesis. Earlier that day he had signed his autograph on an album sleeve for Chapman, but he showed no sign of recognition. As Lennon started to enter the building Chapman stepped sideways, pulled the pistol from his pocket, held it straight in front of him with both arms outstretched, and fired all five bullets at his hero. The two bullets that hit Lennon in the back caused him to spin round, and two more ripped into his chest. One went wide of the target.

The most famous pop star in the world staggered up five steps to the Dakota office, where he collapsed in front of the night-duty man. The man who was about to become one of the most famous assassins in the world dropped his gun and stepped back into the shadows. He did not try to run away, but calmly pulled out his well-thumbed copy of J. D. Salinger's *The Catcher in the Rye*, and started to read it while he waited for the police to arrive and arrest him.

The news of John Lennon's death flew electronically around the world, and everywhere there was a reaction of shock. The Dakota was besieged by fans and inundated with flowers, radio stations played Lennon music for twenty-four hours a day and a worldwide ten-minute silent vigil was held six days later.

But while Lennon fans were stupefied by the death of the man they regarded as the next thing to God, others around the world were shocked by something else: the man who had murdered Lennon was one of his fans. The killer was a devotee of his, one of those who claimed to worship him. To those outside the closed world of megastardom, it seemed preposterous. Kennedy and Martin Luther King had both been assassinated, but there was some perverted political sense to their killings. It would have been easier to comprehend if Lennon's killer had been bent on attracting international attention to some cause or other, if the murder had been a kamikaze publicity stunt. But the only thing that Chapman wanted to draw attention to was himself.

The risk from deranged fans had been known for years to those in the public eye. They received nutty mail in with the thousands of genuine, innocent adoring fan letters; they received death threats, they felt uneasy about certain persistent hangers-on at their gates. But it was Lennon's death that publicly marked the extent of the risk, and brought celebrity stalking into the open. It was Lennon's death that floodlit the dark, strange, obsessional world of the fanatical fan.

Mark Chapman's decision to kill his hero John Lennon may have been triggered by a perceptive article in *Esquire* magazine, published in October 1980. The piece examined Lennon's life, which was that of an eccentric semi-recluse, dominated by his Japanese wife Yoko. Their married life was bizarre, their relationship with their son Sean (born by Caesarean operation so that his birth date was the same as his father's) was unconventional. The magazine article examined how Lennon's life measured up to the peace and love philosophy that he had expounded for so long, and found it wanting. He did not emerge as an idealist who put his money where his mouth was, but as an extremely rich 40-year-old who watched daytime television and amused himself speculating in property.

Many devoted fans must have read the article and rejected it, others will have felt betrayed by Lennon. Critics of John and Yoko will have felt vindicated. But Chapman went further. He felt so deeply upset by his icon that he decided to kill him. It took a few weeks, but he managed it — one of the few times that

Mark Chapman lived up to his own expectations.

Chapman was twenty-five at the time he killed Lennon. He was an unremarkable-looking young man who had managed to conceal the full extent of his mental disturbance from a lot of people for a long time. The son of a nurse and an ex-army sergeant, who divorced when he was still a child, he was born in Texas and brought up in Atlanta, Georgia, alienating his family in his early teens when he adopted a hippie lifestyle and experimented with marijuana, LSD, amphetamines and barbiturates. He acquired a criminal record for minor offences, most of them connected with drugs. During these years he idolized Lennon. At seventeen he cleaned up his act after he claimed to have met Jesus Christ, who came into his room and stood by his left knee, starting a tingling which spread 'from the tip of my toe to the top of my head'. Chapman became a smartly dressed, clean-shaven, short-haired Bible freak, conventionally dressed apart from the large cross he always hung around his neck. He dropped out of school – where his record had not been good – to follow Christ. He joined a Pentecostal church, and walked the streets accosting passers-by and trying to convert them. His Christianity was fundamental: God represented the forces of good and the devil represented the forces of evil, and the world was a battleground in which the two sides fought each other. His feelings about Lennon became ambivalent; on one hand he still listened to and enjoyed the music, but on the other he suspected Lennon of being the anti-Christ because he had said the Beatles were more popular than Jesus.

Chapman became involved with the YMCA, and attended their summer camps, acting as a counsellor to young children. He felt a great rapport with children, and was popular with them. When he felt his Christian calling was bigger and that he should be doing something more dramatic for his faith, in 1976 he went to Beirut with a group of other volunteers from the YMCA, but was rapidly recalled back to the States because of the war in the Lebanon.

At this stage Chapman was, by his own lights, doing well. He had an attractive, bright girlfriend who shared his evangelical Christianity. He was very well thought of by the YMCA bosses, and it was at their suggestion that he went, with his girlfriend, to college in Tennessee in the hope of getting some qualifications so that he could take up a full-time post with the organization. But he hated academic work, and before the first term was over he had had a breakdown, walking out on the course and his girlfriend. He blamed the staff and the other pupils, describing them as 'phoneys' – the favourite description used by Holden Caulfield, the main character in *The Catcher in the Rye*, for his enemies. The book, a seminal work about teenage alienation from the adult world, spoke to Chapman at a deep level, and he identified with the hero who believed that childish innocence was more precious than maturity.

His family were not sympathetic after he dropped out and Chapman, twenty-one years old at the time, found a job as a security guard to support himself. He was given some rudimentary training in the use of a pistol; Chapman proved to be a good marksman. But being a security guard was, he felt, only a stop gap, and in a desperate bid to get some better qualifi-cations he enrolled once more in college. When he failed to keep up with the academic work once again he felt a complete failure, and decided that he would end his own life. But he wanted to do it in style and in his own time; he had read somewhere that the Hawaiian islands were as close to paradise as you can get on earth, so he decided to commit suicide only after he had visited them.

Six months later, having travelled all around the islands, he decided that the appointed time had come, and fixed a hosepipe from the exhaust of his car. But he was no more competent at suicide than he was at college work; he was found and taken to hospital. After his physical problems were sorted out he was transferred to a psychiatric ward where he was treated for severe neurotic depression, a diagnosis which shows how clever he was at masking the extent of his symptoms, because by this time Chapman was certainly psychotic. He was preoccupied by the fight between God and the devil, which he hallucinated about constantly. He believed his brain could pick up the commands of the opposing armies, so that he refused a confusion of signals urging him to do good and then to do evil.

Perhaps he recognized his own need for help and treatment: when he was discharged he took an unde-manding clerical job in the hospital and worked as a volunteer in the psychiatric unit. He saved his earn-ings assiduously, and started to plan a six-week holi-day, in which he intended to see as much as possible of the world. The travel agent who helped him plan his holiday, which started in Tokyo, was a Japanese girl working in a Honolulu agency. She was the daughter of a prosperous baker. While he was away Chapman sent her postcards, and when he returned they started going out together. Gloria was a Buddhist who believed in fortune-telling and astrology, a combination at odds with Chapman's born-again evangelical Christian faith, but theirs was a genuine romance and in June 1979 they were married.

Gloria had a comfortable life; her father was wealthy and she had her own salary. Chapman, who was still working at the hospital, began to enjoy a lifestyle he had never previously aspired to. He harboured dreams of grandeur, seeing himself as an art connoisseur. But his taste in pictures was esoteric and no doubt governed by the religious battleground his brain had become; he coveted a Salvador Dali representation of the crucifixion of Christ overlaid with the assassination of Abraham Lincoln. Death was becoming a fixation of his.

By the time he had been married for six months, Chapman had walked out on his job at the hospital in a fit of pique because he did not get a promotion he wanted. He became a security guard again: it was a job which gave him less responsibility and paid him less money, and he recognized it as a downward step. Money was no problem, though, because he had access to a shared account with Gloria.

For the whole of 1980 Chapman's behaviour was odd, although obviously not odd enough to alert anybody. He bullied Gloria, was inordinately possessive about her, and was extravagant with their money, spending far more than he contributed to the household. Opposite the apartment where he and Gloria lived was an office of the Church of Scientology, a cult which recruits with promises of self-improvement. Chapman disapproved of the organization, and could be seen marching up and down repeatedly outside their offices, muttering to himself. The office began to receive threatening phone calls, sometimes as many as forty in a day. The phone would ring, the receiver be picked up, and a male voice would whisper 'Bang, bang, you're dead.' Chapman later admitted he was the caller.

At home Gloria was becoming increasingly worried about him. He had always played lots of Lennon music, but the signs were there that he was developing into more than a fan. In August he wrote to a friend, said he was going to New York on a mission, and gave his address as the Dakota. His beloved Bible had an addition that he had scrawled in himself: 'The Gospel According to John' became 'The Gospel According to John Lennon'. He read everything he could get his hands on about the star. After reading the *Esquire* article in October, his attitudes to Lennon hardened. He would sit in a darkened room, naked, in the lotus position, listening to speeded-up Beatles and Lennon tapes, and chanting 'John Lennon, I'm going to kill you.'

'It was hideous,' he said later from his prison cell at Attica, 'I would strip naked, gritting my teeth and summoning the devil and wild things into my mind. I was sending out telegrams to Satan, "Give me the opportunity to kill John Lennon."'

He had, he would reveal later in prison, already thought about and discounted killing Jackie Onassis, Ronald Reagan, David Bowie and Elizabeth Taylor, among others. But once he hit on Lennon, everything he read and heard about the man whose music he revered confirmed that Lennon was 'a phoney'. There was a time when Chapman's delusions made him believe he *was* Lennon: when he gave up his job on 23 October he signed off as John Lennon, then scored the name out. But more telling, and more fundamental, was the belief that he was Holden Caulfield, *The Catcher in the Rye*.

Four days after finishing at work, Chapman bought a gun. It was not hard. He walked into a shop in Honolulu where the slogan above the door said 'Buy a gun and get a bang out of life' He paid $169.00 for .38 calibre pistol, which he chose because it was small enough to conceal in a pocket. He flew to New York on a one-way ticket, telling his wife Gloria that he was going 'to make things different'. Arriving on 30 October, he became Holden Caulfield, retracing his fictional hero's steps through the city with his well-thumbed copy of *The Catcher in the Rye* in his pocket. He went to the spots in Central Park that Salinger mentioned in the book and he went to the Museum of Natural History, another place Caulfield visited.

In between his pilgrimages, he joined the small knot of fans who hung around the Dakota building, hoping for a glimpse of their idol. He moved hotels, to be nearer to his stakeout, never giving any clue to the others that he was any different from them in his devotion to the star. He was even 'normal' enough to go out on a date with a girl he met in Central Park, where she worked in a café. The only clue she had about his state of mind came when he angrily lashed out at New York gun laws: he had discovered he could not buy bullets in the city. He contacted an old schoolfriend, a policeman back in his home state, Georgia, who agreed to supply him with ammunition. He flew to Atlanta to collect five hollow-nosed dumdum bullets.

Back in New York, Chapman was listening hard to the warring factions in his head. One side told him to kill Lennon, the other told him not to. The first victory went to the goodies: he phoned Gloria in Honolulu and told her that coming to New York had been a mistake. He revealed to her that he had been on a mission to kill Lennon – it was the first she had heard of his plans – but that he had won 'a great victory' and was on his way home. For three weeks he sat around the Honolulu apartment watching television. On the wall of the apartment was a plaque inscribed with the Ten Commandments, and as he walked past it Chapman saw 'Thou Shalt Not Kill' leap out at him; a sign, he believed.

But the battle was still raging and he needed to get back to New York, to be near Lennon. He told Gloria that he had thrown the gun and the bullets into the sea, and that she was not to worry that he would do anything silly. He even made an appointment with a psychotherapist who had treated him before for depression, but he never turned up. When he should have been getting professional help coping with his delusions, he was on a plane to New York.

He stayed at the YMCA for the first night, staking out the Dakota during the days. His second day in New York was, probably more by coincidence than planning, Pearl Harbor day, the anniversary of the

Japanese attack on the American fleet which led to the US entering the Second World War. Both Lennon and Chapman had Japanese wives. That night, the eve of Lennon's assassination, he went into his Holden Caulfield role-playing mode again. He moved from the YMCA to a hotel, booking a room for seven nights on his Visa card. On a table he laid out his must valued possessions: tapes by the Beatles and by guitarist Todd Rundgren, his New Testament in which he had written 'Holden Caulfield', a picture of Dorothy from *The Wizard of Oz* and some photos of himself when he worked at YMCA summer camps with young children. Then, like Caulfield, he hired a prostitute and re-enacted a scene from the book: talking to the girl, massaging her and being given a massage, but not having sex.

The next day, on his way to the Dakota, he bought a new copy of the book. On the title page he wrote 'This is my statement.' He took a copy of Lennon's new album, *Double Fantasy*, and was mingling with the other fans by lunchtime. He had dressed carefully for the cold New York winter, wearing long thermal underwear, a coat buttoned up to the neck and a Russian fur hat. With his chubby cheeks he looked as though he might be a refugee from behind the Iron Curtain. The first member of the Lennon clan who he saw was Sean, John's 5-year-old son, who came out of the Dakota with his nanny. Holden Caulfield liked kids, so did Mark Chapman. It was another fan, one of the regulars, who introduced Sean to Chapman, who knelt on one knee before the little boy and put his hand in the child's. He told Sean he had come all the way from Hawaii, and that he was honoured to meet him. Then he added that Sean should take care of his runny nose. 'You wouldn't want to get sick and miss Christmas,' said the man who was planning to make sure there would be no happy family gathering in the Lennon apartment on Christmas Day that year. Afterwards Chapman described Sean as 'the cutest little boy I have ever seen'. It was 5.00 in the afternoon when Lennon first appeared, and all Chapman did was thrust his copy of *Double Fantasy* in front of the star for an autograph. 'John Lennon, December 1980' was scrawled across the cover. An amateur photographer, Paul Goresh, who was hanging around hoping to get some good pictures, took one of Lennon with Chapman in the background; it would later appear all around the world.

The other fans got tired and drifted away. At 8.00 p.m. Goresh, who had been chatting with Chapman, said he was calling it a day. Chapman tried to persuade him to stay: 'You never know, something might happen. He might go to Spain or something tonight – and you will never see him again.'

It was as near as he could get to inviting Goresh to record on film the murder of John Lennon. The photographer did not pick up on it, and missed the scoop of a lifetime. For a couple of hours Chapman chatted with the Cuban doorman at the building. He seemed, the doorman said later, sane and normal. It was ten minutes to eleven when the Lennons returned. A few seconds later mayhem broke loose. Lennon, blood pouring from his mouth and chest, staggered into the building. Yoko screamed and screamed. The night-duty man hit a panic button, and within minutes two police cars, sirens screeching, were at the scene. John was taken to hospital, barely alive. He died shortly after, despite the desperate efforts of a seven-strong medical team.

Chapman, while all this was going on, had taken off his coat and hat to show the police officers that he was no longer armed. He waited quietly for them to arrive, exchanging a few words with the devastated doorman, the Cuban to whom he had been talking earlier, who shook the gun from his hand and kicked it into the street. Chapman even apologized for what he had done, and when a woman who had heard the shots came running up, he told her to get out of there for her own sake. Then he took out his copy of *Catcher* and started to read. Not surprisingly, when the police arrived they went to arrest the wrong man, turning towards the young night-duty man, not fifteen-stone Chapman who was hanging back in the shadows.

Chapman's original intention was to say nothing and hand over the book, with the inscription 'This is my Statement' to the police, but his resolution failed him when the police grabbed him.

'Please don't hurt me,' he pleaded, reassuring them that 'I acted alone.'

In the police car being taken into custody one of the cops asked him if he knew what he had just done. He replied: 'I'm sorry, I didn't know that he was a friend of yours.' He was just as polite and restrained when he phoned his wife Gloria in Honolulu. He gave her concise and clear instructions about getting the police to protect her from the journalists who were already gathering outside the apartment. She said she loved him and he said he loved her.

He later explained the conflict that went on in his mind at the time of the killing, by seeing himself as two people, a child and an adult. He said the child and the adult went together to the Dakota that day, and the adult wanted to get in a cab and go home.

'Then the child screams "No! No! No! Devil! Help me, Devil! Give me the power and strength to do this. I want this. I want to be somebody."'

He placed great emphasis on the fact that neither Yoko nor John spoke to him, as if a smile and a 'hello' might have saved John's life. In his disturbed state he did not see Lennon stagger into the building, and when he realized there was no body in front of him he was not sure that he had actually done it.

'I was kind of glad that he wasn't there because I thought I had missed him or didn't kill him or something. I just wanted the police to hurry up and come.'

The death of the pop icon caused such an uproar that police insisted Chapman wore a bullet proof vest before his trial, and they painted the windows of his cell black so that he would not be shot by snipers. He refused to plead an insanity defence at the trial, instead admitting his guilt. The trial was therefore over quickly, with Chapman sentenced to between twenty years and life, with an order that he should receive psychiatric treatment. Because of the crime and the emotions it stirred up, it is likely that life will mean life. His own lawyer asked the judge not to impose a minimum sentence (after which Chapman could have been released) because, he said, 'All reports come to the conclusion that he is not a sane man. It was not a sane crime. It was . . . a monstrously irrational killing.' When Chapman was asked if he wished to say anything in his own defence he read out a passage from *The Catcher in the Rye*.

Chapman lives in Attica Prison, New York, segregated from the other inmates. Attica is notoriously violent, and amid its shifting population there are always some who would relish the fame of being the man who killed the man who killed John Lennon.

Gloria, Chapman's wife, has not divorced him. For three years she lived near the prison, visiting him regularly. But she then moved back to their Honolulu home; he has said he no longer wants her to visit. She sends him money regularly.

In a television documentary, shown in Britain in 1988, Chapman showed no remorse for killing Lennon, only regret that the star did not die immediately and that Sean was left without a father. In a television interview in 1992 he said that when he shot Lennon he did not believe he was killing a real person, he was killing an image, a record cover. He said he had undergone an exorcism performed by a priest in his prison cell, and that his demons had left him. He said he did not expect to ever be forgiven for 'taking away a genius'.

A psychiatrist involved in his care diagnosed Chapman as exhibiting 'the symptoms of virtually every malady in psychiatric literature'.

Astonishingly, Mark Chapman, who stalked and murdered John Lennon, now has his own collection of would-be stalkers, weird letter writers who mail him their assorted fantasies. He gets plenty of straightforward hate mail from Lennon fans, but he also gets love letters from women he has never met, and letters applauding what he did.

He spends a lot of time answering them. He also spends a lot of time reading *The Catcher in the Rye*.

If the death of Lennon put stalking into the public eye for the first time, it was the shooting of President Reagan by a Jodie Foster fan four months later that proved to the world that Lennon's murder was not an isolated tragedy. The cliché 'the price of fame' began to have real meaning to a public which had smiled cynically every time a celebrity complained about invasion of privacy or harassment by fans. To those on modest incomes who helped their idols amass million-dollar bank balances by buying their records, watching their films or getting hooked on their TV soap characters, the stars' whinges had always been a bit hard to take. Now, within four months, the real fear that stalked the stars had been brought out into the open. When celebrities complained about fans it was not, as their public had imagined, out of frustration at autograph hunters disturbing them in the middle of restaurant meals, or because they were unable to walk down a shopping mall without being mobbed; it was an ever-present knowledge that somewhere out there was a mentally deranged fan who had them in their sights. All they could hope was that the sights were not attached to a rifle.

John Hinckley, who shot Reagan in the chest and seriously injured his press secretary James Brady, as well as wounding a policeman and a secret service agent, did it, he claimed, for Jodie. In his shabby motel room in Washington police found a letter to the star:

Dear Jodie

There is a definite possibility that I will be killed in my attempt to get Reagan. This letter is being written an hour before I leave for the Hilton Hotel [where Reagan had been lunching]. Jodie, I'm asking you to please look into your heart and at least give me the chance with this historical deed to gain your respect and love. I love you forever,

John Hinckley

At the time Jodie Foster was eighteen, in her first year at Yale University. She was a well-established actress, having shot to fame as a child in films like *Bugsy Malone*. Hinckley's attempt on Reagan's life largely mirrored the plot of one of her films, *Taxi Driver*, in which she played a teenage prostitute. The other star, Robert de Niro, played a character described in the publicity material for the film as 'a loner incapable of communicating' who spent 'his off-duty hours eating junk food or sitting alone in a dingy room'. When the taxi driver is rejected by the prostitute, he sends her a letter before setting out to assassinate the President. There's no doubt that Hinckley had seen – and been influenced by – the film, because about six months before he shot Reagan he wrote to the film's scriptwriter, asking for an introduction to Jodie Foster. The actress also knew his name well before she heard it on the news bulletins about the shooting; he had been pushing letters under the door of her room at Yale.

Hinckley, who was twenty-five at the time of the shooting, was a desperate, deluded and dangerous misfit. Unlike Mark Chapman, he had never really established any long-lasting adult relationships; one of the most telling comments about him came from his landlord when he was in college, who commented that in all the time he had known Hinckley, he had only once seen him in the company of another human being. But there was nothing in his early life to suggest that the kid from the well-off Texan background would end up a notorious would-be assassin, no signs of deep emotional or mental disturbance in his childhood. He didn't come from a broken home, he wasn't brutalized by poverty. There were some traumas to cope with, like living in the shadow of a successful and popular sister in school, but the majority of youngsters cope with problems of that scale.

Hinckley even managed to conceal his solitariness throughout high school, although in retrospect no close friends stepped forward and claimed to have shared his confidences. But to the rest of his classmates he appeared normal: 'So normal that he appeared to fade into the woodwork,' said one girl who was in his year. After school, though, and after moving away from his parents' home, his life began to gradually disintegrate.

John Hinckley was the third and last child of the family. His father was an oil engineer, who moved the family to the capital of America's oil industry, Dallas, when his son John was two. They were an America adman's dream of a family: good-looking, churchgoing, hardworking parents with three blonde, blue-eyed, attractive children. Even in the looks-conscious environment of middle-ranking Dallas society, the only girl, Diane, stood out for her prettiness. Scott, the oldest boy, seven years older than John, did well at school and at sports and eventually went into his father's business. John, as a child, was very cute, average at his schoolwork, and very good at basketball – the best in his elementary school team.

When he was eleven his parents moved to the most swanky suburb of affluent Dallas, to a large house with a sweeping drive and a swimming pool. He seemed to fit in at high school, again becoming very involved in basketball, and a keen supporter of all the school's other teams. He even joined in with school activities like the Rodeo Club, which organized barbecues, square dances and trips to rodeos. The only shadow over his school career – which was academically undistinguished but OK – was the popularity of his sister, who was three years older than him. She was good at everything: a star in class, head cheerleader, in the choir, in a school operetta production. She was also very attractive. But if John felt oppressed by her presence, his classmates saw no sign of it.

By the time he was fifteen his father had amassed enough capital to start his own business, Hinckley Oil. He was successful, and when his oldest son Scott finished his engineering degree he joined the company. Five years later the company – and the Hinckley family – moved to the town of Evergreen in Colorado, again to a quiet, well-to-do area. By this time John Hinckley was studying for a business degree at Texas Technical University in Lubbock, Texas. He was registered at the Tech for the next seven years, changing from business to liberal arts, but never completed his degree and only attended classes sporadically.

It was at this stage that his life began to fall apart. He did not take part in any of the university social activities, and journalists who trawled through every aspect of his life after the assassination attempt failed to find any friends, close or casual, in Lubbock. Nobody really noticed him, and the only thing he did which in retrospect is revealing was to choose Hitler's *Mein Kampf* and the Auschwitz concentration camp as two of his study projects in his German history course. The room where he lived – where his landlord only once saw him with another person – was always full of burger boxes and ice-cream cartons.

'He just sat there all the time, staring at the TV,' said his landlord. The picture of the De Niro character from *Taxi Driver* was starting to emerge. He dropped out of college in 1976 and went to hang around Hollywood, staying in cheap rooms in the red-light district. He went back to college in 1977, but did not last the year. He became involved with the National Socialist Party of America, a neo-Nazi group, but in the end he was kicked out: he was too extreme even for these right-wing extremists, and when he started to advocate shooting people they decided he had to go. The president of the party later told a journalist that they decided that Hinckley was 'either a nut or a federal agent'.

The American academic system means that students can drop a course and pick it up again whenever they like, without losing the credits they have already gained for previous work. Hinckley, having been away for more than a year, started back at Texas Tech in 1979. In the same year he started to buy firearms; in the small redneck town of Lubbock he was easily able to buy a .38 pistol and two .22 pistols. By this stage his parents must have been aware of the disintegration of his personality, because from time to time, back at the family home in Evergreen, Colorado, he visited a psychiatrist.

He finally left college in the summer of 1980, aged twenty-five, and started a strange chaotic ramble around America, as if he felt that by keeping moving, by never spending too long in one place, he could hold his fragmenting personality together. When he found himself in conversation with strangers he would boast of being a close friend of Jodie Foster's, sometimes saying he was her lover. He turned up at Yale, where she was studying, and left several notes for her. He went to Nashville and was arrested as he tried to fly out to New York; his luggage contained three handguns and fifty rounds of ammunition. President Carter was due to fly into Nashville that day, but Hinckley's name – which should have been passed on to the secret service – slipped through the net. Four days later he was in Dallas, buying two more pistols from a store with the slogan 'Guns don't cause crime any more than flies cause garbage' in the window. He bought the bullets, appropriately named 'devastator bullets' from a store in Lubbock, the town where he had been in college. They cost ten times as much as ordinary bullets and exploded on contact, like dumdum bullets. Seven days after this shopping trip he was in Denver, applying for jobs. Then it was Washington, then Denver again, then back to New Haven (to be near Jodie at Yale), then Washington again.

By the beginning of March 1981 he was sticking more letters through Jodie Foster's door at Yale, and by this time she was so concerned about them that they were handed to the college authorities. Hinckley then returned to Denver. He applied for jobs and pawned his possessions to pay for his motel room. His restless moving around the country continued: he went to Los Angeles via Salt Lake City by plane, only to board a bus back to Salt Lake City the next day. It was from there that he moved on to Washington, and his date with President Reagan.

It took him three days to get to Washington, travelling by Greyhound bus, arriving on Sunday 29 March. He ate a cheeseburger at the bus station, and walked about impatiently; other travellers thought he was waiting for someone to pick him up. Then he walked to a hotel two blocks west of the White House, where he checked into a $42-a-night room. He stayed in the room all day, making a couple of local phone calls. Next day he left early, and returned about noon, asking the receptionist if he had received any telephone messages while out. There was none for him. A chambermaid who tidied his room that morning noticed that among his possessions scattered around the room was a newspaper cutting about President Reagan's timetable. It showed that Reagan would leave the White House at 1.45 p.m., after spending the morning with some prominent figures from the Hispanic community, and would then travel to the Washington Hilton to give a speech.

Hinckley wrote his letter to Jodie Foster and then walked to the Hilton, which was less than a mile from his hotel. He wore a raincoat, and he mingled with the photographers and reporters outside the hotel, giving at least one of them the impression that he was a secret service man. Inside, Reagan, the great communicator, was not on good form. His speech to 3,500 union delegates was not one of his best, but there was one line in it that the newspapers pounced on the following day: 'Violent crime has surged by ten per cent, making neighbourhood streets unsafe and families fearful in their homes.'

As he stepped outside the hotel, violent crime surged again. Turning to wave at the crowd, Reagan smiled broadly. Hinckley pulled out his pistol, aimed, fired. Two bullets, then a pause, then four more. One of the secret service men pushed Reagan into the waiting limousine and dived on top of him, urging the driver to take off. Behind them, Reagan's press secretary Jim Brady slumped to the ground, blood pouring down his face. A bullet had gone into his head, an injury which would leave him permanently disabled. A Washington policeman was shot in the chest and a secret service agent also received a chest wound. It was a matter of minutes before Reagan and the agent with him in the back of the car realized that the President, too, had been shot in the chest.

Hinckley was pounced on and disarmed within seconds, handcuffed to an agent and thrown into the back of a police car. At Washington police headquarters he hardly spoke. 'Does anybody know what that guy's beef was?' President Reagan asked, as he lay in his hospital bed.

Jodie Foster did not know the answer, although she knew she was in some macabre way the inspiration for Hinckley's actions. Twenty-one months later she wrote a perceptive account of how Hinckley's fixation with her, and his subsequent actions, affected her. She had overcome the initial reaction to her when she started at university, the curiosity about her because of her Hollywood background, the resentment of her. She had even, according to one journalist who interviewed her peers, changed her style of dress to blend inconspicuously in with the group. And then John Hinckley had come along and let her know that for her – and for other stars – there could be no normal, no blending in.

Why me? was the theme of the article she had published in *Esquire* magazine. It explored the terrifying events that followed Hinckley's arrest. Jodie was appearing on stage in a college production, and she was determined to go ahead with it. She had been moved from her shared dormitory to a single room that could more easily be protected by security men, there were security men screening the audience for the play, and at Jodie's request cameras were banned. A whole pack of photographers had descended on Yale as soon as the news of Hinckley's obsession with her had broken, and she wasn't prepared to face any more. But a camera did get in; she could hear the familiar rhythmic click of a motor drive in the darkened auditorium. She looked hard at the area of the audience the sound was coming from and locked eyes with a bearded man who was watching her unflinchingly. He was there again the next night, in a different seat. The following night a note was found on a bulletin board: 'By the time the show is over, Jodie Foster will be dead.' It turned out to be a hoax.

But a few days later a real death threat was pushed under Jodie's door. This time the police swung into action and caught up with her second stalker, Edward Richardson, within hours. He was arrested in New

York, with a loaded gun, and he told police that he decided not to kill Jodie because she was too pretty; he was going to kill the President instead. He had also telephoned a bomb threat, demanding the release of Hinckley and secret service agents had to search all the college rooms that Jodie used. Richardson had a beard, just like the man in the audience. A year later he was released, on parole.

After his arrest, Jodie says a great change came over her – or so she was told by those around her. 'I started perceiving death in the most mundane but distressing events. Being photographed felt like being shot. I thought everyone was looking at me in crowds; perhaps they were. Every sick letter I received I made sure to read, to laugh at, to read again.'

She was not sleeping properly, her pride in her appearance went. She felt bitter about the way other students had, she felt, betrayed her by telling journalists all about her and, in one case, selling an article to a magazine about her. In her own intelligent well-written article she describes the pain and anger that she, at eighteen, suffered because of her two stalkers. Her anguish was heightened by the media pursuit of her, but the feelings of isolation, desperation and frustration she felt at being unable to control her own life are common to all victims.

The security that surrounded Hinckley as he waited for his trial was greater than any that Jodie Foster had. The security services recognized that, as with Mark Chapman, Hinckley was a natural target for plenty of glory-seekers. It caused a sensation when Hinckley was found not guilty of attempting to murder Reagan, because of his insanity. But the net result for the American people was the same: he went behind bars, with very little prospect of ever being released.

It was surprising, therefore, to find him being considered for unsupervised release to spend a weekend with his parents only six years after the shooting. His application to be allowed home – he had already been back to Colorado in the company of a nurse – was supported by staff who had been involved in his care and treatment.

At a court hearing to consider his application it was revealed that he had written a sympathetic letter to Ted Bundy, one of America's most notorious serial killers who is on Death Row in Florida. Hinckley 'expressed sorrow' at the 'awkward position you [Bundy] find yourself in'. He had also written to a college student, asking her to kill Jodie Foster for him and to send a pistol by post to him so that he could escape from jail. He then told the girl to hijack a jet and demand that Hinckley and Jodie Foster both be taken aboard it. Hinckley had also received a letter from a woman in jail for trying to kill President Ford; she suggested Hinckley write to Charles Manson. To hear about the networking that was going on between long-term prisoners was almost as shocking to the law-abiding public as the whole idea of stalking.

Hinckley's application to go home alone was turned down, and has been turned down ever since. When Hinckley's application came up again in 1988, the court heard that staff had intercepted a letter from him to a mail order company that was selling pictures of Jodie Foster; his obsession was undiminished. In 1993, twelve years after committing the crime, he applied for parole. The answer was no.

'THE BENEVOLENT ANGEL OF DEATH'

SHE RUSHED OUT of her apartment block in Los Angeles on a fine sunny morning in March 1982, a slim, pretty girl with long dark hair, wearing a sailor-style top and trousers. It wasn't far from the block doorway to her car, which was parked by the kerb. She was on her way to a music class, in a hurry because she was late.

'Are you Theresa Saldana?' a male voice with a pronounced Scottish accent asked, as she was slipping the key into the car door. She knew, as soon as she heard the question, that the man who had been stalking her for the past few weeks had caught up with her. She instinctively turned to face him, and then tried to run. He was very close, and when he grabbed her she knew he was far too strong for her to be able to escape. She spontaneously raised her hands, to protect her face, and as she did so she felt the first searing hot thrust of pain in her chest.

Arthur Jackson, a 47-year-old Scottish drifter with a long history of psychiatric illness, stabbed 27-year-old actress Theresa Saldana ten times with the five-inch blade of a kitchen knife as she struggled with him, screaming 'He's trying to kill me.' Fortunately for her, among the people who witnessed the attack was a 26-year-old bottled water delivery man, Jeff Fenn, who had the courage to tackle Jackson. He launched himself on to the demented Scotsman, not realizing that he was armed. When he saw the knife he was able to get it off Jackson and then hold him on the ground until the police arrived.

'I heard a lady screaming, I ran up the street and tried to break it up,' said Fenn. 'The man appeared to be beating her with a fist, but when I grabbed the guy to get him into a headlock I saw he had a knife. Then I pulled him to the ground while she ran into the apartment. I got the knife out of his hands and threw it into the street. He asked me how long it had been since he stabbed her, but I didn't want to talk to him so I told him to just lie down and be still while I held his arms behind him on the ground.'

While he was being held by Fenn, Jackson told the crowd that gathered that they would find the reasons for his attack in a bag he was carrying.

Released from Jackson's grip, Theresa ran back to the apartment block, screaming that she was dying and needed help. Her husband Fred Feliciano had been called, and he stayed by her side as paramedics gave her blood transfusions and then rushed her to the Cedars-Sinai hospital. She was operated on immediately. Four of the stab wounds had punctured one of her lungs, and there were three other stab wounds in her chest, narrowly missing her heart. The left hand which she had raised to protect her face had been slashed so badly that it required extensive surgery over the next few months. The doctors lost count of how many stitches they had to put in on that first day, but she needed twenty-six pints of blood. Before she was wheeled into the operating theatre for her first four hours of surgery Theresa told them she was an actress and begged them to do their job well and not leave her with too many scars. For four weeks she was on two drips, one in each arm, and she was in hospital for a total of ten weeks.

The delivery man who saved her life visited her in hospital a few days later. Although he had seen her most celebrated film, *Raging Bull*, in which she played Jake La Motta's sister-in-law, only the day before, he did not recognize her at the time of the attack. Theresa had a large trophy inscribed for him with the words: 'To my hero, Jeffrey Fenn. Thank you, thank you, thank you. With much love and gratitude for ever.'

There was no doubt that Jeffrey's actions saved Theresa from death. When police examined Arthur Jackson's belongings, they found in the battered shoulder bag he was carrying a document he had written, describing Theresa as his 'divine angel' and his 'countess angel'. He had seen her in a film called *Defiance*, in which she played the girlfriend of a young seaman caught up in a fight with a street gang. Jackson, diagnosed as a paranoid schizophrenic, was deluded enough to believe that the film was the story of his life, and that Theresa was therefore his girlfriend. He claimed she was too good for the world, and he was on a 'divine mission' as a 'benevolent angel of death'. His mission was to kill her, and he wrote that he was acting under the orders of the 'Knights of St Michael in the kingdom of heaven'.

Theresa, he believed, would be better off dead than with the 'scum' she mixed with on earth, which was probably a reference to her husband.

In the document, which was entitled 'Petition to the United States Government for a State-Imposed Execution', he pleaded for his own life to be ended in the electric chair, so that he could join her. He said he wanted to die at Alcatraz, the famous federal prison which had been closed for some years. He stipulated the execution should take place in Cell Block D, because that was where a convicted armed robber named Joseph Cretzer had died in 1946 while leading an insurrection, and Jackson believed that by dying there he could free Cretzer's soul from purgatory, while rejoining his own 'divine angel' in heaven. He also asked for piped music to be played and light refreshments served while he was in the electric chair. He mentioned Theresa Saldana's name fifty times in the whole document.

He also weighed up the pros and cons of where he should kill her – she had an apartment in New York as well as her home in Los Angeles – but opted for California because it had recently reintroduced the death penalty. He wanted to die, but could not bring himself to commit suicide.

Jackson was first diagnosed as mentally ill when he was seventeen, and had been in and out of psychiatric hospitals in Scotland and America ever since. He had been deported from America twice, but had still managed to get a visa to return. Two days after seeing *Defiance* during the Christmas holiday in his home town of Aberdeen, he travelled 8,000 miles on 'an odyssey to find her and complete my mission'. He funded his travel from his British state benefits; he was classified as long-term disabled. He tried to get hold of a gun, which he described in his writings as 'more humane' but could not get one, despite travelling to several states. About a week before he stabbed Theresa, he had turned up in New York, phoning both her New York and Hollywood agents, and then tracking down and contacting her parents. He told her mother that he was speaking on behalf of Martin Scorsese, who directed *Raging Bull*, and that he wanted to offer her another part. Well-spoken, with a distinctive accent, and perfectly lucid, he convinced her mother into giving him Theresa's address in Los Angeles.

'When he told me he had a very good part for my daughter I got excited and gave him Theresa's address,' Mrs Saldana later told a journalist.

By the time of the attack, Theresa knew she was being stalked. Her New York agent told her of a conversation with a man who claimed to be from the famous William Morris talent agency; a few simple questions had betrayed his lack of knowledge of film industry procedure, and the agent went on the alert, reporting the call to the police. Her mother, too, had called her to tell her Scorsese had another part for her: when no offer came, it was clear her mother had been hoaxed. Not only that, but the hoaxer now had Theresa's address.

'My mom has never, never given out information before,' said Theresa a few days after the attack. 'It's not her fault. She just didn't want me to miss the opportunity. She was excited that Scorsese would be calling me.'

After the warnings from her agent and her mother, she was scared and stayed with a neighbour until her husband came home. After that she took more precautions than usual, making sure that she was rarely alone in her apartment and never alone outside at night. But she did not anticipate an attack in broad daylight on a sunny morning, when she had only a few yards to go from her front door to her car.

'I've always been a trusting person. When John Lennon was killed all I can remember is terrible, terrible sadness, as though a piece of my life had been taken away,' Theresa said seven months after the attack. 'But it didn't really make me afraid for me. Now I do not give my phone number to anyone. I do not let anyone know where I live. If someone wants to reach me for a job, it's strictly through my agent.

'I now do things with other people and I always have someone with me. I'm not paranoid, but I am very, very careful.'

She re-started work as soon as she could, taking parts in three television series in the months between the attack and Jackson's court case. She needed to work: her bills of more than $50,000 for the two and a half months she spent in hospital exceeded the limits of her health insurance. During that time she left hospital in a wheelchair and on an intravenous drip to identify Jackson as her attacker before a court.

She believed that work was therapeutic. 'Some people can't believe I want to go on acting after being stabbed by a nut who saw me in a film,' she said in a newspaper interview. 'But I feel that, though you never forget, you've got to carry on and be active.'

Any spare time she had went to founding an organization to help other victims of violence; she found the support system inadequate because none of the counsellors she met had themselves been through an experience similar to hers. She teamed up with a Los Angeles teacher who had been shot in her classroom, and with the backing of the police and psychiatrists they organized support counselling for other victims.

The only emotion Arthur Jackson expressed while he was held on remand was one of regret – not for stabbing Theresa, but for failing to kill her. Another prisoner told the prosecution that he was distraught when he discovered that she had lived, because that meant he had failed to fulfil his mission. He was tried for attempted murder at Santa Monica Supreme Court seven months after the attack, and found guilty. The maximum sentence, twelve years, was passed on him the following month. Theresa testified against him, saying in court: 'I have had to endure a tremendous amount of physical pain and there will be still more pain in the coming weeks, months and possibly years.'

Because Jackson refused to accept that he was insane – he could have pleaded guilty but insane and been sentenced to a secure psychiatric institution – under the American system he went to prison (in Britain, regardless of his own opinion about his mental state, he would have been assessed and, with his history, almost certainly been sent to a hospital for the criminally insane, such as Broadmoor). The prosecutor, Deputy District Attorney Michael Knight, expressed disquiet after the trial about Jackson being treated as a 'normal' prisoner. He pointed out that, with good behaviour, Jackson would be released in eight years, and although he would be instantly deported back to Scotland 'the son of a gun could be back in this country within a week. He's already been deported twice, if that tells you something.'

Investigations into how Jackson managed to get a tourist visa to return to the States revealed that he had legally changed his middle name from John to Richard two years earlier. He had first been deported in 1961, after entering the States in 1955, for failing to declare that he had a history of mental illness. He arrived as a permanent immigrant, and served fourteen months in the US army, but was then discharged as unfit. He served ninety days in jail for possessing a knife, which was discovered after the secret service detained him for making threats against President Kennedy, and after he came out of jail he was taken straight to the airport and flown back to Scotland. In 1966 he returned as a tourist, and was deported for overstaying his visa, after serving another prison sentence for carrying a knife. At that stage he was treated in a Californian psychiatric hospital.

Jackson's own lawyer had the trial delayed for a month while they collected evidence of his long-term illness from psychiatric hospitals in Scotland and the States. He said he could not think of a stronger insanity defence than Jackson's, and described it as 'a classic example'.

But Jackson, who listed his occupation on his British passport as 'technician in scenario and music', refused to allow him to run it and pleaded not guilty. He rejected diagnoses of his condition, described by a psychiatrist in court as 'chronic paranoid schizo-phrenic', and maintained that he was 'allergic to the world'. It seems that the only time he recognized the degree of his own problems was when he was seven-teen and was voluntarily admitted to a hospital in Scotland, where he asked the psychiatrist in charge of his case to 'go into my brain and scrape the dirt off'. With an insanity defence, his lawyer hoped he could prove that he did not act with premeditated malice – that he was too ill to be responsible for his actions. The prosecutor in the case argued that Jackson's preparations – the journey from Scotland, the purchase of the knife, the research into where Theresa lived – proved that he was capable of what is known in legal jargon as 'malice aforethought'.

The jury took nine hours to decide that Jackson was guilty of attempted first-degree murder, not a lesser charge of assault with a deadly weapon, which would have carried a maximum sentence of seven years.

Theresa Saldana wept tears of joy when Jackson got the maximum sentence. But her relief was tem-pered with the knowledge that Jackson would one day be released. Three years after the Saldana case, a new law was introduced to allow for the indefinite detention on a year-by-year renewable basis of deranged prisoners in California, although Jackson's sentence pre-dated the legislation and it was therefore arguable that he was not covered by it. But before those arguments could even be aired, the law was repealed as 'unconstitutional', to the great dismay of Theresa Saldana and many other victims.

Jackson's behaviour record in prison was deemed

to be good, despite him sending letters and making phone calls to journalists and others, stating that his one aim in life was to fulfil the same mission: to kill Theresa. He was still referring to himself as 'the benevolent angel of death', and in one letter to a television producer he wrote: 'I am capable of alternating between sentiment and savagery, romance and reality . . . Also police or FBI protection for TS won't stop the hit squad, murder contract men, nor will bullet-proof vests.' He was being held in the medical wing of Vacaville prison in California, where the chief psychiatrist considered him 'extremely dangerous. He is still psychotic, still delusional, still elaborately involved with Theresa Saldana, Gregory Peck, Charlton Heston and Charles Bronson.'

But despite all this, after seven years he came up for parole, and the psychiatrist's opinion carried no weight; all that mattered was that he had behaved himself. He was not the first seriously disturbed patient to have slipped through the loophole: the parole division of the prison department estimated that about a hundred deranged prisoners had already been released.

'The law ties our hands on this. Just because someone says they will do something, we cannot make the assumption that they will,' said a department official.

Jackson's psychiatrist believed it was the only assumption to make about him. He was, she said, a meticulous planner, used to waiting, and deeply regretted having botched his attempt on Theresa's life. Shortly after his arrest he had started to write an eighty-nine page letter, in handwriting so tiny that it could hardly be read without a magnifying glass, in which he explained why he wanted to kill her.

It started with 'Dear fondest Theresa' and went on to explain that he was suffering from a 'torturous love sickness in my soul for you combined with a desperate desire to escape into a beautiful world I have always dreamed of (the palaces of gardens of sweet paradise) whereby the plan was for you, Theresa, to go ahead first, then I would join you in a few months via the little green room at San Quentin.'

Another passage read, 'I swear on the ashes of my dead mother and on the scars of Theresa Saldana that neither God nor I will rest in peace until this special request and my solemn petition has been granted.'

As the date for his potential release drew nearer Theresa Saldana reluctantly forced herself back into the limelight to fight it. By this time she had been married to her second husband, actor Phil Peters, for a few months and they were expecting their first child. Their address was a closely guarded secret, their telephone number was ex-directory and known to only a trusted handful of people. She had made a film about her own ordeal in 1984 and was still a little involved with the victim support group, but she was also intent on not letting her whole life be ruled by the horrific attack. 'I got so over-identified with the issues and the cause,' she said, 'I became Theresa Saldana, The Girl Who Got Stabbed . . . the tragedy queen. It's not really me to have all this depressing stuff circling round me. You know, ninety-nine per cent of my life is to smile and one per cent is this miserable situation. There is a part of me that feels really overjoyed to even be alive.'

Yet the prospect of Jackson's imminent release was

so terrifying that she made a public plea for 'logic, decency and common sense'. 'This is my life and I stand for other people as well ... It's so late and, you know, along the years I always believed that something would be passed. There seemed to be so many people working on so many different things. And I kept faith and believed that a law would be passed, and then a law was passed, and so recently repealed ...' she told the *Los Angeles Times*. 'And then even when I got the letter about the repeal they said they weren't going to take it as the final thing. But in the last couple of weeks all we got were very tacit and very, very specific and serious words to the effect of "Prepare yourself because he is coming out on the fifteenth of June. And there is nothing we can do."

'My life is in jeopardy. I'm not saying to kill this person ... I'm' not saying the reason for further detainment is punishment, not at all. I believe that we have an obligation to protect the public's safety.'

Assurances that Jackson would again be deported to Britain were of little comfort to the actress, as she realized how easily he had been able to get back into America on previous occasions. Her pleas received wide publicity, and Jackson's release was deferred when he was given an added 270-day sentence for damaging state property and resisting prison officers. The extra time gave the lawyers an opportunity to put together a new case against him for sending threatening letters to Theresa, and he was sentenced to another five years and eight months in prison.

It was before this second sentence began that Jackson's story took a bizarre turn. From his prison cell he wrote to the *People* newspaper in London, to Scotland Yard and to the British consul in Los Angeles, claiming to have shot a man during a bank raid in London in 1967. Former Grenadier guardsman 33-year-old Anthony Fletcher was brutally gunned down by a single shot at point blank range, after courageously trapping in a cul-de-sac the robber, who had stolen £22 from a Chelsea branch of the National Westminster bank. His bravery led to him being dubbed a 'have-a-go hero' by the popular press, a sobriquet which has passed into common usage for any passer-by who tackles a criminal. Anthony Fletcher was posthumously awarded the George Cross for his bravery. Jackson also claimed to have taken part in another bank raid two years earlier, and said he had information on 'a scheduled mass murderer' in a British city.

This last claim, and his psychiatric history, led to a first reaction of disbelief, but Jackson was obviously in possession of detailed facts about the bank raids, and detectives from London flew out to interview him. They were satisfied that he knew enough to have been involved, and they reopened the case of Anthony Fletcher's murder. After tracing thirty-five witnesses and re-examining the forensic evidence, they believed they had enough evidence to bring him to trial. If Jackson had been deported in 1990, he would have walked straight into the arms of the Metropolitan police.

But Theresa Saldana worried that he would not receive a long sentence in Britain and would soon be released to fly back to stalk her. Her campaign against him was rewarded with his second conviction, and her involvement will keep him in prison without parole until June 1996. Unless the Americans find some other way of detaining him – and Theresa would like him to stay permanently locked up in the States rather than see him handed over to Britain – he will eventually face trial here when he is released.

Friends of pretty 21-year-old American TV actress Rebecca Schaeffer were stunned by her death. Who could have gunned her down? Rebecca, they said, did not have an enemy in the world. When her murderer was arrested the following day it became clear that in his own eyes he was not her enemy but a devoted fan, bent on 'saving' her innocence from the wicked world.

Rebecca was an only child with parents who are a psychologist and a writer. She was doing well at school but was side-tracked into modelling by her own stunning looks. A model agency in her home town of Portland, Oregon, snapped her up at fifteen, and within a couple of years she headed for New York, where she was taken on to the books of one of the big, prestigious agencies. Her fresh-faced good looks made her a natural for teenage magazine covers. Friends from the time remember her as streetwise and confident, not tough but not frightened by the big city.

Not tall enough for fashion modelling and reluctant to limit herself to photographic modelling, she pursued her dream of becoming an actress, signing up for acting and dancing classes. She struggled, as all youngsters in the cut-throat business do; when her agent tried to let her know that she had been given a part in a CBS sitcom, *My Sister Sam*, her telephone was disconnected because the bill had not been paid, and the agent was forced to call at her home and tape a message to the door.

She moved to Los Angeles for the part, and found a quiet flat in a respectable, middle-class area of the city. After sharing with other models in New York she consciously chose to live on her own. But she was not lonely: she was popular on the set, she had girl friends and a few months before her death she was dating an actor who she knew from her home town.

'We'd travel, go to parks, have picnics. She liked to horseback ride or just spend time on a mountain top. She was the only actor I've ever known who managed to become successful and remain unjaded,' he said after her death. 'She was extremely curious and spirited.'

After her exposure in the sitcom her future looked very bright. She landed a good role in a dark comedy, *Scenes from the Class Struggle in Beverly Hills*, and signed to do another feature film, *One Point of View*. She loved the work and the laid-back Californian lifestyle.

Into this idyll stepped a 19-year-old stranger with a glossy publicity photograph of the actress he idolized. Robert Bardo, who came from Tucson, Arizona, traced his idol by hiring a private detective who checked address records at the California State Department of Motor Vehicles. (After Rebecca's death, celebrities successfully petitioned for access to the records to be restricted.)

It was a warm Tuesday morning in July 1989 when Bardo turned up in the street outside Rebecca's apartment block with a large manila folder under his arm, from which he pulled out her photograph from time to time. The curly-haired young man in a yellow polo shirt accosted a few passers-by, asking if they knew where she lived, and asking if the address he had for her was a house or an apartment block. Others who did not speak to him also remembered him – there was a strange and memorably disturbing quality about him.

'He looked weird,' said one neighbour who bumped into him twice. 'It was strange seeing him twice. You think about it for a second, then you go your own way. That's what you do in LA.'

Someone else described him as handling the folder containing the photograph gingerly, as though it were precious: 'It was like it contained food and he didn't want to turn it over.'

Shortly afterwards, another neighbour heard the sound of a shot and two screams, and then breaking glass. Rebecca Schaeffer's body lay slumped on the doorstep of the block. Her intercom was broken, and she had come down in person to see who her caller was. A single bullet hit her in the chest and ripped through two panes of glass. By the time the neighbour reached her side there was no discernible pulse and she was pronounced dead on arrival when her body was taken to hospital. The youth in the yellow polo shirt had last been scene jogging calmly away from the scene of the crime. He disappeared down an alleyway.

Almost immediately, police and friends reached the conclusion that the murderer was a deranged fan. There could be no other motive.

'I can only assume it was somebody who didn't know her but was obsessed with her. I can't imagine that anybody who really knew her would do this. She was so mature and intuitive that she would have made sure this couldn't happen,' said the director of her TV series.

By the following day, Bardo was back in his home town of Tucson, where police picked up reports of a man behaving bizarrely and disrupting traffic at a major road junction. They arrested Bardo. In the meantime LA police had a tip-off from a friend of Bardo's in Tennessee, who knew that the youth had harboured a long-term obsession with the actress, had written to her, phoned her agent several times and had talked about hurting her. A photo of Bardo was faxed from Arizona to California, and the neighbours who had seen Bardo on the day of the murder identified him immediately.

At Bardo's home the police found a collection of videos. He had everything Rebecca Schaeffer had ever appeared in. He had apparently visited her at Warner Brothers studios the year before, to deliver a five-foot high teddy bear to her. He'd confessed his love for her to a security guard, but his desire for her had tipped into hatred when he saw the character she was playing in *Scenes From the Class Struggle* lose her virginity on screen.

At his trial the judge refused to accept that Bardo was mentally unstable, although he had a history of mental illness. The judge, sentencing him to life without parole, said, 'He had different motives from most people, but again most people aren't murderers.'

Before he was given a life sentence, to be served at

the notorious San Quentin prison, Bardo made a long, rambling speech to the court. 'I do realize what I've done and the pain I caused and it was irreversibly wrong,' he said. He admitted stalking his 'goddess' for days, 'hoping to get the chance to say hello to her'. When he finally rang her doorbell and she appeared, he was too tongue-tied to speak – so he pulled out a gun and shot her, laughing as he did it.

'DON'T SAY I DIDN'T WARN YOU'

'WHEN I STARTED out, I didn't have any desire to be a great actress or to learn how to act. I just wanted to be famous.'

It was Katharine Hepburn who said those words, and she was being characteristically honest. There are many celebrities who talk about their vocation, their art, the importance of their work. They are not (necessarily) phoneys: as a breed actors and actresses have a high work ethic. Theirs is a craft that can be worked on and developed and improved, and the good ones are constantly honing their natural skills and talents for the camera or the stage. But few are as ruthlessly truthful as Hepburn; they did not lie in their childhood beds and dream of attending drama classes, voice training, stage technique; they did not fantasize about early morning calls to make-up, about finding their best scenes on the cutting-room floor, about difficult and demanding directors. What they dreamed about was fame. Names in lights, top billing, adulation. Some coveted the financial rewards of stardom, others would (in the secrecy of their adolescent yearnings) have even sacrificed that for the heady taste of public adulation.

Even had they been presented with a true picture of the downside of stardom, it is unlikely that any of them would have abandoned their dreams. Years later, having fulfilled their ambitions, and well-aware of the bitter realities that come with the other trappings of celebrity, a few genuinely wonder whether the chase was worth the quarry; most would still not exchange Hollywood mansions, hot and cold running servants and an eager public dancing attendance on them for obscurity, a nine-to-five job in an office or on a factory production line, and a modest home. They may feel afraid, angry, intruded upon and at risk at different times, but the balance still weighs, they reckon, in their favour.

And then along comes a monster . . .

It's true that all Hollywood stalkers are deranged, but the degree of derangement varies enormously. Some will be content to write long, rambling, non-threatening letters; others will turn up on the doorstep with a knife or a gun. Some celebrities attract more obsessive fans than others, partly because of the nature of the parts they play and their public profile. It's fair to say, although no research has been done into it, that every above-the-title star will have at least one stalker, and some will have many. But there seems to be no way of predicting which star will attract the very dangerous life-threatening stalker – even though there may be ways of assessing which stalker may turn nasty, which star they will be fixated on is in the lap of the gods.

What is it, for example, that makes Olivia Newton-

John such a target for stalkers? Is it her innocent little-girl image, healthy and wholesome but in need of protection? You could just as easily argue that her appeal is the antithesis of the darker edge that seems to attract obsessives. Yet attract them she does.

She first had to step up her security to a 24-hour armed guard in 1983, when a former mental patient who was obsessed with her committed five murders. He had written to her that he heard voices, and that the voices told him that she was a muse (a reference to her role as a muse in the film *Xanadu*) and that she was trapped under Lake Arthur, Louisiana, near to the home where he shot his mother, his father, his 2-year-old cousin and two nephews. The 28-year-old Michael Perry had sent two letters to her before the slaughter of his family, telling her in one of them that there was 'an underground network operating' under the trailer home he lived in, which was parked at the back of his parents' home. He had also twice tried to get into her Malibu beach home. After shooting his relatives at point-blank range, Perry was on the loose for two and a half weeks, and police were very concerned for Olivia, adding their own patrolmen to the security guards she employed. In his trailer home they had found three names on a blank cheque: Olivia, Matt and Judge O'Connor. Judge O'Connor was the first woman to sit in America's Supreme Court, for which achievement she had received quite a lot of publicity. 'Matt' was believed to be a reference to Olivia's boyfriend, Matt Lattanzi. During the hunt for Perry, Olivia Newton-John took refuge back in her native Australia, staying with her father.

Perry was finally arrested in Washington DC,

where his hotel room contained seven black and white television sets, all small ones with twelve-inch screens. On the screen of one of the sets were some strange scribblings, including the names of the family members he had killed. All the sets were tuned in to show nothing but static, and on some of the screens Perry had painted pairs of eyes. He was only caught because staff of the cheap rooming house called the police when he tried to walk out with a stolen clock radio under his arm.

After Perry came Ralph Nau, who stalked Olivia, Cher and British singer Sheena Easton, plaguing all three of them with phone calls through the night to their ex-directory numbers, lurking in the shadows near their Hollywood homes and sending them death threats made from words cut out of newspapers. He showed a dogged determination to track them down, often operating with nothing more than a newspaper photograph from which he matched the background building. He turned up on the set of one of Cher's movies, he followed Sheena Easton back to her native Scotland (where he was turned back before he could enter the country) and he followed Olivia to Australia. He showed amazing energy, sending letters to fifty other female stars, including actress Farrah Fawcett and singers Marie Osmond and Whitney Houston, and a clutch of American soap stars.

In 1984, when he was twenty-nine, he was arrested for butchering his 8-year-old stepbrother with an axe, and burying the body in a cornfield. He believed that the little boy was coming between him and another of his loves, gymnast Nadia Comaneci, who happened to be on television at the time of the murder.

Police suspected he may have been involved in two other murder cases, but there was not enough evidence to charge him. He escaped life imprisonment because he was insane and he was ordered to be held in a secure psychiatric hospital. At his trial a medical report assessed him as dangerously psychotic, with a hatred of women and deep feelings of inadequacy. The stars who had been his victims could at last breathe a sigh of relief – albeit temporary – at his containment.

By the beginning of 1989 Olivia Newton-John was again being seriously stalked, by an unemployed mechanic who had recently been released from prison for carrying a concealed weapon. After inundating her with more than a thousand letters over two years, and after sending her a 75-dollar ring for her daughter Chloe, 27-year-old Randall Gleckler from Ohio turned up at her home and was accidentally allowed through the iron security gates, after passing himself off as a songwriter. A secretary realized immediately that a serious mistake had been made – he had used his own name – and called the police. The star and her 3-year-old daughter hid in a bedroom until he was arrested. Although he was unarmed, he had two bullets in his pockets. He was taken to a psychiatric hospital for evaluation and as the medical staff could find nothing wrong with him he was released four days later.

Although Gleckler did not reappear, Olivia Newton-John's respite was short-lived. Within four months she and her companions in terror, Sheena Easton and Cher (who once received an ear through the post from another manic fan) found themselves facing the prospect of Ralph Nau being released. His case came up for review and he was turned down, but the stars knew that he would be eligible to apply again two months later. The three of them, who shared the services of Gavin de Becker to advise them, took the unusual step of issuing a joint statement, pleading for his next appeal for freedom to also be thrown out: 'He has dangerous delusions about us. For several years he has acted on these delusions by travelling great distances to pursue us. We are understandably concerned about the safety of our families and our own safety.' The statement went on to say that the people of Illinois, the state in which he was tried and held, should oppose any review of his case. 'Illinois is where he killed before and he has a continuing relationship to potential victims' – which meant that he still harboured delusions about his victims, despite five years in hospital.

De Becker revealed that Nau had been writing letters to the three stars, letters which had been intercepted by hospital staff. He had described Olivia as 'an evil impostor at war with me'; Cher was 'a bitch who is determined to see me ruined'; and Easton was 'a woman running from her love for me'. Nau claimed to receive messages on a TV screen in his head, which told him that Olivia Newton-John was dead and that her place had been taken by another woman; once he got this usurper out of the way he would be able to concentrate on his pursuit of Cher and Sheena, his true loves.

Nau's appeal for freedom was rejected, but his case continues to come up for review every six months. The celebrities he stalked can only hope and pray that his case never slips through a net and he is released back on to the streets.

Like Nau, Thomas Jay Luttman had a list of stars he was targeting. Unlike Nau, who confined himself to attractive female stars, Luttman's list was altogether more eclectic and included Jane Fonda, the then US Agriculture Secretary John Block and two soap opera stars, Bill Hayes and Susan Seaforth-Hayes (married in real life.) First on his list was an attorney, who had recently served legal papers on Luttman for defaulting on a loan. To carry out his crusade of death Luttman ordered an Uzi sub-machine-gun, paying three-quarters of the price down and arranging to come back to the store to pick up the weapon when he had the rest of the money. To get it, he broke into a woman's apartment, allegedly raped her and took her bank card. Luckily for the people on his list, the woman broke free and ran naked to a neighbour's. Police surrounded her flat and arrested Luttman, who fired at them with a shotgun. When they took him into custody they found a list of his intended victims. Jane Fonda's name was not on it but under questioning he revealed his intention to kill her because of her opposition to the war in Vietnam.

Although they can be dangerous and devious, stalkers are not usually hard to track down (historically, the problems that the police have are to do with prosecuting them and keeping them in custody for what, in many cases, are individually minor offences.) Many stalkers openly write to the celebrities they are obsessed with under their own names. Others leave easy clues. Stephanie Zimbalist, the actress who starred in the *Remington Steele* show, received 200 notes in eighteen months from a man who signed himself 'Your Secret Admirer'. He threatened, 'I'll get you. I am watching your house. I have in mind some mischief. Don't say I didn't warn you.' But his identity did not remain secret for long when he revealed in one letter the time and date of the flight he would be taking to Los Angeles to carry out his threats, and the hotel where he would be staying. Michael Shields, who weighed thirty stone, was arrested at the airport. The amount he had given away about himself in that last letter suggests it may have been a cry for help, a bid for others to stop his behaviour spiralling completely out of control.

A few stalkers have no intention of being caught, and cover their tracks well. Michael J. Fox, star of *Back to the Future*, expressed the dichotomy of fame when he said that it had 'both brightened and darkened' life for him and his actress wife Tracy Pollan. Fox received 5,000 threatening letters from a shipping clerk called Tina Ledbetter who lived in Camirillo, California; she was upset that he had married. She first wrote to him demanding that he stop dating Tracy. Unusually among deranged fans, she did not imagine that she should be the object of his romantic attention, but instead she wrote promoting the cause of another actress with whom Fox had been involved, Nancy McKeon (both Tracy and Nancy had starred with Fox in a TV series):

Dear Michael

Dump Tracy immediately! Go back to Nancy McKeon. The whole world knows that you've been screwing Tracy. They say you and Tracy are living together. But I know that's not true. Your next movie I am looking forward to. Although, I heard it is going to be a major box office bomb, *Bright Lights, Big City*. Please don't tell me that you are only going to do one more session of *Family Ties*, even the reruns. Go back to Nancy immediately. You made such a good-looking couple.

Your Number One Fan

It was anonymous, it showed classic signs of obsession, but it did not jump out as dangerous among the hundreds of letters Fox received every week from female fans. It was not until his relationship with Tracy reached the engagement stage that her letters became more vitriolic, containing lines like 'Dump Tracy immediately, go back to Nancy or Tracy will be killed.' By the time he married Tracy in July 1989 she was writing:

You are a total asshole for marrying Tracy. She just wants to get her hands on your money. You just made the biggest mistake in your life marrying Tracy. Divorce Tracy immediately or I'll personally kill you. You don't really love her. Go back to Nancy McKeon immediately or I will kill you. I am serious about what I said. I will kill you if you don't divorce Tracy immediately. You better listen to me. I'm serious about killing you.

It was principally because of her that the wedding of Michael J. Fox and Tracy Pollan had more security surrounding it than Hollywood had ever previously seen.

Within weeks, the letters were getting stronger: 'You're a goddamn bastard for marrying that goddamn Jewish money-hungry bitch. So if you don't want to die, divorce Tracy immediately.' They arrived at the rate of several a day, and the pressure mounted.

'I'm coming after you with a gun and I'm going to kill you if you don't divorce Tracy immediately. You are dead if you don't divorce Tracy immediately. You better listen to me because you are dead if you don't. Beware of the audience at the tapings of your show because I am out there watching you . . .'

After the announcement that Fox and his wife were expecting a child, Tina Ledbetter's anonymous letters went off the scale: 'You're a goddamn fucking bastard. I know where you live and I'm going to kill you and that goddamn fucking bitch and that goddamn fucking baby. You shithead, you bastard.'

Fox had put the case of Tina Ledbetter in the hands of Gavin de Becker from the moment the letters became more than normal fan letters, and the detection of the anonymous letter writer and her subsequent prosecution is a testament to the professional expertise that he has developed. At first the letters did not raise too much alarm: the writer was not psychotic; the letters were not full of delusions. She knew who Fox was and she did not see herself as his wife or his lover. The women she wrote about, Tracy and Nancy, were real women and she saw them in appropriate relationships to Fox. (She may not have approved of his marriage to Tracy, but she recognized it. Her preference for Nancy was based on reports of his previous relationship with her.) She also expressed her hostility to Tracy, and eventually to Fox himself, openly. According to Dr Park Dietz, expressions of hate are far less worrying than expressions of love. Hate mail carries with it its own catharsis; love for a celebrity is destined to be unrequited and therefore unsatisfactory. Judged by de Becker's computer program, Tina Ledbetter did not constitute a real threat until the anger in her letters, and the threats, escalated out of all proportion.

She was skilful about avoiding detection, posting her letters from different areas, but she finally betrayed herself when she sent a box of rabbits' droppings to Fox's publicist (it transpired that she bred rabbits). Although she had concealed it, de Becker's office was able to make out part of the reference number of the parcel firm and through them he was able to trace her address. He was also able to describe to the police the sort of person they would find at the address: a woman, unattractive, possibly overweight or too thin, possibly untidy in her appearance. The psychological profile from which he worked showed that she would be someone of very low self-esteem. As soon as they saw Tina Marie Ledbetter, they knew they had the right woman, and this was confirmed when they found the typewriter which matched the letters. They also found a butcher's knife in her bedroom.

She was held in custody for ten months pending trial, and was then sentenced to four years, suspended. She was ordered to have counselling and to stay away from Fox.

Tina Marie Ledbetter's obsession with Fox was triggered by his role in *Family Ties*, a long-running US TV series. Actors and actresses who appear in soaps and series, playing the same character over months and sometimes years, are the most likely to attract stalkers. Even for genuine and harmless fans, the reality of their existence as actors becomes confused with the parts they play. Stars of any soap grow tired of being told that their wives or husbands are being unfaithful, or being given advice on how to handle situations which apply to their character, not to them. If normal people can become confused, those who are already having clinical problems with their grasp on reality are even more easily affected.

One of Fox's co-stars on *Family Ties*, Justine Bateman, attracted a stalker who was physically more of a threat to her than Ledbetter ever was to Fox. John Smetek believed he had made love to the actress on a beach seven years before his arrest in 1989. He believed that he was destined to marry her and in pursuit of her he held a loaded revolver against his own stomach, threatening to shoot himself, outside a theatre in Berkeley, California, where she was appearing. He held police at bay for three hours. Smetek, who was thirty-nine, had been stalking Justine for six months, sending her flowery love letters, phoning her and tracking her to restaurants and to the health centre where she regularly exercised.

She, too, is a client of Gavin de Becker, and de Becker had tipped off the police after discovering that Smetek had bought tickets for a preview performance of the play and that he had been hanging around outside when she was attending rehearsals. Approached by the police, Smetek had handed the tickets over because, he said, he did not want to upset Justine. But at about 10.00 a.m. on the day of the first performance he was seen sitting outside the theatre with his gun. Eventually police and mental health workers were able to persuade him to surrender the weapon. Smetek's mother blamed the Hare Krishna cult, which she said had brainwashed her son so that he could no longer recognize reality. Smetek occasionally used a Hare Krishna name, but had been kicked out of a sect community. Despite a whole range of delusions, including a belief that he was a member of the Bavarian royal family, Smetek was charming and could attract friendship, although it was usually short-lived.

'He tells everyone Justine Bateman will be his wife,' one friend told a journalist after his arrest. 'He says her father was a dear friend of his and had offered to introduce him . . . But John felt if that happened Justine would lose interest. "Who would marry someone their father introduced them to?" he would often say.'

He claimed to be a regular in the audience for the taping of the show *Family Ties* and told another friend that he had seen her playing a love scene, and that she had looked straight out into the audience and into his eyes. He said he had met her backstage after the show, and although she hadn't said anything to him he knew she had arranged the meeting. There was even, he said, a taped marker on the floor where she stood with an initial J on it, a sign that she had worked out the encounter in advance.

His friends were convinced that he really did know the actress 'but not that they'd ever had a sexual relationship – only spiritual'. He believed that in a past life she was a Hindu god and his religious guide, and that it was part of their pre-ordained cosmic lives to marry and be together. The fact that she had a regular boyfriend, actor Leif Garrett (to whom Smetek bore a remarkable resemblance), did not appear to worry him, as he explained that it was simply something she had to do before they could be together. Ninety per cent of all his conversations revolved around her.

Justine Bateman was quoted as having commented, before Smetek's arrest: 'I feel like a caged animal. I've had to change my lifestyle to avoid that man. I can't sleep, I can't eat, my nerves are so raw.'

Another stalker who held police at bay while she threatened to kill herself was Joni Leigh Penn. Exceptionally, Penn was stalking another woman, the *Cagney and Lacey* actress Sharon Gless. According to Dr Park Dietz, almost all stalkers are fixated on someone of the opposite sex but as Penn is a lesbian who wanted to sexually assault the actress, she still conforms to Dietz's general rule.

She had been pursuing Sharon Gless for over two years when she broke into one of the actress's homes at 3.00 a.m. on 30 March 1990 and holed herself up in there for seven hours with a semi-automatic rifle and 500 rounds of ammunition. Luckily there was nobody in the house; Sharon Gless used it as an office only. Smashing a window to get in, Penn had triggered a silent alarm which sent police rushing to the building. Penn, who was thirty, pointed the rifle at her own chest, retreated into the bathroom and locked herself in. After seeing her weapon, police took the precaution of evacuating families from ten neighbouring houses. Four hours into the siege, Penn insisted on talking to a female police officer, to whom she spoke about wanting to see Sharon and about killing herself. She did not suggest she wanted to harm Sharon. By 10.00 a.m. she was tired and soon afterwards she gave herself up.

Penn, who lived with her twin sister in a rented two-bedroomed flat, worked as a domestic cleaner and impressed her neighbours only with her quietness and orderliness. She first took an interest in Sharon Gless three years before the siege, when she started to turn up on the set of *Cagney and Lacey*, and at first appeared to be nothing more than an enthusiastic fan. She would joke with guards at the set gate, and they thought nothing of her. She occasionally sent flowers and she may have exchanged words with the star she idolized. Then she started writing letters.

'In the beginning they were romantic in tone, but then they turned increasingly hostile,' said Michael Gless, Sharon's brother and also her lawyer. In all, Penn sent about 120 letters. In January 1988 the star received a different letter: this one was from a psychiatrist who was treating Penn. He warned the star that his patient was talking about shooting herself in front of her idol, and although she had no intention of hurting the star there was always a risk. It was nine months after this that Penn turned up outside Sharon's house, and that's when her brother swung into legal action and got a restraining order against Penn, who was forbidden to go within 200 yards of any of Sharon's family, or within 1,000 yards of her home or any of her family's homes. The order did not prevent her from sending an envelope containing three photographs to the star; one showed Penn holding a gun to her open mouth, another showed her holding it to her temple and the third showed what Michael Gless described as 'a kind of shrine she had made to Sharon, composed of publicity pictures and flowers. In the middle she had placed an attack rifle.'

Joni Penn pleaded guilty to burglary charges and was given a four-year sentence.

The celebrities who have been forced to take recourse to law against their stalkers are legion, although many of the stalkers are not physically threatening. Clint Eastwood may play characters like William Munny in *The Unforgiven* who, on celluloid, go ranging for revenge, but in real life direct action is off limits. Clint is believed to have tried it, accosting in person the man who was hounding his daughter. But it was the law that eventually rid Alison Eastwood of her stalker, by having him deported back to Britain. Alison, an actress, was seventeen when Mike Joynson, a 21-year-old drifter from Salford, Greater Manchester, flew into California intent on tracking her down. He had seen her in a film called *Tightrope*, in which she plays a girl who is handcuffed by a psychopath.

To get to her, Joynson jumped a security fence around her father's home, he barged into her mother's home, he sent letters and flowers and even faxes to Clint's office, declaring his love for her. He lived in a tent, which he pitched at different times outside her father's home, her mother's home and her school gates. A restraining order forbidding him to go near her failed to stop him and so did a face-to-face warning from Eastwood. Eventually Joynson was prosecuted for trespassing, put on probation for three years and deported back to Britain.

Another macho hero, Sylvester Stallone, found himself up against an unlikely enemy when an attractive blonde babysitter became fixated on him. Elfie Wade, who was thirty-four in 1990 when Stallone got a restraining order against her, had been dropping as many as ten notes a night into his mailbox for nearly two years, delivering them between 11.00 p.m. and 7.00 a.m. They were threatening, deranged letters: she once enclosed a picture of a burned skeleton and on another occasion a photograph of John Lennon, who had been assassinated by a stalker. 'I'll tie you up if you try to escape from me,' she wrote in one letter. In an interview after getting an order banning her from going within 200 yards of his home or his business premises, Stallone said: 'She claims we were lovers in a past life. That's all I need . . . But this woman is nuts. She wants to hurt me. She'd drop off these bizarre notes and pictures at my Malibu beach house in the middle of the night and my skin would crawl. I've gotten 500 cards and letters from her. They ramble on about all sorts of crazy things – threats against the government . . . pictures of bombs blowing up and destroying things, crazy pictures of George Bush and a lot of messed up religious theories.'

He said his children were disturbed by Wade, and knowing that she worked as a babysitter for other people worried him. He felt it was his duty to expose her. 'When I'd wake up in the morning and see that another of the letters had arrived in the middle of the night I'd get unnerved . . . The fact that she's a babysitter, earning her living that way, is frightening. Innocent children may be falling under her "care".'

In Hollywood it is the stars who don't have stalkers who are the exceptions to the rule. The Jackson family, for instance, have had to cope with them for several members of the family, different stalkers operating independently and targeting different members of the clan. LaToya, Janet and Michael have all been forced to take legal action against obsessed fans. In Michael's case, the stalker bizarrely claimed the singer was the father of her six-year-old twins, and she even took out a £100 million paternity suit against him. She lost.

'HE'S OUT THERE SOMEWHERE'

As she emerges from the theatre where she has been playing to a packed house, the actress looks nervously at the small cluster of fans by the stage door. A hundred years ago she might have hoped to find her own stage-door Johnny, the aristocratic son of a peer of the realm, a wealthy and bedazzled fan who would whisk her away from the grimy boards, marry her, shower her with the family pearls and make her children into honourables.

Today, she does not hope for a positive, but rather for a negative. She hopes that he, her most persistent fan, will *not* be there. She hopes that she will not be asked for her autograph for the hundredth time, she hopes there will be no more red roses from him, no more tortuous, indecipherable letters. Today's actress can no longer bask in the warmth of her fans' appreciation: every declaration of devotion has to be regarded with suspicion, because behind it may lurk a stalker.

The shabby motels of Los Angeles might be the natural habitat of the beast, but the television studios and theatres of Britain have their own sub-species.

No star in Britain has been shot or knifed, nobody has taken delivery of a fan's ear in a box through the mail (as Cher's office did). But British crime patterns run about ten years behind the USA, and it was the 1980s which saw the huge explosion in stalking in America. Whether we will ever reach the situation where a top British-based star has as many as 500 oddballs sending potentially worrying letters is debatable as American stars have international appeal, to obsessional fans as well as to normal ones. But there are already plenty of signs that in stalking, as well as other crime, we are following America's lead.

What Britain does not have is the big-time business in advising stars and providing security for them that exists in Hollywood. Here British celebrities are far less ruthless in their attitudes to the fans whose attentions become over zealous, and take the sort of risks in encountering them, even trying to help them, that would make the American experts' blood run cold.

To date, the stalkers who haunt British stars, although obsessive and of a high nuisance value, are not violent like those the Hollywood stars fend off. But to their victims, their presence is just as harrowing.

Helena Bonham Carter, the delicate English rose who starred in the Merchant Ivory productions of *A Room with a View* and *Howard's End*, expressed feelings of enormous restraint when, after being pestered for six years by a fan who she was eventually forced to take to court, she said: 'I feel sad about the whole business and I feel sad for him.'

She obtained her injunction against Andrew Farquharson in February 1993, banning him from going near the home she shared with her parents or telephoning her. She was twenty-six and Farquharson was twenty-seven years old at the time, and although he had never posed a physical threat, she felt she needed protection from the letters with which he bombarded her. He had first become interested in her career when he was a student, and had over the years become more and more obsessional. What started as polite fan letters degenerated into detailed sexual propositions, the sexual content escalating after he saw Helena playing against type in an episode of *Miami Vice*. When he left home in Scotland to live near her in London, and when he began to appear constantly on her parents' doorstep, the family decided to take action. Helena's parents, her mother Elena, a psychotherapist, and her father Raymond, a retired banker who is seriously disabled and has been in a wheelchair since Helena was a teenager, often had to bear the brunt of his obsession, partly to shelter their daughter but also because she was frequently away from home filming. They always helped her open her post, because of his letters.

The police at Golders Green police station, near the Bonham Carter home, knew all about Farquharson, and had even had him bound over to keep the peace after arresting him on the doorstep, but eventually the family had to resort to a High Court injunction.

'He'd been writing letters more or less every day for six years, and then after about three years he started phoning, day and night,' said the actress. 'His home is in Inverness, but he suddenly arrived on my doorstep, which was just too intrusive. My parents spoke to him but there was no way he could have been persuaded logically to leave me alone. I tried speaking to him myself, but he was completely unfazed. He wanted to be my friend – what can you say to that? I said, "I don't want you to be my friend." He said, "Why not – we could have a lot in common," and it just went on and on.

'I never felt physically threatened but it was just exhausting . . . I'd see him waiting outside the house and that upset me, because I really do want to lead a normal life. I'm not going to lead a hermit-like existence. It seems ridiculous that acting in films should inhibit your freedom . . . I don't think other people would have been as patient or tolerant as my parents were.'

Farquharson's own parents encouraged Helena to take their son to court in a bid to stop him being a nuisance.

The most interesting comment the actress made obliquely expressed the double bind of fame: 'It made me quite angry because I felt that I was being manipulated into feeling like a bad person.' She did not like being forced into the position of taking such trenchant action against someone who had been seduced into believing in her availability (Farquharson said he wanted to fall in love with her and quite openly expressed to journalists a desire to have sex with her) by her film and television roles.

Another star whose desire to stop her stalker pestering her was tempered by a genuine pity for his mental state was Gloria Hunniford. It was 1989 when she went to court to restrain 63-year-old Brian Jennison from following her everywhere. He sent her flowers and notes – nothing threatening or sexual, but enough for the television and radio star to find it 'extremely uncomfortable'.

She got an order banning Jennison from coming within 500 yards of her home or 100 yards of her workplace. When he failed to observe the restrictions, she went back to the High Court three months later and Jennison, who had also pursued Margaret Thatcher and Princess Margaret, and sent letters to the director general of the BBC, faced a jail sentence. But Gloria took pity on the 'sad, old man' after he agreed to make a promise before the court that he would not harass her again and she dropped her case against him.

'It really was a very uncomfortable experience,' she said at the time. 'When he started calling at my house it was extremely worrying. Often I wasn't here, and my son had to get rid of him. In the end I took pity on him. It was my decision to drop the case and not go the full way, which would probably have ended up with him being jailed. I just wanted him to stop what he was doing. I hope he gets treatment for his problem and that he doesn't bother me or anybody else again.'

Despite her pity, Jennison continued to plague the star. 'I don't want the responsibility of sending him to prison. It's horrible and terrifying. It just goes with the job, unfortunately,' said Gloria.

Glen Murphy, star of *London's Burning*, took the same line, even though his stalker – a woman who believed she was having an affair with him – was more threatening. He was blitzed with love letters; the woman turned up wherever he was, even at events which had not been publicized; she waited for hours outside his office and, chillingly, she was able to list in detail the contents of his car. Murphy regarded her presence as part of the territory of stardom, but said he would go to the police if ever she turned up at his home and threatened his wife and four children.

Not all celebrities are able to be so philosophical, because not all stalkers are so easy to live with. However terrifying it was for Gloria, it was many times worse for actress Joanne Pearce, who is the victim of physical threats including threats to kill. She was forced to move house and change her phone number five times to keep a demented woman stalker at bay. The woman, who sent Joanne letters covered with blood splashes, detailed exactly what she would like to do to the actress. Joanne described the situation in an interview with a journalist in 1990: 'Every time I go round a corner I expect to have acid thrown in my face or a knife stuck in my back. Wherever I go she always manages to find me . . . I live in constant fear for my life. It started when she sent a menacing letter to my home. I tried to ignore it but the threats got worse and worse.'

Joanne's parents and brother were also subjected to a barrage of hate mail telling them exactly what the woman planned for Joanne. When the actress bought a new car, within days it was scratched and covered in graffiti. The stalker was adept at plotting her movements, leaving messages on stage doors where she was appearing which threatened to kill her. During one particularly virulent spate of threats as many as ten plain-clothes policemen were drafted in to protect the actress, but her stalker did not break cover.

Joanne opened and read all her letters from the crazed woman, and admitted that she cried at the verbal attacks on her; she read that she was ugly and that was why she was unmarried and had no children, that she was a poor actress. But reading them enabled Joanne to search for clues as to the woman's identity; she even studied books on schizophrenia to help her understand her enemy. Without the support of her family and friends, she said, she would have been driven to a nervous breakdown.

The energy and commitment of a stalker who could track Joanne around the country, could trace each new ex-directory number, could find out and attack her new car within days of her having it, is astonishing, and may suggest that the woman concerned regarded the pursuit of her quarry as a full-time occupation. Another stalker who, like Joanne's, managed to keep his identity secret, and also appeared to have remarkable time and resources to trace his victims, is the man called 'Hugh' who selected a bevy of middle-aged actresses as his target. His attentions are obscene, rather than physically threatening. It was only when Diana Rigg went to the police with the latest in a ten-year sequence of letters that it became clear that her stalker had also been sending letters to Lynda Baron, a singer turned actress who starred with Ronnie Barker in *Open All Hours*, Isobel Black, star of the 1960s TV series *The Troubleshooters*, Nyree Dawn Porter, most famous for her role in *The Forsyte Saga*, actress Dinah Sheridan, mother of Conservative Party Chairman Jeremy Hanley and TV presenter Jenny Hanley, and the American actress Lauren Bacall. When an envelope addressed to Diana Rigg by 'Hugh' was published in the *Daily Mail* in 1992, Lynda Baron and a friend of Lauren Bacall's made contact to say that they instantly recognized the familiar curly handwriting. Isobel Black, who had received a letter only the previous day, fished the envelope out of the bin and compared it to the one in the newspaper: there was no doubt, it was the same man. Dinah Sheridan and Nyree Dawn Porter had gone public about the stalker five years earlier; they were receiving letters in the same handwriting, post-marked from Bolton, near Manchester, like all the others. The only difference was that in the early letters to these two, the stalker signed himself 'Janet' but expert opinion, both on the handwriting and the content of the letters, suggested it was a man writing them.

Diana Rigg went to the police when her correspondent started to include obscene references to her teenage daughter Rachel in the letters. Until then she had regarded the letters, all full of graphic sexual references and sometimes including packages with offensive contents, as the downside of her fame and fortune, something that she had to accept as part of her working life – she did not regard 'Hugh' as dangerous. But she sought help when Rachel was threatened. Similarly Dinah Sheridan had reported her letters to the police because they, too, always contained references to her daughter, Jenny Hanley.

All the actresses 'Hugh' targets get a flurry of letters whenever they are appearing on stage. The letters arrive addressed to the theatre, which suggests that 'Hugh' may well be doing his research from *Stage*, the newspaper for the acting profession, which regularly publishes details of who is appearing where.

'He is only in evidence when my name appears on theatre marquees,' says Dinah Sheridan. 'The letters started when I was working in the West End, at the Haymarket Theatre. They were obscene, disgusting, and they always implicated my daughter Jenny. After receiving a few I asked the company manager to tell the police. I was interviewed, and the police pointed out the characteristic way in which he always printed my name, with the word 'actress' after the name, which appeared on both sides of the envelope. The postmark was always Manchester. I was told that if I recognized one of these letters, I was not to open it because there might be fingerprints inside. I gave them to the police for the run of the play. Since then I have received them only when he was apparently able to locate me, because I was appearing on stage.

'On the one occasion after talking to the police that I did, without realizing, open one, it was a padded envelope containing a small phial – I did not investigate the contents, but passed it on to the company manager for the police. When I am not appearing at a theatre I do not hear from him.'

One clue to the stalker's identity is his preference for women of a certain age.

'He obviously has a thing about middle-aged actresses,' said Diana Rigg. 'We are all of the same generation, give or take a few years. Clearly he is very sick. I don't think he is dangerous, but anyone who has regularly been receiving these will tell you he should be stopped.'

Nyree Dawn Porter likened receiving one of the

John Lennon (*top*) and the two faces of the man who killed him, Mark David Chapman, as a schoolboy and shortly after his arrest in December 1980.

John Warnock Hinckley (*right*), whose failed assassination attempt on President Reagan in 1981 was designed to win the affections of the actress Jodie Foster (*below*).

Left: Rebecca Schaeffer, the 21-year-old American TV actress gunned down by Robert Bardo, a 'devoted fan'.

Below: Robert Bardo, left, on trial for the murder of Rebecca Schaeffer in July 1989.

Theresa Saldana (*below*), the American actress who still bears the scars of the frenzied knife attack by Arthur Jackson (*right*) and who lives in fear of his release from prison.

Tina Marie Ledbetter (*right*)
wrote some 5,000 letters to
film star Michael J. Fox (*above*),
ordering him to go back to a
former girlfriend and
threatening to kill both him
and his wife if he did not.

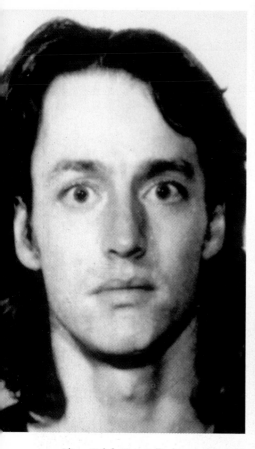

Above: Ralph Nau stalked several female celebrities with a dogged determination, plaguing them with phone calls and death threats. He was finally committed to a secure psychiatric hospital after murdering his 8-year-old stepbrother.

Right: Olivia Newton-John (*top*), Cher (*centre*) and Sheena Easton (*below*) have all suffered the unwanted attentions of obsessional fans, including those of Ralph Nau.

Clint Eastwood's 17-year-old daughter Alison was stalked by a British fan, who even went as far as pitching his tent outside her school gates.

Helena Bonham-Carter (*above*) was pestered for six years by Andrew Farquharson (*right*), and eventually obtained a court injunction against him.

letters to being 'mentally raped': 'You feel because you're a woman and inclined to receive guilt easily that maybe it's something you are doing that has provoked it. But when they keep coming at you, you realize it's nothing to do with you at all.'

She took the opportunity when appearing on ITV's daytime *The Time – The Place* programme to speak directly to the anonymous letter writer. 'I'd like you to know that I haven't read one of your poems since 1986, but lots of policemen at Rochester Row police station have,' said the actress, who has been a target for the letters since 1982.

Most stalkers are not as successful as 'Hugh' (or 'Janet' as he still calls himself to Nyree Dawn Porter and Dinah Sheridan) at keeping their identity secret – they don't want to remain anonymous. Their delusions bind them intimately with their chosen victim, either in love or in hatred, and they see it as a two-way traffic. They believe the celebrity is interacting with them, often imagining signals being sent to them in the most bizarre and delusional ways: the way a newsreader smiles at the end of a bulletin, the time that the lights go out in his or her bedroom, whenever a certain song is sung. They don't want to be anonymous. Most of them do not believe that their behaviour is threatening.

Although the 20-year-old man from Leicester who stalked actress and singer Debbie Gibson did not put his name on the obscene and threatening messages he sent to the *Grease* star, he left enough clues for police to be able to track him down easily. He had been writing to her at her American offices for some time, and when in 1993 she flew into Britain to co-star with Craig McLachlan in *Grease* at the Dominion Theatre, he began to write to her there. But he needed to advertise his obsession: he also sent a package of pictures and a six-line letter threatening to kill Debbie to the *Sun* newspaper. The pictures were similar to ones he had posted to the star herself, with her head superimposed on pornographic magazine material. Police inquiries showed that the same writer had been in touch with Debbie's British fan club – and had provided the club with his name and address. He was traced and arrested. For Debbie Gibson it was a frightening echo of a more serious incident in America, when a crazed fan had turned up outside her home with a loaded gun. He was given a six-year jail sentence.

The man who stalked *Darling Buds of May* star Catherine Zeta Jones, although far less of a threat to the actress, also felt a compulsion to advertise his attentions, but he did it rather more subtly. When a letter was published anonymously in an agony aunt's column the actress felt sure it was her stalker who was writing about his attempts to get to know her: 'I was able to find out where her family live and have driven past their house. I have sent flowers to her and had flowers delivered but have had no reply. All I ask is for a chance to meet her. How can I make her take notice?'

The actress knew that a man had turned up on the doorstep of her parents' home in South Wales, carrying flowers and declaring his love for her. Her father had given him short shrift, but Catherine, whose new found stardom had attracted a massive wave of media interest, was very concerned.

'It is very worrying when you get a man, a complete stranger, knocking on the door of your family home to tell you he loves you. It's not a normal way to behave and it makes me shiver to think what was going through his mind. It's chilling to know he's still out there.'

The Frenchwoman who followed Phil Collins for two years actually believed he was trying to kill her; unfortunately for the star, that belief did not encourage her to stay as far away from him as possible. She turned up on his doorstep on a regular basis, pressing the doorbell at all hours. She had seen him play at Nîmes and her relationship with him started with a few predictable fan letters. These became more intense as she was swept along by her delusions about him. She believed that every song he had written with a letter 'a' in the title were written for her, because that was her initial.

'She's a psychiatric nurse by profession, which is a bit scary, isn't it?' Collins said. 'Ten o'clock at night she'll ring the doorbell and when we get to the door it's like "Oh Christ, it's her again." I say: "Will you please go away?" One time I ended up pushing her and she fell over. I think she understood at that point that I was really fed up with it. I had to restrain myself.'

Collins's instinctive way of handling his stalker would not meet with the approval of the American experts. They would argue that he is applying rationality to an irrational person. He thinks that by pushing her he got through the message that he is fed up; it is more likely that she misinterpreted his action completely, turning it in her mind into evidence that he really is trying to kill her, or even that it was a loving gesture. Gavin de Becker would be horrified at the thought of a star of Collins's standing opening the door personally to deranged fans.

It is predictable that rock stars like Collins will attract stalkers. Sting, George Harrison, Rod Stewart – they have all had more than their share of strange fan mail. Stewart actually had to fight off a female stalker who had been threatening to kill him. The attack happened in his Los Angeles home when the 5-foot 2-inch blonde managed to penetrate the security round his home in 1989, after following him for three years. She had been standing outside the gates and had seized a fortuitous opportunity to get up the drive and through the open front door of the mansion. Luckily she was not armed. Stewart had been sunbathing by his pool when she got in, and had just retreated to the cool of his sitting room. Suddenly the door swung open and in came the woman whose letters and phone calls had put all his security staff on alert. She had been sending messages combining a love for the star with a desire to kill him, the combination that is potentially the most dangerous frame of mind for a stalker.

The woman flung herself at Stewart shouting that she loved him and clawing at him with her fingernails. The singer managed to throw her off and run, and his staff restrained her until the police came.

'Rod was very lucky,' said one of his employees later. 'The girl had come to the house scores of times. She had made verbal and written threats to kill him. Once she brought her own bodyguard, the man she said was going to "take care of business for me". She began to show all the signs of the obsessed fan who stalks her prey until she gets him. Rod could have been dead there and then. It certainly scared him.'

Stewart himself admitted to being 'petrified'. He said, 'I'm making bloody sure it doesn't happen again.' When he married model Rachael Hunter he ensured that their £13 million LA home had the most advanced state-of-the-art security, as well as making sure his British home was well protected.

Ex-Beatle George Harrison has learnt to live with fear since John Lennon was shot, and has spent a fortune protecting his homes in Oxfordshire, Hawaii, France and Australia.

'The death of John brought out a lot of crazies,' he said, ' but you have to take care in case there is the odd one – like Chapman – who will act upon his madness.'

Police were so concerned by one threat that targeted Harrison soon after Lennon's death, they provided him with a seventeen-man escort. In recent months his main threat has come from an American who has threatened to burn down his home. The threats have been received in phone calls; the man has, with persistence that is characteristic of so many stalkers, tracked down the star's ex-directory phone numbers at his homes and offices around the world, and left a succession of chilling predictions. He has also made contact with hotels where Harrison has been booked in anonymously, and with offices he has visited for business meetings. Now Harrison has installed video cameras and 24-hour security patrols at his British home.

One obsessed British girl drove Sting to call in the

police, after she persistently bombarded his home and his office with phone calls. Although compared to some stalkers her behaviour was mild and she was never threatening or obscene, she, too, had managed to get hold of a series of unlisted phone numbers. The girl, Elizabeth Griffin from Exeter, had even changed her name to Roxanne Sumner – Roxanne for one of Sting's songs, Sumner because that is the star's real surname. The police confiscated a diary listing the star's numbers and warned her about her behaviour.

Actor Martin Shaw's stalker knew a lot more about him than just his telephone numbers. She knew his bank balance, when his TV licence was due and a whole chronicle of far more intimate details, because for a whole year she had all his mail delivered to her home. She opened it, read it, resealed it and then hand-delivered it to the former *Professionals* star – and all achieved by simply signing a re-direction form at the Post Office, the standard procedure anybody uses when changing address.

'I never knew the woman,' said Shaw, 'but all of my mail for a year was delivered to her first.'

The most common delusion suffered by stalkers is that they are having an affair with the star of their choice. Actor Dennis Waterman was pursued in his *Minder* heyday by a 20-year-old girl who followed him all over the country, making public scenes because he did not acknowledge her. Both Waterman and his wife Rula Lenska felt a great deal of sympathy for the girl, but her attentions eventually became more than they could handle. After she threatened to kill herself they called in the police, more for her own protection than theirs.

Much more threatening were the letters received by Patsy Kensit and her rock star husband Jim Kerr, so much so that Patsy felt sufficiently frightened to go into hiding shortly after the birth of her baby son James in 1992. Jim Kerr had been pursued for three years by an American woman who claimed to be his lover. She had even changed her surname to his. When the baby was born her letters changed in tone: she began threatening to knife Patsy to death. 'The sword of truth', she wrote, was going to 'annihilate' the actress. One letter was even delivered to the hospital where the star gave birth.

Television presenters and newsreaders seem to form another natural category of attraction for stalkers, probably because of the regularity of their appearance, making them almost as likely candidates for obsessional fans as soap stars. Selina Scott, Zeinab Badawi, Carol Barnes, Kirsty Wark, Sarah Hogg, Michaela Strachan: they've all starred in the sad fantasies of pests who have been unable to control their own behaviour. GMTV's Amanda Redington had a more frightening encounter than most when she was pursued around Europe by a Dutch fan. At the time she was living in Holland and presenting a European pop programme.

'For five years he pursued me. At first it was obscene letters and items of clothing. One night when I was doing a show in Oslo he discovered where I was staying and came to my hotel to find me. When he saw me come in and go to the lift he actually leapt out on top of me and pushed into the lift with me. The lift gates were closing, leaving me inside alone with him.'

She knew from his letters that he had violent fantasies. Luckily she managed to hit the 'open' button on the lift control panel. 'The staff pulled him off me . . . It still makes me shudder.'

Children's TV favourite Michaela Strachan received 2,500 letters from her stalker, who was eventually prosecuted under criminal law because his letters contained overt threats to kill her, and he was detained for psychiatric tests. Michaela was fortunate that the law was able to help her. Ben Elton was forced to use civil law to get an injunction against the woman who made his life a misery, and even had to go back to the High Court when the stalker transferred her attentions to his mother.

Janette Tough, the tiny half of the Krankies comedy duo, was stalked for over three years by another woman who became obsessed with her. Janette, who on stage dresses and behaves like a naughty schoolboy, was followed around Britain by the woman from Derby, who hitch-hiked between theatres where the Krankies were appearing. The stalker, who is also tiny, suffers from the same glandular disease which stopped Janette from growing to normal height, and obviously identified with a star who had not allowed her size to hamper her career.

'She started writing for advice but then declared her love,' said Janette. 'She quickly became twisted and confused, wanting to live with me one moment and kill me the next.'

The stalker tracked down the address of Janette's husband's parents. Scared, Janette and Ian contacted the police and the social services department for the Derby area where the stalker was living with her parents. They were told there was nothing that could be done.

'We even spoke to her parents. They seem nice but they don't seem able to control her,' said Janette.

Actress Julia Sawalha, who plays Jennifer Saunders's daughter in *Absolutely Fabulous*, did not bother to contact the police when she received a letter telling her that she was top of a list of 666 women that the writer intended to kill. The letter, which was sent to her parents' address, said she would die painlessly, with chloroform.

'I suppose I should have gone to the police, but my uncle is in the force and he said I should wait and see if I get another letter ... It shook me up a bit just to think that there is this kind of weirdo out there. But you have to put it to the back of your mind. If you started worrying about that sort of thing then it would drive you mad. He obviously needs treatment but there is nothing I can do so I try not to think about it.'

Kate O'Mara did go to the authorities when a prisoner who was writing to her suddenly announced that he was about to be freed. The glamorous fifty-something actress had received a stream of letters from the man, sometimes bombarding her with proposals of marriage and sometimes assuming that she had already agreed to wed him. When he announced that he was going to be released the following week, and that all the arrangements had been made for the wedding ceremony, she got in touch with the prison authorities – and to her relief was told that he still had many years of his sentence to run.

The area of entertainment that most attracts

stalkers is, inevitably, the soap opera. Because the characters portrayed are meant to be ordinary, accessible people, legions of fans identify with them. Viewing figures peak and trough according to the degree of this involvement, so the writers, producers and actors are all striving for the very ingredient that triggers so many cases of stalking: a confusion of identity between the fan and the celebrity. Soaps also bring with them a sheer volume of exposure for the main characters that guarantees they will pick up a substantial number of obsessed fans.

British soap stars are therefore in the vanguard when it comes to dealing with fans of all descriptions, and particularly potentially dangerous ones. They know the golden American rule: the less you say about it, the less chance there is of sparking others into it. Yet at the same time, it is their front-line experience which could provide invaluable help to other celebrities, to those working to understand the minds of stalkers and to those trying to frame or enforce laws limiting their unacceptable behaviour.

One soap star who agreed to be interviewed for this book with a guarantee of anonymity sums up the feelings of many victims when she says that it is 'the constant insecurity' that is the most debilitating fear.

'He's out there somewhere. I don't know where, I don't know anything about him. I don't know if he's a weedy little man who sits at home watching the telly all day and having lonely fantasies, or whether he's a real sicko parked round the corner with a knife in his pocket. The only thing I know is he's out there somewhere.

'And I also know he is tuned in to my soap

religiously, because he writes in detail about the characters. He seems in some ways to be able to distinguish between me and my role, but in other ways he confuses the two of us completely. I get between three and eight letters a week, and they've been coming for over two years. They started out reasonably politely, although they were definitely love letters. Then, as time went on, they got more and more sexually explicit. Something happened to my character in the series, she was involved in a sexual situation, and that seemed to open the floodgates for him. From then on, I was fair game: he could write any kind of filth and stick it in the post to me.

'I don't read them now. At the beginning I did, but as soon as I realized they were coming too frequently the office started to deal with them. The police have been informed, but we do not know his identity. The postmarks are from all over the north-east, and sometimes from other areas. That's frightening: it shows that he moves around the country.

'The worst fear of all is the uncertainty. I think if I knew who he was, had a picture of him in my mind, I could cope better, even though it would not make him less sick. It is the constant thought that he might be out there. When I go to public events and I'm signing autographs and shaking hands, I glance around and wonder if one of them is him.

'I wonder if he has a wife and family? I've decided that he can't have, because they'd surely be suspicious. Does he have a job? He always puts first-class stamps on the letters, as if it matters how fast that rubbish gets here.

'I've occasionally had flowers delivered to the

studio without any message. They're probably from genuine fans. But I always ask one of the staff to see that they go to a hospital – I don't want them, because they may be from him.

'It would be way off beam to say that I think about him all the time. But there's never a day goes by when I don't, even for a few seconds, think about him. What right has he, or anybody, to worm their way into my life like this? Yet how can he be stopped?

'I don't think it's because I'm in a soap. I think that is what has focused him on me, but if it hadn't been me it would have been someone else. The man is ill, and he'd have found someone to be obsessional about, whatever. In my most charitable moments I almost feel sorry for him, although if you saw the perverted dross he writes, you wouldn't. But I also feel, occasionally, that it is probably better that he is writing this stuff to me, because if he wasn't he might be doing horrible things to women he met. At least he's getting something out of his system.

'Most of the time I just wish he'd go to hell.'

At Granada television studios in Manchester, where *Coronation Street* is produced, security men keep a close look out for faces which appear just too often among the knots of fans who gather, or appear just too keen. When 'Street' star Amanda Barrie, who plays Alma Baldwin, was involved in a storyline about a telephone stalker, a real-life pest began to show up regularly at the studio entrances and had to be warned off by the police.

Despite all these cases, the British experience is still, thankfully, light years behind the American one. One regular soap actress in the States, Andrea Evans, took a long hard look at the title of the show she had been appearing in for ten years – *One Life to Live* – and decided to act on it. She realized that she did only have one life to live and that she was simply no longer willing to cope with the exhausting strain put on her by the constant problem of stalkers. 'I was fainting at work. I couldn't eat, I couldn't sleep,' she said. She quit the soap.

'YOUR NUMBER ONE FAN'

IN THE 1960s Andy Warhol famously remarked
that 'in the future everyone will be famous for fifteen
minutes'. He later got bored with hearing the same
line quoted back at him and amended it to 'in fifteen
minutes everybody will be famous', a more compli-
cated view of modern society. His original thesis is
the one that has gone into the books of quotations,
because it is an idea whose time has, more or less,
come. We live in a celebrity culture, dominated by a
voracious media which has the technology to pump
entertainment and information into our homes
twenty-four hours a day. To compete – and television,
radio, newspaper, magazine, book and film industries
are relentlessly competitive – they need to instantly
grab the attention of the consumer. There can be no
slow burn to kindle the imagination; the goods on
offer have to shriek their novelty value. And one thing
that the media bosses know and understand is that
people like people. They can deal with facts, abstrac-
tions, philosophies, they can even be fascinated and
intrigued by them. But what they like, really enjoy,
is hearing about people. The gossip over the garden

fence has gone global. As local communities have broken down and populations become more mobile, families more isolated, the media has stepped in to fill the void left because so many people no longer know the neighbours on the other side of the real garden fence.

So all popular media coverage is personality-led. Politicians, generals, clerics: no one can expect to be judged purely on his or her work or aspirations, they must know that every aspect of their personality and lifestyle is up for grabs when they reach the public eye. And popular is not a synonym for lowbrow. The 'heavy' British broadsheet newspapers compete with each other for the number of by-lined personality columns that they run; they create their own celebrities, all vying to tell us interesting and not-so-interesting facts about life *chez eux*.

Not quite everybody has achieved their fifteen minutes of fame, but a far greater proportion of the population than might have expected it when Warhol first made his remark thirty years ago. Anyone who can flip a pancake over can line up to be a television cook – provided the smile is right, the presentation quirkily off-beat, who cares about the culinary skills? Any Church worthy who can work a good joke into his sermon can expect a slot on TV or radio. Any sports star who can run faster, score more goals, or even fail with a shrug or a tear which catches the popular imagination can be guaranteed large sponsorship deals and a trail of cameramen behind him or her.

Celebrities are no longer just the actors and actresses or pop singers who set out to be stars. Fame can be the by-product of any walk of life: we have computer whizzkids, political pundits, clothes designers, 'super' models, financial wizards, media medics, authors who tour the chat shows to promote books. They are all introduced to us by name and we are invited to know more about their lives. They have the same pseudo-intimacy with the public as film and TV stars, and as a result they, too, attract the unwanted attentions of obsessive fans. You don't have to be a movie star to have a celebrity stalker.

Dr David Nias says: 'There was a time when celebrities were remote, glamorous figures. Teenage crushes were rites of passage based on mystery, fantasy and ignorance. Now celebrities are happy to be our friends. They invite magazines like *Hello!* into their homes and spill out their intimate thoughts to the tabloids. But in an alienating society, where normal relationships are difficult to form, it is easy to understand how affection is transferred to these accessible stars. So for many, a glimpse inside the kitchen can quickly be transformed to a hopeful step towards the star's bedroom. There is now a very thin, blurred line between public and private life, fact and fantasy – reality and virtual reality.'

It was like the stark climax to a Stephen King horror novel. The setting was a small, quiet town on America's east coast. It was the middle of the night. The wife, alone in the large Victorian house because her husband and son had gone away to watch a baseball game, heard the sound of breaking glass downstairs. When she went down to the kitchen she confronted a skinny, bearded man with wild eyes, who she later described as a 'Charles Manson looka-like'. He was brandishing a box, which he told her was a home-made bomb.

Barefoot and wearing only a nightgown, she escaped and fled to a neighbour's to call the police. The intruder roamed through the house, eventually finding his way into one of the Gothic turrets above the third-floor attic. When he was finally brought out by the police, the 'bomb' turned out to be a collection of springs, pencil stubs, erasers and batteries which were not connected to anything.

For the world's most famous author of horror stories, what happened in his own home that night in 1991 was 'the price of writing books that are near the edge'. The intruder who was dragged out of Stephen King's attic was a man called Eric Keene, who told the police a wild story about wanting revenge on the author because, he claimed, King had stolen the plot of his book *Misery* from Keene's aunt in Texas. *Misery* is the story of a novelist held pris-oner by a psychotic fan who has been following him and who is on the scene to rescue him when he has a serious car crash in appalling weather conditions. She takes him back to her isolated home and her initial devotion to him is gradually eroded by the twisted and unreal relationship she has with the characters from his books. Unable to escape because his legs are broken, the novelist is ultimately subject to appalling mental and physical cruelty. As with all King books, the strength of the story is in the writing: he is able to create settings and characters so power-fully that he achieves the essential 'willing suspension of disbelief'. King novels are set in ordinary towns with a cast of recognizably ordinary people, to whom the most horrific things eventually happen. But the build-up is slow, the tension mounts imperceptibly, credibility is only seen to be stretched in retrospect. He has a massive and avid following, and in *Misery* he was on top form, writing about two worlds he knows well: small town America and the precarious relationship between an author and his fans.

So it is, perhaps, unsurprising that it was *Misery* that triggered this close and frightening encounter with a deranged fan. Keene, while claiming that his motive was to right the wrong of the imagined plot theft, also professed to be a great Stephen King enthusiast, to have read everything King had ever written and to be his 'number one fan', a sobriquet familiar to any celebrity who receives fan mail. It was as 'your number one fan' that Tina Marie Ledbetter signed her obsessive stream of hate mail to Michael J. Fox. King himself gave the words a chilling resonance in *Misery* and the film of the novel, which stars Kathy Bates, ends eerily with yet another woman admirer introducing herself to the novelist by that description.

'Keene expressed great love for my books and wanted me to pay back for this imagined theft of a plot from his aunt by writing the story of his life, basically to explain to people why everything was wrong with him and somehow make it right,' says King, who has three other persistent stalkers.

'Having the house broken into was the most extreme and frightening example of what's happened to us, but the feelings that Keene expressed seem to be common. On the one hand these people love what you do and on the other hand they feel that it some-how renders them invalid. They love and hate you at the same time, which is what *Misery* is about.'

He believes that the type of book he writes is in some way responsible for the type of fans he attracts – although, interestingly, the fictional novelist in *Misery* was writing romantic books, the antithesis to Stephen King's own output. It made the story more powerful: the deranged fan with the dark and sinister psyche was devoted to the pure, virginal heroine of the bodice-ripping romantic fiction she devoured. Instinc-tively, King may have hit on a truth. The fact that Olivia Newton-John scores so highly on the stalking scale shows that opposites are at least as likely to attract as those with a more obvious appeal to the dark side of the soul. Rationally, though, he accepts that 'The kind of books I write have more of a tend-ency to attract the nutters.'

He says, 'I'm sure that rock and roll attracts more nutters than chamber music, and even within rock and roll there are levels. Ozzy Osbourne, Ritchie Blackmore, Angus Young will gather more nutters than rockers like Rod Stewart, who would get more of the "I wanna go to bed with you" letters than they would.

'I've accepted that I have stalkers. I'm not philo-sophical about it, but I accept it in the same way that you accept a disability like a club foot. I have very bad eyesight and I might as well accept it. Do I like it? No, I don't, but as I can't change it I get on with it.

'I don't like living behind a fence. I go round and check the doors at night, sometimes I go round and check the doors twice at night. On the other hand, would I trade my life on the basis of a few cranks? No. Do I think I'm actually going to get killed? I think the odds are long. I do live in Bangor, a small town, so it's not as bad as it could be. What I don't like is if I'm out walking the dog and a car swerves to the kerb ahead of me, the thought goes through my mind, "That may be somebody who's got the idea that I'm a satanist or something, and I need to be killed."

'And I worry for my family. It isn't the ultimate case, the Mark Chapman who comes out of nowhere and kills somebody. You can't think about that. But we worry about kidnapping, and we worried a lot more when the children were younger. We worry about the effect celebrity has on their lives. There are a lot of people out there who are unbalanced, who may decide they want to take out on the son or daughter what they can't take out on the father.'

King, who has three children, has found his life so intertwined with that of one of his stalkers, a man who has never exhibited any violent or threatening behaviour towards King, that he conversationally refers to the man by his first name, and says that he almost regards him as a friend. 'In a way he's a friend. I'm a part of his life and he's a part of mine. Maybe one day we'll be free of each other, but I'm still keeping tabs on him. He's been in my life for a long time now, since not long after John Lennon was killed.'

The man, Steve Lightfoot, travels America in a camper van which he plasters with handwritten posters about his current obsession. He parked the van in Bangor, King's home town, for about six months in 1992, spending his days playing his guitar in the streets and haranguing passers-by about his theory that it was Stephen King, not Mark Chapman, who shot John Lennon. 'Photos prove it is Stephen King, not Mark David Chapman, getting John Lennon's autograph,' said the placards.

'He believes it was me, Richard Nixon and Ronald Reagan who headed the conspiracy to kill Lennon, and that we communicated with each other through key phrases in American news magazines,' says King, who hired a private detective to investigate Lightfoot.

'I wanted to know how dangerous he really was, whether or not he had firearms. The detective told me he is like a barking dog in someone's yard – if you express fear and worry about him he may bite, but he probably won't. The detective said that as I live in a small town, there was a good chance that one day I would come face to face with this guy. He advised me not to show fear. So one day I went to get a pair of pants tailored and he was there on the corner playing his protest songs on his guitar. I walked by and I said, "Hello, Steven." He gave me a look, but I sensed no recognition in his eyes. After I finished in the shop the guy who runs it said Steve was still there, and asked if I wanted to go out the back door. I actually thought about it and then I said, "No, I won't go out the back door. This is my town not his town."

'So I walked past him and as I did so I said, "Take care." That's all. Later that day he plastered the town with his "newsletter" saying I threatened him. He said I grabbed him around the neck and said, "Take very good care, Steven, because on some dark night

I may come and get you." That's a total psychotic distortion of what really happened.'

King's detective tracked Lightfoot when he left Bangor. 'We know he went from here to New York and spent some time playing his guitar outside the Dakota building where Lennon died. Then he went to England, to Liverpool, to visit Lennon's birthplace. After that he was seen outside the Los Angeles night-club where the actor River Phoenix died. He was claiming the CIA killed River Phoenix because of his opposition to meat-eating.'

The state of Maine, where King lives, is putting through an anti-stalking law. 'I'm one of the reasons why. There aren't enough legal ways to pin these people down here. But in a sense, it doesn't matter whether there is a law or not. Steve may on one level be completely out of touch with reality, but on another level he is street smart – no, he is more than that. He is celebrity smart. And so are a lot of these really dedicated stalkers. Steve went to Kennebunk-port, Maine, when Bush was president and was on holiday there. The guys who protect the president, the secret service, knew he was coming, because they certainly keep tabs on people like him. But he knew they knew and he played his own game. He knew where to park and where not to park, he knew what he could say and what he couldn't. They didn't bust him; he didn't break the law. In the same way, he knows there are certain things he cannot say or do or I will have a suit against him for harassment, and he stays within those bounds. So with guys like him, the law is almost irrelevant.'

Stephen King first hired his detective, a local retired

police officer, in 1990. He chose him because he was 'plugged into the local scene'.

'Tim, my detective, comes into my office and my house on a regular basis. My secretary Shirley flags any mail she thinks is peculiar and he looks at it. With Steve, because Tim is local, he was able to go up to the guy, get talking to him like he was interested in his rap, buy him a couple of beers, find out his story. I was able to find some things out about Steve from other people, because this is a small town. I coach Little League baseball with a guy who works in the post office, who was able to tell me that Steve was receiving quite large amounts of money which were mailed there. I was interested in how he was able to support himself because he was clearly quite well-heeled. It turned out his father was killed in a plane crash and there was a very large settlement from the airline company, a lot of which went to Steve.'

As well as Lightfoot, the detective keeps tabs on two women who write to the novelist regularly.

'He's identified these two women as potential problems. They're "repeaters" – security experts worry most about the ones who write a lot. And they worry most of all when "repeaters" stop writing: while the letters are coming, you know where they are and what they are doing. When the letters stop there's always a risk that they are putting their fantasy into reality.

'There's a lady from Princeton, New Jersey, who has made a couple of pilgrimages up here to stand outside my house. She claims I've stolen her ideas by telepathy. We have an eye kept on her because she's clearly odd in the head. And there's another lady in Pennsylvania who has written to me five thousand times in the last ten years. I get very full reports on her; I know about her menstrual problems, her boyfriend troubles, the most intimate stuff.'

King believes that stalking is a modern phenomenon, born of the cult of the celebrity, which he dates back to 1974 and the birth of the American magazine *People*.

'It was the first magazine entirely devoted to celebrities. It was no longer enough just to be a glamorous Hollywood starlet, you had to share every detail of your life with the readers. We've turned celebrities into royalty. Everybody becomes a celebrity; we have celebrity ice-cream makers, celebrity computer bosses, even celebrity children. And that's when you see the sexualization of young children, which brings with it a host of other problems. There are a lot more celebrities out there, and a lot more people curious about them. It also makes becoming a celebrity more desirable and, in a sort of way, more accessible. There's this feeling I have about Steve Lightfoot, that the whole Lennon thing is just a sidebar issue. There's something in him that says to you: I wanna be famous. You have what belongs to me. He thinks it is his right, his turn to be a celebrity, and that he is blocked by people like me who have fame and *are* celebrities.

'There's now a cannibal press here in the States — and certainly over there in Britain too — that feeds on celebrities. In fact, in that way the British press is further down the road than we are. But let's stand back and look at this: John Lennon gets gunned down, an actress gets killed, another gets slashed with a knife, a model gets acid thrown at her. Only four or five serious physical attacks have happened to all those thousands of celebrities. They get magnified by a press which devours anything to do with the famous, but if you calculate the risk of it happening to you, it is not that great.'

With their long, exposed limbs, their healthy outdoor complexions and the fabled wealth of their bank balances, girl sports stars are obvious fuel for the fantasies of armchair fans. Female tennis stars are particularly vulnerable: they compete as individuals (or never more than a doubles team), which means they get a lot of individual attention from the cameras; they usually have great legs; they are in a sport which gives them (almost) the same exposure as their male counterparts. Tennis is big on television and girls who are big in tennis will inevitably attract a lot of fans, some of them the obsessional sort.

When Guenther Parche stuck a knife into Monica Seles on the centre court at Hamburg in April 1993 he brought tennis stalking – an occupational hazard that had been known about for some years by the players and their entourages – into the open. Parche was doubly obsessed: he 'loved' Steffi Graf, a fellow German, and had fixed his 'hate' on Seles who was challenging Graf's position as the world's number one woman player. Parche, a lonely bachelor who lived in a small room at his aunt's home near Leipzig, which he had turned into a shrine for Graf, felt so badly when his idol lost two important matches to Seles that he later described it in court as his world beginning to crumble.

'There was an earthquake inside of me . . . something within me broke. I was deeply affected. I just did not want to live any longer. It was just unimaginable.'

He had first become obsessed with Graf in 1988, when he was working as a fitter in East Germany. Because he neither smoked nor drank and never went away on holidays, the small, balding fan, who was thirty-eight when he plunged the knife into Seles, was able to save enough money to dedicate his life to Graf. He sent her anonymous letters and cash gifts, and travelled to watch her play when she was in Germany. Above his bed he hung a life-size picture of her, which he rolled up and took with him on his mission to injure Seles because he could not bear to be parted from it. He kept a library of video recordings of all Graf's games, which he played over and over in his room. He had no social life and had never had a girlfriend. 'He sat in front of his TV day and night waiting for Steffi's matches,' his aunt said. 'He recorded them and played them over and over. She was his idol. He talked only about her wonderful figure.'

In court, Parche himself said Steffi was 'a dream-like creation with eyes that glisten like diamonds and hair like silk . . . She has the gift of God and never again will someone be created like her.'

When he saw Monica Seles beating Graf, Parche felt helpless and distraught, and devised his appalling plan to help her. He took a turquoise-handled kitchen knife with a three-and-a-half-inch blade from his aunt's drawer with him to the tournament at Hamburg and managed to get through the security round the court and attack Seles as she sat at the net between games.

He planned, he told the court, to injure and not to kill 19-year-old Seles, and for that reason 'did not use all my strength'. He wanted to stab her in the arm, but because of the angle at which she was sitting he struck her shoulder.

'It all happened so quickly, I don't remember anything,' he said.

For Seles there was a similar brief moment of unreality. 'I didn't realize what had happened. I couldn't breathe. The pain came when someone pressed their hand on my back. It was like a fog, somehow unreal, and I thought maybe I would be dead. I was lucky because I bent down a little to reach my towel when the knife hit me.'

To the horror of the Seles camp, Parche was only given a two-year suspended sentence for the crime. It was not just tennis fans who were outraged: Parche had to be held in custody after the court case to save him from the angry mob that gathered outside when news of his sentence was announced. The court had accepted that what Parche needed was psychiatric help, and that sending him to prison would not solve his – or any stalker's – problem. But although it may have been the right sentence for the offender, it fell far short of offering the consolation of retribution to the victim. Seles, after all, was a very young girl who had suffered an awful physical outrage as well as an assault on her fundamental sense of security. She described the verdict as 'sick' and said she was 'shocked and horrified' by it.

'He gets to go back to his life, but I can't because I am still recovering from this attack. I have been punished more than this man.

'Every night in my dreams I see knives. These fears come back again and again. I don't think I will ever get over this, it will never come to an end. I have woken at nights bathed in sweat, unable to sleep again. My mother has sat on my bed for hours holding my hand, trying to calm me.'

Long after the knife wound had healed, the girl who had seemed to have everything – good looks, great talent, massive earning potential – could still not get to grips with what had happened to her. She was so unstrung, not just by the physical attack but by the deranged reasoning behind it, that she could not get herself back on to the professional tennis circuit.

Behind tight security at her Florida home, she spent months disconsolately practising for a few hours a day, unnerved not just by the risk of another attack but by a disintegration in her confidence. In a sport that requires single-minded dedication, a year after her attack Seles was wondering whether she would ever again be able to summon that will to win.

'Before I was stabbed I always lived for tomorrow – my next match, my next tournament. But if I've learned one thing from all that's happened to me, it's that if you would know what tomorrow brings you may not want to live it,' she said, a world-weary, jaundiced view of life from a 20-year-old. 'It is bound to come back to my mind when I step out on a tennis court. The guy who attacked me got what he wanted [Graf's return to the number-one spot] and he was let out free. No matter how you look at it, the message sent out is that what he did to me was OK. Anybody in my situation could have a big problem with that.

'When you go home after enduring something like what happened to me, the single, absolute thing you have to be is clear with yourself. I want to give something back to the game, so the players coming up can feel safer on court – or know that they have a pension plan. There is still a lot I want to accomplish ... I don't just want to be the one who got stabbed.'

Her wish to make things safer for the other girl players was instantly achieved. Security at every subsequent tournament on the circuit has been reappraised and increased, in most cases more than doubled. But the nerve-jangling effect of a stalker actually getting on court and stabbing the world's top player, coupled with the high profile presence of police and private security men ever since, has made life on the women's circuit even less attractive than it previously was. (Apart from the lure of fame and big earnings, there is little to recommend the life of a professional tennis player, especially a woman. The men often have wives and families who travel with them but few of the female players are able to carry normal life around in their suitcases.)

Parche's attack on Seles flushed more tennis stalkers out into the open. The Pavlovian reaction of the media turned the spotlight on the other obsessed fans who travelled the circuit in pursuit of their particular favourites. Theo Dunkelberg spent two years trailing Anke Huber, the German number-two player, having latched on to her when she was only a 16-year-old. He tracked her down to hotels, even managing to find out her room number and get up to her door. He tried to get into lifts with her. He sent flowers, letters and gifts of blue satin underwear. Although

Dunkelberg has never threatened violence, the young tennis star is afraid of him.

'I really fear what he will do to me – I am scared he will do something terrible . . . It is a terrible situation. Every time I play I see his eyes on me. I am not to blame. In Hamburg, he was in the hotel. He was once on the same floor and he was going to the elevator with me to speak to me,' said the player. 'I am very scared by him but what can I do? I have done nothing to encourage him. He is at every tournament. I have tried to be friendly and said he should leave me alone, but he doesn't listen. He walks behind me all the time. I don't know what I can do.'

Not only did she not know what she could do, but neither did the police. Dunkelberg was held and questioned during Wimbledon 1993, but he had broken no laws and could not be charged. After his release he said: 'I am no nutter. I am a real fan.'

If Huber needed advice on how to deal with Dunkelberg's presence, she could at least turn to her fellow countrywoman Steffi Graf, the object of Parche's obsession. Graf has experience of stalkers, and not just Parche: there is something about the German number one that has made her the target of more loony fans than any other woman on the circuit. One of them actually got into the grounds of her home in April 1989 and found her practising on the tennis courts. In front of her he slashed his wrists because he had read that she had a boyfriend. Another, Kurt Zum Felde, pestered her for over seven years, and is well-known to the police in Frankfurt, where he lives within a few miles of Graf's home in nearby Bruehl. He has been arrested in her garden, having somehow cleared a high security fence; he has been arrested after spending five nights sleeping in his car outside her gates; he has sent her letters – one as long as twenty-seven pages – and presents. At the same time, his adoration of her can swing into hatred. He was ejected from Wimbledon in 1993 for shouting 'You are responsible for everything!' from the front row of the Centre Court. His taunt was presumed to be a reference to the attack on Seles; a few weeks earlier, at the French Open in Paris, he has shouted 'You are guilty for Monica Seles!' The 6-foot 2-inch tall science graduate, twenty-nine years old at the time, also shouted during the Wimbledon match, 'You cheat, you are not even injured, you bitch!'

He was referring to the fact that Graf had been suffering from a widely reported foot injury. Turning towards him Graf said, 'Oh God, it is him again.' She broke between points to speak to the umpire, asking him to shut the man up. After the match, Zum Felde was removed from the tournament by police. He told them he was in love with Graf and that his volley of abuse was intended to stop her playing so that she would not damage her foot. But despite this protestation of devotion, the next moment he said he was annoyed with her for taking advantage of Seles's lay-off.

'I like tennis but I am not a fan of Steffi's,' he said. 'I was shouting at her because I thought she was making up her injury. She is just a liar – a complete liar and a cheat. It's rubbish for her to say she has a bad foot. If she's so badly hurt how can she win her games so easily?'

He said that he was obeying 'voices' in his head

which told him to yell at Graf. Police were unable to hold him – he had broken no laws – but he was banned from Wimbledon for the rest of the tournament. Ever since the Seles stabbing, Graf has been an even greater target than before for mad fans.

Chris Evert, once the women's tennis world number one and now an established commentator on the game, was also the victim of a stalker. In 1990 a judge in Florida ordered a man who had been bombarding her with sexually explicit letters to stay away from her Florida home. The star had received a telephone death threat and her home had been broken into. She later revealed that, chillingly, a stalker had once succeeded in entering her home and living undetected in a wardrobe for three days.

Tennis stars may be prime targets, but girl skaters are also manna to nourish the obsessions of deranged fans. Like the tennis girls, they compete individually and therefore attention, from the television audience and the crowd at the rink, is focused exclusively on them. Like the tennis girls, they wear short, revealing skirts and, in the case of the skating queens, the yards of leg on show are coupled with a deliberately glamorous presentation. Katarina Witt, the German star, was forced to initiate legal action against Harry Veltman, an American (although he claimed German ancestry) who bombarded her with sexually explicit letters and nude photographs of himself. The letters were enough to strike terror into any soul: 'Don't be afraid when God allows me to pull you out of your body to hold you tight. Then you will know there is life beyond the flesh,' he wrote in one, which opened with the terrifying words:'I'm coming to get you.'

In 1992 in his home state of California, Veltman was sentenced to thirty-seven months in a psychiatric unit and three years' probation for harassing the star. He had followed her whenever she was in the USA, and had sent sixty-eight letters to her address in Germany. He had even thrown sexually threatening notes on to the ice while she was performing. The judge who dealt with Veltman described him as having grandiose delusions and being out of touch with reality.

Women sports stars are not the only ones who attract stalkers: male stars are just as likely to have obsessional fans. Racing driver Alain Prost has been pursued around Europe by a blonde who is determined to get close to him. Sex symbol soccer stars all have their coterie of 'inappropriate' letter-writing fans. Snooker players have found big billing and big money as sports personalities since media interest in their game took off, but the downside for them is that they, too, have become obvious fan fodder. For most of them it means a handful of groupies struggling to get closer to them and a stack of innocent mail; for Stephen Hendry it means something much more unnerving. He is the subject of Gillian Vincent's fantasies (see p. 308). He drew the short straw – out of the legions of girl snooker fans, he attracted the one who, although her behaviour was never threatening in any way, certainly allowed her devotion to cross the bounds of acceptable behaviour.

Inevitably the Royal Family have their own stable of strange followers. One of the first recorded cases of erotomania in Britain was a woman who, in the

1930s, thought King George VI was in love with her, and was able to pick up messages confirming this by watching for curtains to be closed at Buckingham Palace in the evenings. The modern royals, with so much greater media exposure and so much less mystery attached to their private lives, are as vulnerable as any show business stars. Prince Andrew, the Duke of York, gets regular letters from a woman who cannot understand why he does not return her affection: what is more worrying about her than the many others who write regularly to all members of his family is that she shows a detailed knowledge of his movements, plus her letters have assumed a very threatening tone. The one big advantage the royals have over other celebrities is that they have a professional and experienced protection service provided by the police. But as one member of the Royal Protection Squad commented, 'The nutcases are more worrying than the terrorists, because they are so unpredictable. You can't anticipate where one is going to turn up, nor can you know which of them are dangerous – at least you know that all terrorists are dangerous.'

For secretary Louise Hobkinson it really was a question of being victim to her own fifteen minutes of fame. An ex-model, 25-year-old Louise made headlines when she joined the staff of MP Bill Cash as his personal assistant. The tall, leggy blonde became the focus for newspaper features along the lines of 'Would you trust your man with this secretary?', as all the sexy poses she had ever struck as a teenage model were dug out of the darkrooms and splashed across the tabloids. Louise was showered with fan letters, flowers were delivered to her and there were quite a few requests for signed photographs.

Among the letters were some very disturbing ones. Dale Morris, a 27-year-old prisoner serving a two-and-half-year prison sentence for burglary, had latched on to Louise. He was writing to her three or four times every week, sexually explicit letters with an underlying theme of violence that gradually escalated. Over the four months he wrote to her she was translated in his fantasies from being an unattainable idol into someone he believed he was closely involved with. He accused Louise of being unfaithful to him, and when he read that she had a boyfriend the letters became threatening, to both Louise and her solicitor boyfriend. 'He wrote how he would make sure I had a loveless life. He threatened to kill all my boyfriends and said he was in communication with John Major and Bill Clinton. He was an agent, he said, licensed to kill,' Louise told the *Mail on Sunday*.

Whatever composure she was able to retain snapped when the police contacted her to tell her that Morris had escaped from prison. He remained at large for over a month, and during that time a series of obscene telephone calls was made to the office Louise shared with three others. Although the men on the staff volunteered to monitor her calls, eventually the disruption to office life was so great that Louise left what had been her dream job. Terrified at the prospect of her stalker being on the loose, she fled abroad until he was recaptured.

She described vividly her horror after first hearing he was out. After the news sank in she told herself determinedly to get a grip and calm down. To give herself a few moments to think she went to the toilet – 'Then someone came in. I got down on my hands and knees to peer through the gap at the bottom of the cubicle, just to check if the shoes were male or female. I was absolutely terrified.'

Out in the street, she said, any sound of footsteps behind her made her jump.

'He threatened to destroy my life,' she said, 'Well, he's made a pretty good start.'

PART TWO

You Will See
a Stranger

'I'VE HAD ONE OF THOSE CALLS'

THERE IS A SHADOWY figure at the garden gate, night after night. There is a strange voice on the end of the telephone, whispering obscenities. There is a car, always parked in the same spot, the driver's gaze focused in the same direction.

Stalking by a complete stranger is the most unpredictable and unnerving of all stalking. It is beyond any attempt at rationalization. The stalker who gets fixated on a celebrity at least has their public persona on which to build the flawed edifice of his affection; the stalker who vaguely knows his victim also has some impression, probably distorted but real to him, of the personality of his loved one. The ex-partner who stalks comes closest to being understood and comprehended by the rest of society.

But the stalker who selects a complete stranger as a victim? What motivates his behaviour? If he chooses her because he has seen her, fancies her and wants to get to know her, he is closer, in his psychological profile, to the celebrity stalker than to the other groups. He has projected his own fantasy on to a flesh and blood person, he ascribes to her all the characteristics he wants in an idealized partner. He pursues her, and when she rejects him or fails to live up to his ideals, he may become dangerous and threatening.

If, on the other hand, the victim is selected completely at random – a phone number found by trawling through the directory until a female voice answers – the motivation is different. The telephone stalker who never sees his prey wants power. He gets sexual thrills from knowing that he is terrorizing a victim, he gets a kick from the fear and confusion he can cause. He is like a rapist: he experiences sexual stimulation from subjugating and petrifying his victim.

The following pages look at both these kinds of stalker and at the stories of the women who have been their victims.

Beverley Ashworth is a celebrity, but she is not included in the celebrity-stalking section of this book because her stalker hit upon her purely by accident: to him, Beverley was nothing more than a female voice on the end of a telephone, an ear into which he could pour a succession of obscenities. Although her case does not rank alongside the more extreme examples of stalking, to her it was totally unacceptable. Fortunately Beverley, a presenter on Granada Television, is a strong and determined young woman, who made sure that her stalker was brought to justice. It took guts.

When she finally confronted him in court, the look on his face as he recognized her – Beverley is seen by millions in the North-west every night, as she introduces programmes like *Coronation Street* – confirmed that he had no idea who she was. It was a sweet victory for Beverley, one of very few women to see her telephone pest prosecuted and punished, but the inadequate punishment he received infuriated her and she has campaigned ever since for stiffer penalties.

Beverley's problems started in January 1991, when she was thirty-one years old. She was at home during the day talking with a friend when the phone rang, Beverley remembered. 'Whooo! It was fairly explicit. It was like the soundtrack from a blue movie. It shook me. I put the receiver down and said, "I've had one of those calls." I didn't know whether to laugh or cry. I was half-expecting to know the person on the other end of the line. I remember feeling that this could not really be happening, not in my own home. I wondered if it was a sick joke.'

When the phone rang again ten minutes later Beverley's friend answered it for her. It was the same caller, and the message was, if anything, worse.

'She was shocked and slammed the phone down,' says Beverley. 'They were both seriously obscene calls. A few days later it happened again. At first I was shocked, and then I began to seethe with indignation, exploding into rage. I was determined he would not terrorize me, so I contacted the police who in turn contacted British Telecom. Neither seemed initially very helpful. BT were unable to put a trace on my line because the exchange I was on was the wrong type – I felt that was a bit like British Rail complaining about the wrong kind of snow. Whatever their excuse, the result for me was the same.

'They asked me to log and try to tape the calls.

They suggested I could change my number, but I did not want to do that: why should I have the expense of changing? [It costs £28.50 but, if the level of malicious calls is high enough BT will do it free.] Why should I be fined for being a victim? When that thought went through my head I immediately checked it: I told myself that I am not a victim. That would give him a victory, if he made me feel like a victim. I determined to treat it as an inconvenience. Why should I have the inconvenience of letting everyone near to me know my new number? Why should I have the inconvenience of changing all my stationery and business cards? People need to reach me: I have a career, a life. I was not going to let some dirty-talking pest upset it, because that would be a victory for him.'

Although Beverley was determined not to be frightened by the calls, she was unsettled. 'I was very concerned because my number is ex-directory and I am a single woman, living at that time on my own. Who could it be? Everyone became a suspect. I listened to see if I could recognize the voice; it was soft and silky , well-spoken, educated. I did not know it. But at work I looked harder at my male colleagues, and at friends – I even wondered about people I passed in the street.

'Because of my television job, I am known to millions. But I soon decided that he did not know who I was: the calls only came at home and he never used my name. That made me feel safer, gave me strength. If he had said "Hello Beverley" I might have cracked.

'And although I was determined not to be a victim, I found I was putting the answerphone on more and more, which made me feel angry, because it was like hiding in my own home. If somebody I didn't like had come to the door I could have seen who it was and I wouldn't have let them in, but on the phone you can't do that. I felt tested.'

Although Beverley was sure her stalker was not pursuing her because she was a celebrity, she felt her position in the public eye made it more important that she should do everything possible to track down the obscene caller.

'I may be only a regional celebrity, but I have some clout and I felt I wanted to use that clout to get this man so that he could not frighten other women. I knew other colleagues at work who had had persistent callers, and there are people who hang around outside the studios to follow their celebrity targets home. I get letters myself, as all people who appear on television regularly do. Sometimes viewers send gifts; often the letters are sweet, but sometimes the attention goes beyond the normal boundaries. They tell me all about their lives, they ask for dates. If I met them at a dinner party or in a wine bar I might find them attractive and want to go out with them, but I'm worried about anybody who makes the first approach by writing to a stranger. Especially if the letter comes from Strangeways!

'So I felt that this was not just my problem, that it went wider than that, and if I ignored it I would be letting other women down.'

The police initially gave Beverley some advice about handing the calls: they told her to lay the receiver down and allow the caller to get everything out of his system, and then gently replace it. This would not provoke him, nor would he be ringing back straightaway. Beverly reported all the calls to the police, and after two weeks, in which the frequency was stepped up to several times every afternoon, they began to treat the matter as serious.

'I only received one call that was out of office hours – and thank goodness I did, because that is what eventually nailed him. He was obviously ringing me from somewhere quiet at his office, although God knows where if he was doing what he said he was. The calls were always male masturbatory fantasies, and he would let me know what he was doing. He did not need a response from me, it was as though I wasn't really part of it, but at the same time he needed to know I was there because he rarely spoke on my answering machine. The calls were not life-threatening, they were bizarre. But it was obviously essential to him to have a woman listening in fear at the other end.

'I became suspicious of so many people. I could only tell a few close girlfriends what was happening, because any man could be the one. I even looked sideways at the detectives: after all, they were blokes. It was hard to keep a balance between my sense of humour and rising feeling of paranoia.'

Three months after the calls started, BT modernized Beverley's exchange, putting her area on to the computerized digital system with which they can trace calls instantly. Beverley still had to log her calls to cross-reference them with the print-out of numbers calling her. The BT investigators immediately tracked the calls to a computer company a mile away from her home, but the problem was that there were several extensions in the building and forty men working there.

'I felt a shudder of anxiety when they told me where the calls were coming from. I passed it every day on my way to work. Then I instantly became angry again, thinking, "The bastard's in there."'

After being given the number by BT, the police began an investigation of the staff at the computer company. They had decided that Beverley's caller was not an amateur: there was something about his delivery, as though he had rehearsed his lines, which convinced them he had pestered other women. It was in September, nine months after the calls began, that detectives went into the computer company, disguised as council workers in order not to arouse suspicion. While they were there, the calls were still coming and Beverley tried to keep her stalker on the phone as long as possible, to get a good voice trace. The police were pleased, because it gave them a better profile of the caller; they decided that he sounded as though he was in his thirties.

With the help of the company secretary they went through attendance records, to see who was in the office at the time of the calls. There were never any times when Beverley's stalker was alone, there were always at least two men in the building. Eventually a shortlist of half a dozen was drawn up, and then it was narrowed down to three. Beverley was shown all the names, in case any of them seemed familiar to her. They didn't.

One call had been made when the prime suspect was not in the office, and this was the only one Beverley had received which broke the previous pattern. It had come at 2.00 a.m. on Valentine's Day, instead of in the afternoon, and it had been a silent call. Although it had happened before her exchange had been digitalized, the detectives on Beverley's case went back to the computer company and discovered that the man they suspected had been away on business and had spent the night in a hotel in Telford. They contacted the hotel and were provided with a print-out of the phone calls he had made.

'Bingo! We had him. My number came up on his bill. That was the key piece of evidence – it put him, and only him, in the frame. He was called in by his boss who asked him for the keys of his company car and sacked him on the spot. The police were waiting outside to arrest him. It was very embarrassing for the company, and they were so apologetic and upset that I felt sorry for them: it was no more their fault than mine.

'I felt so relieved I went on holiday to celebrate. Meanwhile, he was asking the arresting officers, "How did you get me? Which number was it?" which suggests he had been ringing other women. He had been cynical and clever about it, never ringing when he was alone in the building. He was smart. He made only one slip-up, and that was to ring from a hotel.'

Beverley came face to face with her caller when he appeared before Macclesfield Magistrates Court in January 1992, a year after the calls started. He was charged with making malicious telephone calls and pleaded guilty. Beverley did not have to go to court as the case was not contested, but she was determined to do so.

'I wanted to be there, I wanted to see justice being

done. It was a very strange day; the court was so small I was quite close to him. I met him face to face as we went in – that was when he realized that I was a familiar face from his TV screen. He looked shocked. He was a total stranger to me, but I wanted to know what he looked like. When I saw him I went cold, it was a very odd feeling actually seeing this man.

'He was a 34-year-old computer consultant, not your idea of a dirty old man in scuffed shoes and a raincoat. He looked Mr Respectable Office Manager: smart suit, glasses, moustache and well-combed hair. I glared at him.'

Because her stalker pleaded guilty, the details of the calls made to Beverley were not presented to the court. She was disappointed and angry.

'I would have liked every shameful detail to have been paraded in public. I wanted him to be humiliated in the way he had tried to humiliate me and possibly other women. It was all very genteel, the magistrates were spared all the sexually explicit dross that I had to listen to. He looked the picture of misfortune and the mitigating circumstances that his defence offered were, in my opinion, pathetic. They said he had lost his job – so he should. They said he needed medical help – too true, and I'm the one that knows it. And they said – can you believe it – that he would suffer because of the adverse publicity. He should have thought about all that before he picked the phone up.'

Beverley's stalker was fined £300 and ordered to pay her £100 compensation– £2 for every week of his uninvited presence in her life. Because her stalker had lost his £24,000-a-year job the magistrates were told of his problems paying the fine. Apparently he had commitments to a mortgage and other household bills.

'I wanted to jump up and down and yell. Nobody was asking what I earned, how I felt, what financial problems I might have, everything centred on him. I felt it was completely cockeyed. I wanted him to suffer more.

'It was not perfect justice. He deserved more. Malicious phone calls are classed in law as a nuisance – he could have been given a tougher sentence if he had wrecked a phone box, because that would be classed as criminal damage. Yet people like him can wreck lives.'

Since the court case Beverley has been campaigning to have penalties for malicious calls increased. She has written to the Home Office and to MPs, and she now gives awareness classes to Greater Manchester Police, helping policemen to understand and deal with victims of stalking.

'I'm lucky,' says Beverley, 'I was strong enough to take it, but even I felt vulnerable and at risk. All I suffered was a few sleepless nights. I refused to think of myself as a victim and I have never asked for, or needed, counselling. But stalking is an invisible crime, it rarely leaves visible scars. It is about fear, about nasty mind games. It gives warped men perverted kicks and victims can suffer for years as a result. It should be punished much more heavily.'

'A BLIGHT ON OUR LIVES'

LISA GRAYSON IS a small, very pretty girl who once had a golden future in British gymnastics. Tragically, injuries to her ankles prevented her continuing as one of the country's top gymnasts. Even more tragically, she has been left with a dangerous legacy from her brief fame: a stalker who has pursued her relentlessly since 1988, when she was sixteen.

Lisa's stalker has not been violent, he has not sent her obscene or pornographic material, he has only twice turned up in person outside her home. Yet, in many ways, his presence in her life is more disturbing and more worrying than many of the cases where more obvious harm has been done.

Robert Wall has insidiously and inexorably taken over Lisa's life, and the life of her parents. Since he became obsessed with her, Wall has written over 5,000 poems and hundreds of songs which he has dedicated to her. These have been delivered through the Grayson family letterbox in an unnerving rhythm. Every three months there is a spate of letters, lasting for a week or two, then everything goes quiet. Until they recognized the pattern, Lisa and her parents were more than once lulled into a false sense of security, thinking that their persecutor had lost interest. The scrawled capital letters spelling out Lisa's name on yet another brown envelope soon dispelled their hopes.

Nothing, not even a prison sentence, has stopped Wall. He does not respond to reason, to pleas for compassion, or to the law.

Lisa's natural talent for gymnastics was discovered when she joined a local club at the age of seven. It was not something her parents, Stan and Christine, pushed her into; her friend's sister was a member and Lisa wanted to have a go. It did not take the local coach long to realize that she had exceptional potential and within weeks she was training with youngsters much older than herself. By the time she was a teenager she was winning medals and trophies by the score, and life in the Grayson family revolved around chauffeuring her to competitions and training. She was the youngest of the family's three children: her brothers Peter and Mark are eight and four years older than her respectively, which meant that her parents had more time to dedicate themselves to helping Lisa with her sport.

By the run-up to the Seoul Olympics in 1988, Lisa was well-known in British gymnastic circles. It was her involvement with the Olympic team that put her photograph into Fleet Street newspapers and her name on to national television and radio news bulletins.

Lisa's hopes that she would be selected for the British team were dashed because she was not fully fit from an injury. The family had arranged a holiday in Devon, and they were told by the team coach to go off and enjoy themselves, but to ring every couple of days to check that Lisa was not needed.

Then there was a sudden crisis, caused by injury to another gymnast, and the team – already out in Seoul – was one competitor short. Lisa *was* needed. But she and her family had gone off to Paignton Zoo for the day, and nobody knew where they were. At the instigation of the Minister for Sport, Colin Moynihan, appeals were broadcast on radio throughout the day, particularly on the local Devon networks, and a description of the family car and its number plate were given. As Lisa and her mum and dad were about to leave the zoo car park, they were flagged down by an estate agent who had heard the appeal. He broke the news to them that Lisa was needed in Seoul.

The next few hours were a whirlwind of activity. A police car whizzed them to Exeter Airport, a heli-copter was on standby, a businessman offered them the use of his private jet, frantic phone calls were made to fix up flights to Korea. The national press descended on the airport: for them, it was a great story, a sixteen-year-old girl being tracked down on holiday to represent her country. Stan Grayson found himself being interviewed live by Sandy Gall on ITN news.

In the midst of all the fuss, the Olympic team coach consulted the doctor who had been treating Lisa's injuries and to her lifelong disappointment he again pronounced her unfit to compete. It was a terrible anticlimax, but Lisa was young enough to look for-ward to the next Olympics, and the flurry of press interest had been exciting for both her and her parents.

Among the millions who read Lisa's story and saw her picture in the papers and on television was Robert Wall, an unmarried painter and decorator in his thirties who lives with his mother about sixty miles away from Lisa's home in Redcar, on Teesside. His fixation was born.

It started with a phone call, and then came the letters, a stream of badly spelled, incoherent ramblings. At the beginning he regularly sent gifts, usually to Stan and Christine as well as to Lisa. On one occasion he sent a make-up box to Christine, three CDs to Stan and a gold watch to Lisa. Another time they all received small brass clocks, and Lisa received a fax and telephone answering machine. In the early days there was no name on any of the letters or gifts, but after a while the name Robert started to appear, and finally the family learned his surname and address when he sent a cheque for £50. A personalized passport cover he sent to Lisa included her middle name – proof that he was going to some lengths to find out details of Lisa's life.

By this time the family were very worried. 'We didn't like it, not from the very first presents that arrived,' says Christine, who works in catering. 'We could sense there was something odd about whoever was doing it. It wasn't just a fan. But we did not expect it to go on, we thought he would lose interest and stop.'

When he rang, Christine told him in forthright terms to leave the family alone, and that if he did not she would go to the police. He accused her of being a wicked mother, and one of the constant refrains of his letters since has been that Christine is blocking his contact with Lisa. He appears to believe that Lisa secretly wishes to be with him, but that she is thwarted by her family, particularly her mother.

When he wrote a poem about her nineteenth birthday he enclosed a note with it: 'I was going to send this poem for your birthday but your mar would of send 19 rolling pines [sic].' Another poem refers through three verses to Lisa's 'mar' not letting her go out to play and ends, chillingly, with the line that she cannot come out to play because 'she's getting buried this day'.

His attitude in letters to Stan was friendlier – he took the line that all men were victims of women, and he seemed to expect fellow feeling from Lisa's father. In one letter to Stan he wrote: 'Why do women torment us men?'

Wall, who is half-Maltese, signs many of his letters 'Robert Wall Goggi', which the Graysons presume is his mother's Maltese surname. He also calls himself 'The Maltese Falcon' and 'The Falcon Boy'. He refers to Lisa constantly as 'Walter Mitty'. In the early days he would occasionally promise never to contact them again. He'd write, 'This is the last time you will hear from Robert.' But they soon learned to disregard these promises. They also learned to refuse to accept parcels from him, which they recognized immediately from his spidery handwriting.

Until 1991 Lisa was still competing at international level in gymnastics; she came second in the British Championships in 1988 and won the title in 1989. She competed in the Commonwealth Games in 1990 but was forced to retire in 1991 because of stress fractures to her ankles. Nowadays, although she can no longer compete, she helps coach other young gymnasts. She also works part time as a shop assistant.

While she was still actively involved in the sport, her parents shielded her as best they could from Wall's attentions. To compete at top level in any sport requires single-minded dedication and Chris and Stan were determined not to let a stalker ruin Lisa's chances.

'We hid the letters from her. And she was away from home for weeks at a time training, which at least meant that we could bear the brunt of it without her knowing,' says Stan.

'Every time Lisa was on television with her gymnastics, Wall would write criticizing her performance. We shudder to think now that he may sometimes have been in the audience watching her.'

By 1991 they had withstood three years of Wall's attention, and by this time Lisa had stopped competing. She was at home on a regular basis, and Stan and Christine could no longer shield her. The family had tried complaining to the police, but had been told that nothing could be done as the letters were not abusive and there were no threats of violence. One policeman actually pointed out to them that the letters were complimentary to Lisa, as though that made them less worrying. They were told that the only way they could stop Wall from pestering them further was to take out a civil injunction against him: when that was in force the police would be able to arrest him if he broke it.

The Graysons went to a firm of solicitors in Redcar, Richard Knaggs and Company. They were lucky on two counts: they found sympathetic and committed legal advisers, and Lisa, a student at the time, qualified for legal aid. Had the family been forced to pay their own legal bills, the total over the next three years would have been over £6,000.

But even with these factors in their favour, they were to find that the law is ill-equipped to deal with cases like theirs. Their legal victory against Wall was hard won and ultimately unsatisfactory, as this diary of their battle shows.

They had their first meeting with their solicitor, Ian Merrett, on 30 July 1991. Before anything else happened he took the reasonable step of writing to Wall, telling him that unless he stopped communicating with Lisa, legal action would be taken. In reply, he received the first of several letters from Wall. The letter purported to come from Wall's secretary, but it featured the same incoherent style, erratic grammar, punctuation and spelling as those that the Graysons had received. For several months the solicitors' offices received as many letters as Lisa did – Wall would photocopy all the poems and songs he sent to her and send copies.

Wall visited the Graysons' home twice, luckily both times when Lisa was out. The first time was a Wednesday evening, when Stan, a sales supervisor, and Christine were getting ready to go out to play badminton. Lisa was due to meet them at the sports centre.

'The doorbell rang and I answered it,' says Chris. 'He was standing there, and I knew it was him before he spoke. He said, "Is Lisa in? It's Robert." I ran upstairs to get Stan, and then I came down and said, "You've never met her, she wants nothing to do with you." He tried to leave some presents, but we refused to take them.'

Stan was very tempted to hit him. 'From the very beginning I've wanted to thump him, but I know that if I did, I'd be the one who ends up in trouble. I've had friends offer to go round and sort him out, but I know we must not do that: it's very tempting, but it would put us on the wrong side of the law.'

Chris and Stan rang Lisa and told her not to walk round to where they were going to meet, but to wait and be picked up by them in the car.

A week later it was Stan's turn to open the door to Wall, and he told him forcibly that Lisa wanted nothing to do with him. Again, Wall had brought gifts, which Stan refused to take.

'I told him that if he didn't want trouble, he would go away,' he says.

At this stage the family again called the police, who came round and took statements. Because the injunction proceedings were not complete, though, they said they had no power to arrest Wall. Turning up on the doorstep and asking to see Lisa was not illegal. But a message was passed to Wall's local police station, and a policeman called at his home. It failed to deter him – his next letter to Lisa asked, 'Why did you send the plonkers to my house?'

'Knowing that he was coming to Redcar was very frightening,' says Lisa. 'Before that, I was worried but I could cope with it. The feeling that he might be here, watching me and following me, is the worst feeling of all.' On one occasion a bouquet of flowers was delivered to their home for Christine. When she asked at the florist about who had ordered them, the description fitted Robert Wall to a tee. Knowing that he is a racing fan, they checked and discovered that there was a race meeting that day at Redcar.

'Now we are especially nervous on race days,' says Stan, 'It would only take about fifteen minutes to walk to our house from Redcar racecourse.'

Among the packages that continued to arrive for them, they would find train and bus tickets which showed that Wall had been in Redcar on certain days.

It was obvious that legal action was going to have to be taken.

In March 1992 an application for emergency legal aid was made on Lisa's behalf and was granted. Emergency legal aid is normally restricted to those applicants who need it for an imminent court appearance, or for those in an obviously threatening situation. The Legal Aid Board, having been given evidence of the level of harassment she was suffering, clearly reckoned Lisa's case to be in that category.

The first injunction hearing at Middlesbrough County Court took place on 15 April 1992. Lisa's solicitors had already encountered another problem that they would face again and again in their dealings with Wall: it was extremely difficult to serve legal papers on him. Nobody answered the door at his address, although the process servers could see an old lady looking at them from the window. Papers pushed through the letterbox were pushed back out again. They were forced to wait and serve the papers on Wall when he came home.

Robert Wall turned up at court without a solicitor or barrister and the district judge, who took the hearing in chambers (not in open court), went to great lengths to explain the procedures to him. He was told that, as an alternative to an injunction being imposed on him, he could give an undertaking not to harass or pester the Graysons, or to send them any communications. The case was adjourned to allow Wall to take legal advice.

At this hearing, Wall was sitting on the opposite side of the table from Lisa and her parents – and he admitted then that he had never seen her in the flesh before. He said that when he saw her on television he had believed she was a girl he had previously met at Redcar racecourse, but he now realized he had been mistaken. The Graysons and their solicitor left court hopeful: they believed that the brush with the law, plus the realization that Lisa was not the girl he had originally had in mind, would mean an end to their nightmare.

Their hopes were soon dashed, as the letters continued to arrive, both at their home and at the solicitors' office. Legally, Lisa and her family had the option of applying for damages from Wall, but eventually decided not to. Although they could already see that Wall was unlikely to honour any undertaking he gave in court, they could also see that it would be pointless to pursue him for money.

The date for the full hearing in open court was 16 July 1992. Between the initial hearing and this date Wall sent a flurry of letters to Ian Merrett, Lisa's solicitor. Although he briefly had a firm of solicitors representing him, he ignored all protocols and corresponded directly with Merrett. His semi-literate letters were riddled with obscure and unexplained legal references and he frequently referred to himself in the third person: 'Please also find the questions Mr Wall will ask your plaintiff and a statement in true form of the calling to the Graysons household. Pass on statement to your client so they are well preserve in advance . . .' and 'The court must sit up and take note of three jactitations . . .' [a jactitation is an obsolete legal term].

In a reference to Lisa's affidavit about the publicity surrounding her at the time of the Seoul Olympics, he wrote: 'The Warner Brothers she would make a fortune . . . she never left British soil . . . to boot or not to boot, that is the question.'

About his own affidavit he wrote: 'As shower as your flag is red white and blue this is a true statement . . .'

In his 'true statement' he accused Lisa of telling 'so many lies', and claimed that she was the one who had initiated contact with him. He said she had been to his home twice and had also tried to leave a message on his answering machine. 'She'll never come clean until yous back away,' he wrote to Lisa's solicitor.

On the day of the hearing, in open court, Wall again represented himself. The judge accepted his undertaking that he would not harass Lisa or her family.

Within weeks he had broken the undertaking, and both Lisa and the solicitors' office had received bundles of correspondence from him.

Ian Merrett had left the firm by November 1992,

and Lisa's case was now in the hands of Juliet Critchley. She started enforcement proceedings on 18 November on Lisa's behalf. She detailed all the breaches Wall had made of his court undertaking. Once again, the firm had great difficulty serving the papers on him.

Wall was in court again on 12 January 1993. Lisa's legal team were asking for him to be committed to prison for breaking his undertaking. Wall took the opportunity to tell the court that he was hoping to negotiate a contract with EMI for the songs he was writing; the judge kept a straight face, although others in the court room found it difficult. When Wall said he was going to leave Britain and live in Malta, the judge's comment was 'Good'.

He passed a twenty-one-day prison sentence on Wall, suspended for twelve months, and in summing up he stressed that if Wall breached his undertaking to leave Lisa and her family alone at any time during that twelve-month period, he would go to prison for longer than three weeks.

'Although we hoped it would do the trick, I think we all knew in our heart of hearts that it was a faint hope,' says Juliet Critchley.

The next round of legal activity was initiated by Wall, who decided to appeal against his sentence – even though he was not serving one. The Court of Appeal is in London, but Wall, handling his own legal case, lodged an appeal in Middlesborough. The court and Lisa's solicitors were confused, but court officials, bending over backwards to be fair to a man who was representing himself, gave him a date for a 'leave to appeal application', a hearing in Middlesborough that would give Wall the go-ahead to appeal in London.

The hearing took place on 6 April 1993 in front of the same judge, Judge Bryant, who had imposed the suspended sentence. He told Wall that he did not need leave to appeal but could appeal whenever he wanted to – in London. Wall argued, insisting that there was a court of appeal in Middlesborough. The judge looked around the room and under the bench and then told Wall that he had been coming to Middlesbrough for years, but had never seen a court of appeal. Wall agreed to withdraw his application.

Lisa knew that as far as he was concerned, the whole charade had been a ploy to get her into the same courtroom as him again. 'He likes it. It doesn't do anything to deter him: he likes the attention and he likes having me there. He just sits and stares at me. He even writes to me afterwards criticizing what I was wearing or the way I did my hair.'

The harassment continued. The Graysons changed to an ex-directory phone number after one awful Friday evening when Wall rang their number and left his phone off the hook, playing music down the line to them. Three tunes were played over and over again: 'I'll be Watching You' by Sting, 'Nothing Compares to You' by Sinead O'Connor and 'Starship'. By 11.00 p.m. the family had had enough, and went to a neighbour's house to ring the police – their own line was blocked. The music stayed on the line until the following morning, so Wall must have run up a huge telephone bill, but that was no consolation to Lisa's family. Another futile call was made to Wall's home by the police the next day.

More letters arrived and both Lisa and her solicitor were sent pens stamped with his business name 'Maltese Decorators Ltd' and 'The Falcon Boy'.

The details of all Wall's breaches of his undertaking were sent to court in August 1993, with an application to have him committed to prison. The hearing took place on 1 November, but due to a mix-up by court staff as to the type of hearing, the Graysons were not in court. Neither was Robert Wall, so the committal hearing was adjourned. Stan and Christine Grayson then received a letter from Wall, asking for their daughter's hand in marriage.

On 8 December Wall again failed to turn up for the hearing, having rung the court to say that his car had broken down. The judge, Judge Briggs, ruled that the hearing would go ahead without him. After hearing all the evidence, he sentenced Wall to three months in prison (three months for each of the three breaches, to run concurrently) and another three weeks to be served for the suspended sentence. The judge also imposed an indefinite injunction on Wall not to communicate with Lisa, her family or her solicitors.

The best news for them was that the judge said that he believed Robert Wall was deranged and ordered that he should have a psychiatric assessment while in prison.

'We really felt this was the answer,' says Juliet Critchley. 'We did not expect a prison sentence to achieve anything – nothing else had. But we thought he would be given the medical help he clearly needs. I believed he would be released from prison into a psychiatric hospital, or that, if he did come back into the community, it would be with the support of a psychiatric social worker, and perhaps with medication that would help him.'

For Lisa's parents there was a feeling of 'huge relief'. 'We knew that three months and three weeks in prison was not very long, but we felt someone would finally do something about him,' says Stan.

Lisa was more cynical. 'He'll write to me from prison,' she said as they left the court. She was right.

The communications that Wall sent from prison were to do with another appeal he decided to launch. He wrote to Lisa once and to her solicitor once, and also phoned Juliet Critchley, becoming abusive on the phone and telling her to get the wax cleared out of her ears.

'It was a difficult situation: he had been ordered not to communicate with us, but on the other hand we had to take legal matters seriously ,' says Juliet Critchley, who now has a file twelve inches thick on the case.

She was worried about the change in tone. Wall had not previously been aggressive or threatening, but now he was writing from prison things such as, 'I'm going to get the plaintiff for her lies.' He called Judge Briggs 'a hanging judge' and attached another of his poems, this one entitled 'Injustice', which included the lines, 'If there be a day so true, Hanging Judge Briggs will go to hell too.'

Juliet Critchley wrote to the governor of Home House Prison, where Wall was serving his sentence, pointing out that Wall was breaching a court order by sending letters to Lisa and to herself. By the time she received a reply it was too late for the prison to do anything: on the day her letter had arrived on the governor's desk Wall had been released, having served only half of his sentence.

Alarmed that Wall was out, Juliet Critchley made inquiries with the prison medical staff about the psychiatric assessment he had been given. She was told that medical staff thought there was nothing wrong with him.

'When I gave the doctor a brief run-through of some typical aspects of Wall's letters – he refers to himself in the third person, he believes he is the victim of persecution, he makes lots of Biblical references – he said they would have another look at Wall. I had to tell them it was too late, he was out.

'This is the most disappointing aspect of the whole case. I realize that he is ill and that his actions come from the derangement of his mind, but that is no consolation to the Graysons. I feel so sorry for them, and I feel a lot of suppressed anger towards him for what he has put them through.

'I'm sick of him, I hate dealing with him and his letters. How much worse must it be for them?'

The Graysons describe what has happened to them as 'a blight on our lives'.

'We haven't been able to live normal lives since he came into them – and for Lisa that means she's not been able to grow up without this constant fear and worry,' says Christine.

'It's awful that it has to go this far before anything gets done. Lisa is one of the lucky ones because she has been able to get legal aid – God knows what would have happened without it. We could not have afforded constant court cases.

'You never imagine things like this can happen to ordinary people. You read about it with celebrities, but you don't dream it could be you. Even when it starts, you feel sure it will soon be over. You have no idea that it can keep on and on and on.

'He's taken away so much from us. Lisa's getting engaged, but we feel we can't make a big announcement about it and celebrate it like other families would, because we don't want to let him know. What's going to happen when she gets married? Maybe that will tip him over the edge and make him worse. We've given up hoping that anything will make him better.

'We live with a certain amount of permanent fear. If Stan's not home, I have an arrangement with a neighbour that I'll call her if he ever turns up, and she'll bring help. Why should we have to live like that? We've thought of getting our son Mark, who lives in London, to write to him, telling him that Lisa has moved down there to live. But why should we have to hide her away, pretend she's not here?'

Although the Graysons can laugh at some of the things Wall says in his letters, they no longer feel any pity for him.

'I hate him,' says Lisa, 'I really hate him. I don't feel a bit sorry for him. Maybe he's ill, but that doesn't give him the right to ruin my life. I try hard not to think about him and in the lulls between his letters I can almost manage it. But the minute I see his handwriting on an envelope I feel sick.

'When we first heard that he was out of jail I did

not sleep. I was awake every half hour, thinking there was someone in the room with me. I was waiting for the post every morning – and sure enough, the letters started coming.'

The family are continuing to take legal proceedings against Wall, but they do so with little enthusiasm.

'It feels like being on a horrible treadmill, as though it will just go on and on forever,' says Lisa.

'THE NIGHTMARE WAS REAL'

EVERY NIGHT AT 9.00 p.m. Judy Barclay checks that all the doors and windows of the house she rents are locked, packs sandwiches and drinks and nappies, and barricades herself and her two young sons into an upstairs bedroom. The three of them sleep huddled together in one double bed. At least once during the night Judy's older son James, who had to have major surgery for a brain tumour in 1993 when he was three, will wake up screaming in terror and will have wet the bed again. He believes there is 'a bad man' outside trying to get him – and it is not just childish imagination. James has seen his 'bad man' and he knows he exists. His nightmare is real.

Life for Judy, James and Ryan, who was born in 1992, is appallingly limited and miserable. Ever since September 1993, when Judy first realized she was being stalked, the family have lived in abject terror. The level of persecution they have suffered has escalated from having underwear stolen from the washing line to their home being gutted by fire in an arson attack. There is no evidence that it was her stalker who torched the house at Christmas 1993, but it came as the culmination of three months of intensifying fear, as her life became more and more circumscribed by the watchful presence of a stranger.

Judy is a strikingly pretty divorcee who until the fire lived with her two sons in a three-bedroomed Victorian house in the small village of Mortimore, near Reading, in Berkshire. Although her marriage to Rob, an insurance manager, had broken up, she was determined to make the best of life for herself and her two young sons. Before she became the victim of a stalker she was well-balanced, outgoing and had lots of friends, even though things were not easy – James had been in and out of hospital all year after major surgery to remove a brain tumour and his health was still at a critical stage.

The stalking all started in what Judy describes as 'a silly way'. 'I was doing the ironing and I couldn't find any of my underwear. I rang my mum to see if she had taken any of my things home to wash, but she hadn't. Something spooky – a tingle – went down my spine. My things, and only mine, had vanished. Friends advised me to put an old bra and pair of knickers on the washing line to see if they disappeared, and when they did I rang the police. To my dismay they thought it was a huge joke: I had a knicker-nicker. Ho, ho, ho!'

Judy was very worried. It was not the loss of her clothing, it was the awful thought that somebody was taking it for his own perverted needs, getting into her garden and removing it without her seeing him. She tried not to let her sons see her fear, but from the first day that she realized what was happening, that is the emotion that has pervaded most of Judy's waking hours: fear.

'The police came round and I had to tell them what sort of undies I wore. I explained they were standard Marks and Spencers – nothing special, nothing sexy or provocative, just ordinary M & S, the sort that millions of women in Britain wear every day. I think they mentally dismissed me as a neurotic woman living alone, which I'm not. I'm a strong person.

'By the time the police came my stalker had visited me again. I had heard noise in the garden at about midnight, and I had put it down to a fox rummaging about. The next day I had found the children's toys all thrown around. Later I was told he was probably deliberately noisy and messy: it was his way of letting me know that he was there.'

Judy stopped hanging her underwear outside when she washed it. Then she and the boys went away for a break to the seaside resort of Clacton. They spent a few days there at a home for children recovering from cancer, to help James recuperate after his operation. Judy tried to put all thoughts of the thefts from her garden out of her mind, and hoped they were just silly pranks that would have stopped when she returned home. But when she got back she found that her home had been burgled.

'My sister had to climb through the broken glass in the window to get in, because the burglar had locked the front door from the inside. The police came, and they could see that it was a very odd burglary: all that had been taken was more of my underwear and a selection of the boys' toy cars. The TV, video, radio – all the normal things that burglars take

– were still there. The only things that had been taken had been in my bedroom. Now they took the knicker-nicker more seriously. The laughing stopped.'

The police installed surveillance equipment, two cameras in the kitchen to monitor the garden. Judy's stalker was caught on film, but unfortunately he only appeared in outline. A more powerful infra-red camera got a better picture, but only of the back of his head. When a camera was installed in a neighbour's house that overlooks Judy's garden the film was better: this time the stalker's face could be seen.

The police told Judy they had little grounds for prosecution apart from the law of trespass, as all the film proved was that a man was in Judy's garden at night.

Then Judy saw her stalker. It happened at 4.00 a.m., when Judy arrived home after going to a Bon Jovi concert in Milton Keynes. She got caught up in the regular problem of emptying the car parks after events at Milton Keynes arena, and she was made even later by a hold-up on the motorway.

'As I stopped the car I spotted somebody at the end of my garden. I sat in the car and the man walked away and went into a phone box. He spotted me and ran towards the car, but I got out and made it to my neighbour's door. My neighbour called the police, but by the time they arrived he had gone. Again the police said there was nothing they could do. I sensed that they were wondering what I was doing out at 4.00 a.m., and that once again they felt I was a hysterical woman.

'I bought security lighting for the house and garden,

and began developing a siege mentality. I felt we were living in a fortress.'

He had been watching and noting the comings and goings at her home so thoroughly that he knew the back garden was a trap, rigged with lighting and cameras. He never went in there again. It was just before Christmas when he broke into the garage at 8.00 one evening while she was in the house alone with her two sons.

'I was petrified and this time the boys picked up my fear. I had struggled all this time to keep from them how terrified I was of this man, but I could no longer keep up the act. We could hear him moving about in the garage. At first I tried to rationalize it; I thought it might be my ex-husband, Rob, coming back to pick up something he had forgotten. He had visited us earlier, but I knew he would not just walk into the garage without letting me know he was there. I had heard the garage door creak open, and when I looked outside I could see no car lights.

'I dialled 999 and we clung together, me and the boys, in abject terror. James was screaming, "He's here, he's here." He was so frightened he was wetting himself. His nightmare, the nightmare lots of children have about a monster or a bogeyman, was real, and there was nothing I could do. I felt helpless.'

The police arrived very quickly, within minutes of Judy's call, but her stalker had gone. They used tracker dogs but in the darkness he had got away into nearby woods.

Then Judy went away again, deciding on the spur of the moment to take the boys to visit their grand-mother, Rob's mother, in Bath. At the same time Rob was also away, because his stepmother had died in Spain and he had flown out to be with his father. Judy and her mother-in-law took the boys to see a pantomime; it was a normal, happy, family Christmas outing.

But while they were hissing and booing the fictional villain on the stage, something much more frightening was happening at home. At around midnight that night a fire started, and by the time the alarm was raised at 8.00 a.m. the next morning by neighbours – who heard the radiators exploding – the place had been gutted. They had lived in the house, which was worth about £120,000, for four years, and throughout that time Judy had been busy decorating it, getting it the way she wanted it to be. Everything was ruined.

'My dream home was destroyed. We were left with just the clothes we were wearing and James's battered old teddy bear. Furniture, the boys' toys, and – worst of all – all the irreplaceable mementoes of our lives, including all the family photographs of the boys, were gone.'

A forensic team spent four days sifting through the embers, looking for evidence. All they could conclude was that whoever started the fire did not break into the house with that intention, because no petrol, spirits or paint (the standard equipment of arsonists) had been used. Instead, the fire had been started, they believed, on Judy's bed, where a bonfire of books, letters and magazines was set alight.

When Judy returned home she could not bear to look at the mess. She saw the devastation on her children's faces and she turned away from the ruin of her home, pulling them with her. All three of them had tears running down their cheeks. It was Christmas. Inside, she says, she was 'as burnt up as the floorboards of my home'.

Judy and the children moved in with her parents for the Christmas holiday, and although in many ways it was the worst Christmas of their lives, they were very moved by the help and sympathy they got from all their family and friends.

'They picked us up and carried us through,' Judy says.

Nobody was charged as a result of Judy's fire. The police had no evidence. Whoever or whatever was the cause of the fire, it was a tremendous blow to Judy at a time when she already felt very vulnerable.

The refurbishment of Judy's home is being paid for by her insurance company and she has had nothing but help and courtesy from them. While the work is carried out she lives in a rented house paid for by the insurance company, terrified that her stalker will find her. She does not want to move back to her home, but she cannot move. 'It is a Catch 22 situation. I would never be able to get a mortgage, because at the moment Rob is paying the mortgage as part of his maintenance, and building societies will not accept that as guaranteed income, like a salary. I've asked the council to re-house us, but they are unsympathetic because we have our own house. The only alternative is to declare ourselves homeless and the council will put us into bed-and-breakfast accommodation, which would be awful. I don't think James would cope with being shut in a one-room hostel. None of us would cope with it: it would be like being in a prison cell. Why should we be punished, we have done nothing wrong. I have a home and that's where we are going to have to live.

'The classic advice we get from everyone is move on, move away, build a new life. But we can't. I have thought about getting a guard dog, but both boys are asthmatics. I can't take a male lodger because James is now terrified of men. If I lived in America I would carry a gun.

'Rob, my ex-husband, feels guilty about us being on our own, but it would not be right to get back with him just for protection and it is not his fault. It is not my fault: I never dressed provocatively in short skirts or tight dresses. After he started watching me I even dyed my hair darker and dressed down. I became very conscious of how I looked, and that is wrong, too. I should not have to feel like that. I don't lead the sort of life that would make him, or any other man, think I am available. Since my marriage broke up I have had a couple of dates with other men, but when they meet the kids that's the end of it – my children are now both quite disturbed, and very nervous and difficult with men. Ryan is too young to understand, but I had to tell James the truth. He saw me low and depressed so often. He has constant nightmares and wets the bed. Ryan stopped talking. He was a very bright little boy of fifteen months when we had the fire, very advanced for his age, beginning to talk. But he completely stopped for four or five months, and it was hard work giving him the reassurance he needed.'

Before her children were born, Judy worked as an accountant. She knows she will not be able to go back to full-time office work because the boys need her around, so she is training at college two days a week to be a beauty therapist, a job she hopes she will be able to do from her own home.

'There is no other solution. James's health problems, and the emotional problems he now suffers as a result of all this, mean that I have to be here for him. This man has affected every area of our lives, and even if he disappeared tomorrow it would take us years to get over the damage he has done. Our only hope is that he switches his obsession to somebody else.

'We are trapped. The law cannot help, it seems.'

The police have fitted an alarm, a panic button wired up to the local station, at Judy's rented home, and her neighbours know about the problem. They are all protective of her. But the children find it very difficult to settle to sleep without Judy with them: their fears are too great.

'So every night at nine I take food and drink and nappies and we all climb into the double bed in my room. We are woken up several times by James screaming and wetting the bed. I comfort him, and then change the bedding; it's tiring constantly changing sheets in the early hours, but I can cope with that physical side of it far better than I can the mental pressures. I have tried to work through my worries with James's psychiatrist, but things that seem OK during daylight hours become terrifying at night. We cling together, the three of us, for love and mutual reassurance. I feel desperate: I don't see a future for us.'

PART THREE

WHEN FRIENDSHIP
TURNS TO FEAR

'WHEREVER I WENT, HE FOLLOWED'

No MAN IS an island, entire of itself: every day we all make and renew contact with other people. Much of the dealings we have with others is slight: we nod to shopkeepers, exchange a few comments about the weather with fellow commuters, discuss last night's telly with colleagues. It is not the stuff of intimacy, it holds no promise of commitment or closeness; it is nothing more than the oiling of the wheels of society. We do not think more than fleetingly about the people we speak to, we have no reason to expect they will dwell on us.

Or will they? Will the smile and the kind word be interpreted as something much deeper than they really are? Will some casual brush with an acquaintance trigger a response out of all proportion to our intentions? Will some sad, lonely and essentially disturbed human being latch on to our bland niceties and magnify them into an entirely different kind of exchange?

The odds against it are long, but for a few unlucky people it really happens. They meet someone through their work, through their social life, through mutual friends and suddenly, for no readily available reason, they become the focus of that person's life. They take on a starring role in the fantasies and life-plans of an individual they hardly know. Before long, they realize they have acquired a stalker.

In many cases their role in the life of the stalker has been paternalistic: they are the doctor who has treated them, the bank manager who has listened to their financial problems, the boss who has given them a job, the lecturer who taught them in class. The route to obsession is, if not understandable, at least comprehensible. In the lonely, empty inner life of the stalker their small kindnesses have assumed enormous proportions. Usually the involvement is sexually-motivated. The stalker sees the person they are fixated on as the answer to all their physical and emotional frustrations, and for that reason the vast majority of stalking is across the genders: men stalk women and women stalk men.

But there does not always have to be a sexual element. Sometimes the stalker sees his victim representing a life he believes should be his, and his tortured thought processes persuade him that by insinuating himself into that person's life, he can acquire from them the status he needs. Sometimes a whole family or a couple are stalked by someone who longs to be part of their lifestyle. When Senator Bob Krueger first decided to run for a seat in the US senate in 1984 he employed a pilot to fly him around the state of Texas on his campaign trail. The pilot, Tom Humphrey, became an integral part of the fight for Bob's seat, identifying completely with the cause and the campaign. When Bob lost the election, he and his wife Kathleen were very disappointed, and so were the rest of their staff – but Tom, the pilot, was devastated. He took the defeat personally. He cried and grieved and told the Kruegers that the year he had spent with them had been the best of his life.

After spending hours talking to him, counselling him, trying to help him come to terms with it, the Kruegers eventually had to distance themselves from him a little. From that moment on, and for nine years to come, they had a stalker. Tom left long rambling letters on their doorstep, he phoned them continually, sometimes as many as 120 times a day. He watched them from the house he rented across the street from theirs. He stood on their doorstep, just staring at the door, for twenty minutes at a stretch. His emotionally demanding letters turned into threatening ones and eventually he was imprisoned on three separate occasions for threatening to kill Bob. He claimed in one letter to have hired a killer who would put a bullet through Bob's brain as he lay sleeping next to his wife. Every time he was released from prison, the stalking pattern resumed.

Kathleen, who gave birth to two daughters during the years her family was being stalked, said: 'It's always when I've been at home, where I'm often in the house alone, that I've felt the most frightened. That's what stalkers do – they hold you hostage in your own home.'

The Kruegers know a great deal about Tom Humphrey's unhappy personal background. They started out with immense sympathy and understanding for him, but as his interference in their family life became progressively more terrifying they came to see him as nothing more than an enemy. It is a feeling most stalking victims have in common; most of them realize that their persecutors are mentally ill and in need of help, but all vestiges of compassion are ultimately lost in a desperate fight for their own sanity and self-preservation.

This chapter and the four that follow deal with this most common of all kinds of stalking: stalking by an acquaintance, someone who has a genuine, if tenuous, link with the life of his victim.

When Claire Elliott's family changed their phone number to avoid calls from her stalker, he hung around outside her 14-year-old brother's classroom offering a bribe to any child who would get him the new number. It worked: the phone calls started again. For Claire there was that sinking feeling of helplessness common to stalking victims. No matter what she did, he would always find her, always be there to plague her. He was, she began to feel, a permanent fixture in her life, an affliction she had to learn to live with. And like hundreds of other victims she asked herself the same question over and over: why me?

Claire is a bright, very attractive girl who hopes to take a degree in law or accountancy. She left school at sixteen with a clutch of good GCSE grades, to set up her own perfume business. A year later, in 1991, she met Garry Bush at a local snooker club. Claire's a keen snooker player, playing the women's game competitively at a local level. Garry, who was five years older than her, was a reasonably good amateur player, and he was part of the regular social group who met at the club in Finchley, north London.

Although he was part of the crowd, he was a solitary figure who never, as far as Claire knows, had a girlfriend.

He became very attached to Claire. She was going out with another of the boys in the group, and Garry knew this, and never actually asked her out. He simply appeared to need to be close to her at all times.

'He wanted us to do everything together. He was madly jealous – he would slag off my boyfriend, wanting to get us to finish. Wherever I went, he followed, wherever I sat, he sat next to me. He squeezed into the tightest of spaces to be near me – or if there was no space he would crouch beside me on the floor,' says Claire.

She and her friends regarded him as eccentric but harmless. They knew he had a crush on Claire, but they all assumed it would pass when he got the message that she was not interested.

'He had no confidence in himself, in his ability or his looks, and he never had a girlfriend. One day he asked me to help him write a letter to a girl he fancied from school. He had bottled up his feelings for her for so long he could not express them. Sadly, she turned him down, saying she already had a boyfriend. But she let him down gently.'

After a few months Claire broke up with her boyfriend. She was no longer running her own business, but had an office job in East London, so she moved away from her parents' home to share a house in south London with some friends from work.

'It was meant to be a fresh start. I had split up with my boyfriend, it was a new job, and I also wanted a break from Garry. I took it for granted that if I wasn't around he'd get the message.'

She underestimated his persistence and the fixation he had with her, which was rapidly dominating his life. He began turning up at her office and refusing to leave when asked.

'When my boss got fed up and tried to get him out he kicked up a real fuss, screaming obscenities. It was embarrassing. I suppose that was the start of the real harassment. That was when I first had a clue that this wasn't just eccentricity, or a crush that he would get over. He was putting pressure on, but not as a friend. He sent me a pitiful letter, and I felt so sorry for him. I felt he was losing direction, losing his grip. He plagued me with phone calls, often giving me the silent treatment – I could just hear the sound of breathing on the line. It would be chilling if it was done by a stranger, but I knew Garry, and I put it down to the fact that he was going through a difficult time. After a letter in which he said he was hearing voices I felt I had to get in touch with him, I was worried about him.'

When she talked to him, Garry put a business proposition to Claire. By this time she had left the job in East London, and needed something to do.

'Although it was not my fault, I felt guilty about the way Garry was, and I let him talk me into working with him. I still had no idea how bad his obsession was, I still expected him to behave normally, and I thought he would soon grow out of how he felt about me. We went into partnership taking survey commissions, doing market research in the street. The plan was for Garry to train up a survey team and supervise them and for me to look after the office administration. It seemed a good combination of talents, because Garry was experienced and good at survey work, and I knew about running a business. It could have worked.

'But Garry would come in late, neglecting his side of the business to hang around the office to be with me. I began to realize he was besotted with me, despite the fact that I had explained to him that I was not interested in a relationship. It made no sense, it was madness. And he had never even asked me to go out with him, although he behaved as though there was an unspoken pact that we were together.'

By November 1991 it was clear to Claire that the business was failing. No survey staff were being trained and the number of commissions was dropping.

'Business was lousy. He was goofing up. The partnership collapsed and I felt great relief, because it had been hell working with him, a big mistake.'

That should have been the end of Claire's association with Bush, and she hoped it would be. She had had enough of his oppressive attentions. But on Christmas Eve he was back in her life, with a vengeance.

'I was having a drink with friends at the snooker club, and he was there. He knew all of us, but he never approached us. He just stood and watched me the whole time, like a man from another planet. If I moved, he moved. It was eerie. It got to us all and we decided to leave and go somewhere else for a drink. He followed us.

'He did not actually approach me until I went up

to talk to my ex-boyfriend, when he moved in between us. He squeezed into every space he could to be next to me, but he never said a word. It was quite unnerving. Then he suddenly threw a glass at me. It missed, luckily. I couldn't believe it was really happening. I remember thinking that I must be asleep and having a bad dream. It was Christmas Eve, everyone was in a great mood, having a good time – and I was the target of an incredibly spiteful tantrum. I was shocked, confused and very worried.

'My friends and I left the pub, but he followed again. We watched him: he was banging his head on lamp-posts and walls, and we felt sorry for him, as well as worried. We walked through Finchley and into another pub, and he followed us inside, again not approaching us. He was looking at me with wild staring eyes, full of hate. Finally he walked across and just head-butted me. I wasn't expecting it and my jaw went through the glass I was holding to my lips. I felt him kicking my legs and then he was dragged off me. It took a few people to restrain him: he seemed to be completely out of control.

'We didn't call the police. It was Christmas Eve, the season of goodwill to all men, and we could see he was having some sort of breakdown. We decided he needed help, not the police, and after the incident he left anyway. I wasn't badly hurt – the glass broke in my mouth but I managed to spit out the pieces without being cut. My head ached from the force of the blow and my shins were sore where he kicked me.'

The following day, Christmas Day, Claire ran into Garry again, at the home of a mutual friend, where several of her crowd had agreed to meet to watch television.

'I was the first to arrive – apart from Garry, who was already there. I just froze. I sat on the settee and stared at the TV while our friend went for a shower. I was praying he would return quickly, or that the others would arrive. It was awful: Garry moved to crouch on the floor next to me, and we sat in silence for a few minutes, me desperately keeping my eyes on the television screen. Then he suddenly pounced, holding a knife to my throat and babbling incoherently. He was so intense and his face was full of hatred. I could not tell what he was saying, but at that moment I wasn't interested in his words. I screamed and my friend came rushing out of the bathroom and wrestled him off me, grabbing the knife from him. Garry just walked across and stood by the bathroom door, glaring at me and muttering. Our friend told him to leave, but he wouldn't.'

Once again, Claire and her mates decided not to call the police because they could see how disturbed Garry was. But for Claire Christmas Day was ruined and she went back to her parents' home – with Garry following her.

'He followed me round all the time after Christmas, crouching by my side like a dog. I was angry and upset. He would ring me up at home, but I refused to speak to him. It was stupid not to report him to the police, but I just could not do it. He'd been a sort of friend, he seemed to be ill. I thought he would get better, but he didn't.'

After Garry stole her handbag and rang her up to let her know he had it, Claire finally went to the police. They asked her to arrange a meeting with him, and they would be there to see how he behaved. But Garry must have sensed that something was going on, because he did not show up.

'I think the police thought it was all a lover's tiff, a routine domestic argument,' says Claire.

By this time the phone calls had stepped up. Claire's mother, grandmother, her friends, the staff at the snooker club and the owner of the snooker club were all receiving calls from Garry, asking where she was. He even rang the owner at his home number. He was being verbally abusive about Claire to anyone who would listen to him, calling her a slag and worse.

'Hi, Slag ... I gave you everything I had to offer and you threw it back in my face. I'm going to kill you in the most painful way I can think of. You'll have to kill me to stop me,' is one of the many calls British Telecom recorded on Claire's family phone line.

Bush also rang other snooker clubs in the area. Claire was by now going out with Ram Vaswani, a professional snooker player, the oldest of three talented snooker-playing brothers. Ram is in the big league, making it as far as the fourth round of the world snooker championship, and a star in the local snooker clubs of north London. 'It was embarrassing for me and could have been embarrassing for Ram, having my name blackened around all these clubs. The phone calls were continuing at home, so we arranged to have our number changed.'

It was then that Garry stood outside Claire's brother's school, asking classmates if they knew the new number. Claire's father, Achilles, a shoe designer, was beside himself with anger when he realized that Bush was involving his young son.

'My father lost thousands of pounds worth of business during this whole saga because he would not go abroad leaving his wife and children alone with someone like Garry on the loose. My mother Heather was desperately upset all the time – I'm her daughter, she'd like to wrap me in cotton wool and protect me, but there was nothing she could do. She has suffered as much as I have.

'Garry finally bribed one of the schoolkids into telling him our new number – and the calls began again. British Telecom put a trace on our line, after my solicitor had approached the police about what was happening, and in the meantime we went to court to get an injunction to stop him harassing us.'

Because by this time she was a student and not working, Claire qualified for legal aid. Bush was banned from coming near her or communicating with her, but within days he had broken the court order.

'My car was damaged, for a second time. It cost me £700 to have it repaired. He taunted me about it. He knew I could not prove it was him. One day when I was driving up to the snooker club he jumped out and lay in the path of my car, and I had to swerve to avoid him. Yet he later claimed to the police that I had mounted the pavement and tried to run him over. On another occasion we were outside the club and he came up, swinging a bottle over his head and shouting obscenities. Ram finally told him to get lost and there was a scuffle. Eventually Garry ran off, only to return with the police. He had accused Ram of starting the fight, and Ram was charged by the police, but when it came to court, the case was thrown out.

'But it was more hassle, more unnecessary grief, and it hurt me that Ram had to be involved in all this. Everyone was involved. My family had had their lives completely disrupted. The more mischief he caused, the more delighted Garry was.'

In June 1992 Bush was in court for breaking the injunction, and he was sent to prison for three months. To Claire's astonishment, he managed to persecute her from his cell, sending her a letter from prison.

'I thought it was wonderfully ironic. He'd been sent there for harassing me, and yet he was able to contact and upset me. I gave the letter to my solicitor. When he got out of prison after serving six weeks of his sentence, everything started again, and if anything it was worse. He was more cunning and streetwise. Where at one time he had admitted to many of things he did, he now denied them, or he slapped in a counter-accusation against me. If he was once frightened of the police and the law, he feared nothing now. If he was once sad and pathetic, he was now dangerous. Anyone who tried to help me was damned: he waged war against them, too.'

The letters he sent to Claire and her family and friends – including Ram's family now – were rambling, incoherent, full of colloquialisms, poor spelling and grammar. His handwriting was as messy as his thought processes, and the same sick sentiments were expressed as he used on the phone. He boasted to Claire about taking young girls to raves to corrupt them. He said it made him feel better to make them feel bad.

In June 1993, Garry Bush went to work in Tenerife. Claire made a mental note never to go there on holiday and settled down to get on with the rest of her life, convinced that distance would cool Bush's obsession with her. Within days she was receiving letters and phone calls from the Canary Isles.

Then the harassment stepped up a gear, and another member of Garry's family became involved. Claire had appeared on a television programme talking about her ordeal, and his family felt she had in some way betrayed him – despite all the anguish he had subjected her to over the years. Eventually Claire had to threaten to take legal action to halt the flow of abusive letters coming from his relative.

'I felt like Alice in Wonderland, living in some strange fantasy world. I'd had to take endless threats to kill me, threats to kill my family, Garry had threatened to rape Ram's mother and his younger brother, he had said that if I ever had children he would be standing at the school gate waiting for them. The level of threat and abuse, and the language used, had been horrific. Yet I was being branded a villain for speaking out against him. I was being treated as though I was victimizing him. I feel sorry for his mother. She is a widow and it must have been hard for her witnessing what happened to Garry, and she did not write to me. But for anyone else, however close they are to Garry, to start doing that is unbelievable and unforgivable.'

Although the letters from his family stopped, the calls and letters from Bush did not. There was one chilling moment when Claire picked up the phone at a friend's house, only to hear Bush's voice on the line, calling from Tenerife. He did not recognize her voice, and she handed over the receiver.

Over the 1993 Christmas holiday period she received a series of phone calls which were traced back to the Birmingham area, where Bush has friends.

Claire believes her life has been blighted by Bush. 'It's taken its toll on me. I don't like going places on my own. I need people I know around me. I am uncomfortable with strangers and, where I once took people at face-value, I no longer trust my first instincts. My first instinct was to be sorry for Garry, and look where it got me. I am now more suspicious, more wary, more guarded. It has hit my confidence. Three years ago I would have played at a strange snooker club without a second thought. Now my concentration wanders beyond the next break. I am always watching behind me.

'I feel he took advantage of me. I took so much nonsense from him because he was part of the gang and he was going through a difficult time. I let pass two assaults in a pub, a knife-point attack at my friend's and a series of embarrassing scenes before I did anything. I didn't deserve it: the letters, the vandalism, the sheer venom and hate. And my family, Ram's family and all our friends did not deserve it.

'Looking back I believe he singled me out to attach himself to because when he met me I appeared to be super-confident, running my own business and in a relationship, my life all the way he would have liked his to be. He was a weak guy who used his obsession to suck the confidence out of me, as if by doing that he could infuse it into himself. It was as though he believed he could take what he lacked from me, use me to build up his own self-esteem, feed off me to build up his own strength. I've had a lot of time to try and figure him out, I've thought about the fact that he may have been affected by his father's death, all sorts of things. I believe his family always spoiled him, but he may have been bullied at school.

'Yet none of that explains the sheer vitriol of his attacks. What would tip anyone into threatening to kill another human being? I have tried to blank out the death threats, but the one thing that he has said, more than once, that really haunts me is the threat that he will be at the school gates waiting for my children. I go cold every time I think of that.'

Although Claire qualified for legal aid, she believes the whole protracted ordeal has cost thousands of pounds in lost earnings to various members of the family. 'But you cannot calculate the cost in money, you cannot put a price on fear, worry, constant heartache. I know that I have been very lucky to be surrounded by some strong and loyal people. It was not my fault, any of it, but it would be understandable if other people found it hard to be dragged into it. But Ram, his family and my family have all been great, and without them I would not have kept going. They have all had to put up with some really sickening abuse.'

Like all stalking victims, Claire believes the law has been demonstrated to be totally inadequate. 'It's badly in need of reform. It's mixed up. Years ago it was designed to protect men from lunatic women. Now it offers little protection at all. If he had been my husband, my ex-husband or my boyfriend, the police could have acted. Because he was just a pal, I was helpless.

'I had to endure months of threats to kill me before he came to justice, and then it was under civil law not criminal law. It is wrong, fundamentally wrong, that you have to pay for justice – I got legal aid, but if I had been working I would not have qualified, and it still cost us money. That's unfair, unreasonable and unacceptable today. This is almost the twenty-first century, not Victorian times, not medieval times. At a time when I needed all my concentration for my college studies I was worried about my safety. That's wrong. The law should protect my freedom as much as anyone else's. Hundreds of women endure this kind of hell, and a great many of them cannot afford even the limited legal redress I was able to get.'

All feeling of pity and sympathy Claire may once have had for Bush is now gone.

'I hate him. I hate everything he's done. If I could kill him I would, because it's the only way I can see it stopping. I wish he didn't exist any more.'

'I DIDN'T WANT TO HURT HIS FEELINGS'

'I WAS NOT physically threatened, I was not sexually threatened, my career was not threatened,' says Janey Buchan, who retired in the summer of 1994 at the age of sixty-eight, after fifteen years as a Euro MP. While she recognizes that her experience was much less threatening than many cases of stalking, nevertheless it was, to her, emotionally devastating.

Janey is a tough, indomitable woman who has spent all her adult life battling for the causes she believes in. She is the widow of Labour MP Norman Buchan, who shared her left-wing idealism and her dedication to helping society's underdogs. She has fought relentlessly against apartheid, for homosexual rights, for nuclear disarmament. In the European parliament she has been the scourge of the corrupt and the time-serving, battling against the worst EEC excesses. She once famously calculated that 886 pounds of apples and 1,358 pounds of oranges were being dumped by the Common Market every minute. She has never courted popularity, being quite happy to speak out against the perks of cut-price cars and champagne to herself and other Euro MPs. But she has, because of her natural generosity and her energy, won friends and admirers from all shades of the political spectrum.

Yet despite all her experience as a hard-headed and competent politician, Janey Buchan admits that she was mentally and emotionally devastated by the unremitting attentions of a man who claimed to be a close friend of hers. His first letter to her arrived three days after the death of her husband, and he only stopped writing and phoning her, and her friends and colleagues, three years later, when Janey won a court order banning him from approaching her. It was, in her own words, a time of 'all-embracing, overwhelming hellishness'.

Because she was not followed or threatened, Janey dislikes the use of the word 'stalking' for her case. She prefers to describe the man as 'a pest'. But she was as systematically pursued and harassed as most stalking victims. Her life was as disrupted, and she experienced the same stomach-churning fear every time a letter in the familiar typescript dropped through her letterbox. Her single, huge advantage over other victims is that court action was effective, and the harassment stopped. Her own distress was not so easily switched off, and she wonders if she will ever completely recover.

'I lie in bed and think why did this happen to me, what did we do to deserve this. Now I think it will never end, my resentment will never go away,' she says.

Janey Buchan first met the man who would come back to haunt her life when she was a teenager. She was a working-class girl from a politically active household, and by the time she left school at fourteen she knew her political allegiance. She met her future husband, Norman, who was a student at Glasgow University, when he stopped her in the street to hand her a leaflet, and with him she became active in the Glasgow branch of the Young Communists League and worked as a typist in the Communist Party office. They mixed socially with a crowd of other committed left-wing youngsters, including her future pursuer, who was also a student. It was a happy time full of youthful ideals and dreams of changing the world, which was shattered by the start of World War II. Norman, Janey's first and only boyfriend, went into the army in 1942.

Janey and the rest of the group continued to spend their free time together, going to dances and the cinema. Janey's natural concern for others made sure that the young student was included in their group activities.

'I've been told since that the others were puzzled as to why I did it. A friend has told me since, "We used to hate you for saying 'Come along' to him, because we thought he was such a bore. We wondered why the hell you had to invite him."'

When Janey was serving in the ATS she wrote to many of her friends; she's a compulsive letter-writer. The pursuer was one of many who received notes and letters from her, and when she was home she went to the cinema with him. 'I never regarded him as a boyfriend, and nobody else did – everybody asked me about Norman, who was generally accepted as my boyfriend. But I did go out with this man, as a friend.'

When Norman returned from the war, he and Janey were married. It was November 1945, and she was nineteen. They remained faithful and happy together until his death forty-five years later. 'Neither of us had any other relationships. You could write the history of my sex life on the back of a postage stamp.'

The early years of their marriage were immensely happy. Norman returned to university to complete his degree, and afterwards worked as a teacher. Both he and Janey were immersed in politics. They were well-known in Glasgow left-wing circles, especially as they ran an open house for Communist Party workers and other sympathizers. When Joan Little-wood's Theatre Workshop was in Glasgow, running on a desperate shoestring, Norman and Janey were very involved in finding them lodgings, raising money for them, getting volunteers organized to help them. It was not uncommon to find Janey's sitting room littered with sleeping bags. Her house was described by one friend as 'an office with beds'.

The Buchans bought a house in 1949, and by this time the student she had befriended had almost dropped out of their lives. He visited their home once or twice, but that was all.

'We were all in the Communist Party but he was not in our circle of friends. He knew my brother, and visited us a couple of times. On one occasion he made a strange stilted little speech to Norman about "the best man won" but we thought nothing of it. I can remember after one visit Norman sliding down the wall in a mock collapse of relief. "What a bore," he said. Our group of friends were witty, amusing, into puns and visual jokes; he didn't fit in. We lost touch with him, although I remember hearing from a mutual acquaintance that he had married.

'It was a very, very happy time. Our son Alasdair was the only child among the group. We all went on holidays together as a crowd. There were always stimulating, interesting people around.'

Janey never thought about the man she had known as a teenager. He was still involved politically and from time to time Norman would return from some meeting or other to tell Janey he had bumped into him, but they had a very wide circle of friends and acquaintances, and his name was just one among many. In 1956 the Buchans moved to the house Janey still lives in, and her 'pest' has never been inside it. It was in that same year that the Buchans both left the Communist Party, disillusioned by the invasion of Hungary, and joined Labour. Norman became Labour MP for Paisley South in 1964 and Janey became embroiled in local politics in Scotland, where she first acquired her reputation for battling corruption.

It was not until the 1986 Wapping dispute, when Rupert Murdoch moved his newspapers to the new high-technology plant in Wapping, East London, that Janey saw him again. She and Norman and supporters of the print and journalist unions were handing out anti-Murdoch leaflets in a pedestrian precinct in Glasgow. The day is etched in Janey's memory as a happy one: the weather was good; there was a lot of light-hearted banter with Celtic supporters on their way to a match; there were other amusing incidents with passers-by. Then a middle-aged man and woman came up to her and Norman. She knew it was somebody from their Communist Party past, but could not put a name to the face. After several minutes of polite chat, the couple moved on.

'When they'd gone I asked Norman who it was. He was very amused that I was asking him. Norman was notoriously bad at remembering names and on many occasions I had to whisper out of the side of my mouth to prevent him being embarrassed. Ironically, on this occasion it was him who remembered.'

After that incident in the street, Christmas cards were exchanged, one of them bearing the message 'Remembering long friendship with Norman and Janey.' Janey remembers thinking it was an over-the-top sentiment from someone who was no more than an acquaintance, but thought no more of it.

The illness that led up to Norman's death was a harrowing time for Janey. He became ill in 1989, and Janey and her son Alasdair knew that he had cancer. An operation to remove a tumour appeared to have been completely successful and at first they were cautiously optimistic about the future. It was a time of great tension and stress, as Janey struggled to balance the demands of having a sick husband with her own job. She did not want the details of his illness to be known too widely.

Norman Buchan died in October 1990, in the early hours of a Tuesday morning. The funeral was on the Friday, but before then she had already received a letter of condolence from the man whose letters were to become a major feature of her life for the next three years. Janey assumed it was, like the thousands of others that were delivered, an extension of sympathy from someone who had known her husband. Two thousand mourners turned up at the Linn Crematorium in Glasgow, to pay their respects to a popular and well-liked member of parliament. Among the Buchans' personal friends were the comedian Billy Connolly and Ron Todd of the Transport and General Union.

Two days later, another letter arrived, among a welter of others.

'He said he had been at the service at the crematorium. I hadn't seen him there, but probably would not have recognized him anyway. He talked in the letter about what a marvellous service it had been, what an excellent choice of poetry and music. Then he said, "Poor Janey, you bore up very well but broke down at the end." I didn't break down. much as I may have felt like it, I was very aware of all the people around me, especially my son, who was finding it difficult enough to cope with his own grief.

'When I read the letter I felt it was over-familiar and I was tempted to write and tell him he must have been at a different funeral. Now, looking back, I think, "Why the hell didn't I write?" I'm not sure if a sharp letter then would have saved me endless trouble later, but it may have done. At the time, though, I didn't want to hurt his feelings.'

About ten days later the next letter arrived. This time he said that he was researching the history of our times, and he wanted to interview me about my EEC work. He told me about poetry he had had published and he wanted to know details about when

Norman's books were published. I just remember thinking 'Oh God' and I ignored the letter. Two or three followed in the same vein, and I wrote to him saying I was sorry, at that time I could not cope, but that eventually I would answer his questions. I explained that I was no different from any other woman: I had lost my husband, I had my own job to do and I was trying to get on with my life. I told him that I did not understand what he wanted, but that in the fullness of time I would answer his letters more fully.

'I received another letter straightaway. This one was very apologetic: "*Mea culpa, mea culpa*, how could I have been so crass." That sort of thing. And the letters went on. And on and on. Eventually he sent me a copy of the letter he said I wrote to him when I was sixteen, which was the sort of juvenilia nobody would like to see recycled fifty years later.

'I wrote back and said that I had received it, that I did not know what he wanted but whatever it was, I wanted no part of it. I told him in straightforward language that I did not want him to contact me or any of my staff, as I had discovered that he had been phoning my staff trying to make appointments to see me. My research assistant had been protecting me from him. On one occasion he said to her, when she refused him an appointment, that I must not turn into a recluse. She pointedly told him that I was far from being a recluse, implying that it was only him I was avoiding.

'He took the message not to send letters or make phone calls literally, and instead he started to fax me. A fax came through on my office machine which said, plaintively, "Does this mean I am not to send you a Christmas card?" My normal reaction to anyone else would be to say that of course it didn't, but I instinctively knew that I must give no ground. The emotional events of the past weeks had torn the living daylights out of me and I was still feeling very fragile. I ignored his fax.'

After a short break the letters started again. The preamble to the first one was along the lines of him wishing to respect Janey's views about correspondence, but then it launched into another long and intrusive epistle.

'At this stage I was not keeping them, I was throwing them away,' says Janey. 'Friends all advised me to get rid of them. "These people go away" was the most common piece of advice. One or two of my friends are psychiatrists and retired psychiatrists, and in retrospect they regret giving me that advice, but so little is known generally about how to deal with this sort of problem. The one thing that has come through this experience searing into me, screaming and yelling at me, is that these people do *not* go away. That is the one universal truth about all these cases: it does not get better of its own accord, it gets worse. Each case is different, but it is a myth that people like this eventually stop of their own accord. They do not respond to normal friendly advice.'

The letters continued and Janey was throwing them away, often unopened. In the January after her husband's death a large concert was held in his memory, a lovely occasion that was marred for Janey by a letter she received from the man, saying that he hoped to see her there. She ended up resorting to subterfuge, putting out a rumour that she had already left when she was in fact backstage thanking the actors and singers who had taken part. As the anniversary of Norman's death approached, her pest wrote to her with a draft of an *In Memoriam* notice that he was planning to insert in a newspaper.

'He wanted to know if it met with my approval. I have obviously no objection to people doing that sort of thing if it helps them with their grief and is a comfort for them, but it was not for me, and it had never occurred to me to do anything like that.'

At this stage Janey's son wrote to her pursuer. Alasdair explained that although they could not stop the notice being put in the newspaper, they wanted nothing to do with it. Their feelings were that Norman's friends would remember him anyway, and those who did not would not be affected by a notice in a newspaper. He also stated in very clear terms that his mother was to be left alone.

Over the following few months Alasdair spoke on the telephone to his mother's tormentor on several occasions, and taped the conversations. He relentlessly and politely told the man to leave his mother alone. The man would agree to do that, and then smoothly turn the conversation to a personal one with Alasdair.

'At what point do you think people are off their head?' Janey asks now. 'For a long time I felt he would respond to reason, I tried to treat him as a normal person who could be dealt with in ordinary ways. He is a clever and well-educated man; he had just got his post-graduate degree. But by this stage I could see that he was obsessed.'

As the second anniversary of Norman's death drew near, Janey was deeply upset. Not only had the letters continued, but she had learned that he had been contacting her friends.

'They had tried to protect me by not telling me, and so had my son, who had more dealings with him than I knew about at the time. I was terribly upset when I later found out. He had even contacted two other Scottish Euro MPs and been to see them to discuss EEC policy, but always making references to his relationship with me. He was eating bit by bit into my entire life. A second *In Memoriam* appeared for Norman, which I found upsetting.'

By this time Janey was keeping the letters, although not opening many of them.

'Nobody advised me to do that, it was an instinct. I knew we were crossing a boundary into something that was going to have to be dealt with at some point. I recognized his letters from the typeface, and my stomach would churn whenever one arrived.'

Janey had to warn her friends and colleagues to beware of becoming enmeshed with him. She learned from these third parties that he was claiming to have been very involved in her early life, giving himself a much more prominent position in her circle than he actually ever merited. He claimed to have been involved with the Theatre Workshop project, which particularly angered Janey.

'We were so desperate for friends and supporters at the time, and a lot of the organizing was done from our house. Dear God, I was begging people to help with accommodation. Our friends were grabbed by the scruff of the neck and made to sell raffle tickets, shift props. There is no way I would forget who was there, helping out. For him to claim deep involvement was pure fantasy.'

Colleagues and friends were all targets for his relentless stream of letters, which invariably referred to Janey even when they were not addressed to her.

'One very good friend of mine had letters from him which she ignored. She had been a witness at my wedding, and I at hers, so we go back a long way together, and she was very upset. The trustees of a fund set up in Norman's memory were also harassed. He'd write asking when he, as a contributor to the fund, was going to hear what was happening with the money. The answer was that we were from time to time acquiring pieces for the People's Museum in Glasgow, and these purchases were announced in the press. But it would have been time consuming and very costly to send individual details to the thousands of individuals who had contributed. The two women trustees were outraged at his pursuit of me, and one of them was quite direct and rude to him. Then he started to write to them saying that I live in a mansion (which is not true), and that the collection of books Norman and I accumulated should be opened up as a library for students.

'It was the most appalling cheek. Norman did have 15,000 books but nobody could have been more free about lending them and giving them away than he was. And as for opening up my house for students – I am a running joke among my friends for my free and easy approach to people staying. It was very upsetting.'

She was even more upset when he contacted a blind

friend of hers, one of the crowd who had regularly parked sleeping bags on the floor of her Glasgow home, when she and Norman kept open house for young folk singers, poets, politically committed people and the Theatre Workshop crowd.

'He received a reply from my blind friend, which he photostatted and sent to me. I was deeply upset that he was broadcasting details of another person's life.'

Janey's pursuer was one of the people who left messages on her answering machine, informing her of the death of her blind friend. She agonized whether to thank him for the information. 'Normally I would pick up the phone or dash off a note to anyone who let me know about the death of a mutual friend. One of the most awful things is not finding out until some time afterwards that someone has died. It seemed so graceless not to acknowledge his call, but at the same time I felt that any contact by me would open the floodgates to more letters.'

In the end she got one of her staff to send a short, impersonal thank you. At roughly the same time Janey received a letter from a man in the North of England who was researching a biography of someone he believed she knew. It transpired that Janey was not herself able to help him, but she was able to recommend further areas of research to him – and in the process of sorting this out she discovered that he had received a letter from her pursuer. She asked to see a copy of this letter and when it arrived she was shocked.

'I nearly went through the roof. He said that he and I "had a relationship for many years" – and in today's language that would clearly be interpreted to mean a sexual relationship. I know it doesn't specifically say so, but that is how it would be understood. I was insulted and furious beyond words.

'He also said I had run a "salon" in Glasgow with my husband in the early years of our marriage, which was ridiculous. We kept open house for lots of people who in later years did become famous, but that was never why they were invited in. Looking back, it was an incredible time, but it certainly did not seem so then, and it was never contrived like a "salon".

'Not only that, but he was giving lunatic advice to the man researching the biography.'

It was this letter that determined Janey to take legal action. She had resisted until then because she had held on to the hope that he would stop tormenting her, and she had also reassured herself that although the frequency of his letters was threatening, the content was not. One of his familiar lines was that he and his wife simply wanted to be her friend, that they wanted her to visit them. It was not until she saw in black and white what he was claiming to third parties that she decided to take action.

'I was also reluctant because I knew how difficult it would be. Despite Scotland's Calvinist traditions, Scottish law leans more than English law towards protecting the accused. I applaud that, but I was aware that it would make my case more difficult.'

She had ruled out involving the police because she feared that news of her problem would leak out to newspapers before any action could be taken. She had also struggled to restrain friends who were offering to call round and sort him out.

'Maybe it's a Glaswegian reaction, but there were quite a few offers to take the law into their own hands on my behalf – my brother even phoned from Canada to say he could get some of his friends to take care of him. I had to laugh – and I also had to decline, even though there were moments when I could have cheerfully throttled him.'

Janey took her collection of letters to a firm of solicitors. As they read them one of her legal team commented on how boring they were. But as another letter was opened Janey was asked a question that made her angry and scared at the same time.

'Mrs Buchan, how does he know that you are planning to go to Africa?'

'It was a terrible moment. I realized he must be monitoring the committees that I am on at the European parliament. Anyone can find out those things, but you need to know about the nitty-gritty of the parliament, and that's not what most people would regard as a life-enhancing experience.

'Another letter said he had been to watch the cricket in Glasgow. My house is very close to the cricket ground, and friends going there often park in my drive. He made a reference to having nowhere to park. Yet another letter commented on work being done on the house; he said it was looking very nice.

'When I told one of my friends about these two letters she burst into tears because she was distressed at me being in the house on my own, with him outside. But I still felt he was not stalking me in a physical way, and that he had genuinely only seen my house in passing. As an MP's wife I have grown used to spending time on my own, and I never felt that there was a menacing presence outside.'

It was only when preparing her case with the lawyers that Janey discovered the extent to which he had been harassing her son and others, and the fury of that discovery made her more determined to fight. She knew that the case had to be taken to the Sheriff's Court in the area where her persecutor lived, and she was prepared for failure.

'I knew that it was a difficult one. The sheer volume of letters had been prodigious – I think it was said later in a newspaper report that I received 135 in five weeks, which is an absurd exaggeration, but none the less there were a lot. The sheer energy of the man, writing so often, was amazing. It must have cost him a small fortune in stamps. But the nature of the letters was in some ways a problem. They were not threatening: they were, as my lawyer said, very boring. I was afraid he would stand up in court and repeat what he said in the letters, about only wanting to be friends with me, and that I would appear to be over-reacting and obsessed.

'I decided that if I did fail to get an interdict banning him from communicating with me, I would give a press conference and ask "What good is the legal system if it does not protect you?"

'I told the solicitors that I knew they had a duty to ask me whether or not I had ever had an affair with him. I was able to laugh about it. I said that he had never been across the edge of my doorstep, let alone the edge of my bed, and that if I was going to have an affair with anyone it would have been someone less boring. Maybe I did write a silly, girlish letter when I was sixteen, but Norman was always the person I loved.'

When the writ was drawn up Janey had to decide how to handle the publicity that would inevitably ensue; Euro MPs do not go to court against pensioners who are harassing them very often. She spoke, off the record, to the editors of the Scottish newspapers, as well as to the editors of Scottish editions of London papers. She did not ask them to withhold the story, but simply not to break it before the writ was served.

'I was concerned about him and his wife. I felt sorry for him in a funny kind of way. He was seventy years old, and I knew it would be absolutely awful if he had a heart attack because of it. Despite my misery, I wanted the newspapers to have a care for his life. Hearing about it from a journalist first would be too much of a shock. I also stressed that he was not a stalker – he was an out-and-out pest.'

The writ was served and Janey's pest came before Kilmarnock Sheriff Court in July 1993. He was banned from phoning, writing or sending faxed messages to her, and he has abided by the ruling. But although the harassment has stopped, Janey fears she will never be free from the effects of it.

'What is so awful is that it makes you into a different person. You weigh everything up, become less spontaneous. It makes me blazing mad that I no longer feel free to write letters to all my friends. I was ever a great letter writer, but now I don't want anyone to think that I am obsessed, too. Especially as a widow, I fear people thinking they are lumbered with me because I'm on my own. There are people to whom I have never written the long, good letter I want to write, and I was reluctant to ask for the help I did need from my friends after Norman died because I did not want to burden anyone. I have never really been able to grieve fully for him, because this has dominated my life from so soon after his death. It was a time when I needed to restore myself, get back on an even keel.

'If I find myself talking about it to people and I say to myself, "Stop it, Janey, or they will think you are the obsessed one." But you do want to tell people about the all- embracing, overwhelming hellishness of it all.

'When people first hear about it their natural reaction is to laugh, until I make them realize how serious it is. Often they are embarrassed, because they simply do not know what to say. If I had not been a public figure I might have dealt with it differently. I could have sent the police around. One friend advised me to go round and stand outside his house bawling out what he was doing so the neighbours could hear, which would have been cheaper than legal action.

'I want to tell other victims that they are not alone, but that they will never be able to explain to anyone else how horrible it is. Nobody who has not experienced it will be able to understand the ability of these people to insinuate themselves into your life.'

Janey has found sympathy and understanding from other victims. A friend, a doctor she knows in Brussels, shared a similar experience, and struck a chord with Janey when she said, "It commands you from the top of your head to the soles of your feet."

Janey's social life was obviously going to change in some ways after the death of her husband, but her pest has had an even more fundamental effect on it. She no longer goes to places where she fears she may run into him.

'There was a recent conference on Labour history, which is a subject I have always been interested in, and for which I have more time since my retirement. But I was sure he would be there, so I did not go. I love the Scottish National Orchestra, but I know he goes to their Glasgow concerts, so I do not. I could go to hear them in Edinburgh, but why should my life be so disrupted for him? I find it hard going to the theatre on my own, without Norman, but added to that there is always the fear that I would see him there. Supposing he came across with his wife and I said "Bugger off"? I would feel awful, but I could not bring myself to be polite.

'I have had many sleepless nights, looking back at it all. I don't feel bitter, but I do feel angry. How dare anyone do this to me? What the hell did I do to deserve it?'

'HE'S INVADED MY LIFE'

'IF SOMEONE ELSE had told me this was happening to them, I would not have believed them. I would have thought they were exaggerating.'

Vicky Caldwell's feelings are echoed by many stalking victims. The full impact of the intrusion into their lives is something that is not recognized except by those who are very close to them. When Vicky, who had a nervous breakdown as a result of being stalked, first told a doctor of the trouble she was having, his attitude was that everybody gets a few crank calls, and implicit in this was the suggestion that perhaps she could cope better, perhaps she was exaggerating, being hysterical.

Yet anyone who looks at the scale of her problem, the sheer volume of letters, phone calls and threats she received, would realize it has been a terrifying invasion of her life. It is a tribute to her that despite everything she has been through she has not lost her sense of humour, but she believes her personality has been seriously impaired and she fatalistically accepts that her life has been damaged beyond repair. She cannot bring herself to say the name of her stalker: he is 'that character' or 'that creature' to her.

Vicky was widowed in 1989, after twenty-eight years of happy marriage to her naval officer husband Derek. For the last twelve years of his life Derek was ill, suffering a series of heart attacks. Vicky's days were full: she had to nurse him, helping him come to terms with the fact that he would not be able to go back to sea, and she continued to run the small hairdressing business attached to their sixteenth-century cottage in a picturesque Suffolk village.

At the time, she felt that this was a sad period of her life, as she watched Derek struggling with progressive ill health. In retrospect she regards them as golden days, days when she was what she herself describes as 'a normal person'. It was within months of Derek's death that the stalking began, and life has not been normal for Vicky since.

Her stalker is a man called Jonathan Knight, although he now calls himself Jonathan Caldwell-Knight, having adopted Vicky's name. He lives in a nearby village and met Vicky through her local church. She had attended church regularly earlier in her life, but during Derek's illness she went only when Derek was well enough. After his death, she once again went every Sunday, and centred at least part of her social life around friends she made at church. Jonathan Knight was one of those friends: a casual acquaintance who was invited back to her home along with a group of others. He was secretary of the parochial church council and they met at a coffee morning in January 1990. After that they would nod and greet each other after services, chat about innocuous subjects, see each other at church social events.

Before long Vicky began to suspect he was paying rather more attention to her than to the rest of their circle but she assumed that, given a hint that she was not interested, he would leave her alone. At that stage she simply felt embarrassed that she was going to have to rebuff him, she never imagined that the rebuff would not work. It was a remark Knight made about her music system that precipitated the rebuff; when Vicky commented that it was not working he said he would buy her a new one.

' "It will be my contribution to the household," he said, as if he was planning to move in. I then made it very clear that I was not interested in him romantically. I thought it might be a little bit uncomfortable next time I saw him, but I believed that was the end of it all.'

Instead, it was the start of the nightmare. Knight phoned Vicky constantly, on one occasion 200 times in one night. He bombarded her with letters. He put a rosary and a crucifix through her door. He sent her flowers. He parked his car outside her house all night. He even spent one wet and miserable night sitting on a public bench opposite her home.

He kept track of all Vicky's movements. When she changed her holiday dates at the last minute without him knowing – not because of him – he reported her to the police as a missing person. He rang one of her hairdressing clients to ask where she was, and when the woman replied that she didn't know, and wanted to know why he was asking, he replied, 'We don't want to find Vicky in a pool of blood, do we?'

He claimed to love and care for her, yet on one occasion he reported her to the Department of Health and Social Security, saying that she had no right to the widow's pension she was collecting, and on another occasion (during the days of the poll tax, when local taxes were based on the number of people living in a property) he informed the local council that Vicky had two men living with her. He also rang one of her favourite charities, the Cats' Protection League, to complain that he had been putting £10 notes in the collecting box in her salon which she had not been passing on to the charity. Luckily the organizers knew Vicky well enough to ignore his claim. He made a similar claim about the British Legion poppies that Vicky was selling, asserting that Vicky had cashed a cheque intended for the charity.

'I told the organizer she could check my bank statements and come with me to the bank to prove that I had not stolen the cheque, but I felt contaminated by the accusation.'

Vicky did everything she could to nip Knight's obsession with her in the bud. Soon after it became obvious that Knight had an unhealthy interest in her, she spoke to him. At this stage a stream of love letters had been arriving through her letter box, some inviting her on holiday, one telling her that he had booked a table for dinner at the Dorchester Hotel. Vicky confronted him at church and told him that he was wasting his time, as she was throwing his letters away unread. He replied that it was up to himself how he wasted his time. Next she wrote to him, in January 1991, a year after meeting him. She explained that she still loved her late husband and she did not want a relationship with anyone else. It was a polite, friendly but firm letter, ending with her asking Knight not to phone or write to her any more.

'I still thought he was a normal person when I wrote it. It seems funny now, but at the time I got a friend to read the letter over to make sure that it wasn't hurtful to him!'

It appeared to have done the trick. For a week there were no more calls. Then he rang her again, and told her that he knew she did not mean what she had said in the letter. From then on, the phone calls and letters began to get nasty, although for the most part when the phone rang Vicky would pick it up and hear nothing. Sometimes the line would go dead straightaway, sometimes she would know that someone was listening but they would not speak. When the caller did speak it was to deliver a torrent of abuse.

Vicky's first attempt to get help was when she contacted British Telecom about the phone calls. They told her they could do nothing until she reported matters to the police.

'Going to the police seemed a very big step to take. I'd never in my life had dealings with the police. I can remember if Derek and I were out in the car and we knew there was a police car behind us we would be worrying about whether all our lights worked, that's how law-abiding we were. I thought, "Hang on, everyone gets a few wrong numbers. Perhaps everyone has a few nuisance calls. It will stop." I was going away on holiday and I was convinced it would be over when I returned. When it wasn't, I waited a few days and I went to the police.'

Vicky has no complaints about the way the police

have helped her. Only one of the many officers she has spoken to over the years since Knight began stalking her has ever implied that she might be over-reacting. The others have been supportive and under-standing, even though they have been limited in the help they can give. One officer in particular has fully appreciated what she has been through and has been generous with his time and his help.

'I felt guilty contacting the police. There's part of you which thinks, there are people being raped and murdered, there are robberies being committed: am I just wasting police time with my problem? You feel you are making a fuss over nothing. You worry that the police will think you are just seeking attention. You are violated by what this man is already doing to you and you are violated again by this guilt.'

Not everyone was as quick to appreciate what she was going through as the police were, probably because they naturally found it hard to take on board. Her vicar and other members of the church have ulti-mately proved to be very supportive, but it took months before she could impress on them just how disturbing Knight's attentions were. The first doctor she saw told her that the harassment she was suffering was not unusual, and when Vicky asked him how he would feel if it was his wife who was suffering it, he told her that his wife would cope with it easily. She rarely read Knight's letters, recognizing them immedi-ately because he generally made no attempt to dis-guise his writing. But those she did see veered between being loving and abusive. He told her that he had first seen her when she attended church with Derek and that 'the earth stopped'. She was very distressed when he wrote about Derek's illness, claiming to have known her husband. (Vicky is sure that he and Derek never met.) He also told her that he had been 'in contact' with her late husband, and that Derek wanted them to be together (there was no explanation as to how he had made the contact).

When Knight changed his name to Caldwell-Knight, he sent Vicky and lots of her friends and acquaintances cards proudly announcing the fact. He also put an announcement of their engagement in the local paper, and the first thing Vicky knew about it was when people she knew stopped to congratulate her.

'When he took my name I was so upset that I seriously thought about reverting to my maiden name – I did not want the same name as his on my tombstone. But that seemed unfair to Derek.'

Knight even sent Vicky a typed marriage agreement which appeared to have her signature on it; she believes he forged it, after copying it from a Christmas card sent to mutual friends. There were scores of small but unnerving incidents: she delivered a basket of fruit to the church harvest festival, believing it would be distributed to the old and needy in the parish, only for Knight to turn up at her hairdressing salon with the basket in his hands. She does not know how he got hold of it.

One day when she was working in her salon a subpoena was served on her to appear in court: Knight was on a motoring charge and was claiming that he could not possibly have committed the offence because he was with Vicky at the time, a day eighteen months earlier. Although she knew it was not true,

Vicky did not know how to prove it until, by good chance, she discovered an old diary which showed she was with friends that day. Her friends corroborated the facts, and at the last minute Vicky was released from having to appear as a witness.

Some days Vicky's phone would start ringing at 7.00 a.m. and would go on until the early hours of the next morning. She felt she had to answer it, because of her hairdressing business and because she did not wish to lose contact with her friends. In her salon, clients would often answer it for her. If a man picked it up, Knight would treat him to a torrent of abuse, using strong language.

She refused to open the stream of letters which arrived and which, eventually, she delivered unread to the police. They still arrive, though not as frequently. 'Even picking them up makes me feel contaminated. I have to wash my hands after touching them.'

After the incident in which he sat outside her house overnight, for a week Vicky slept at a neighbour's. She was terrified of being at home on her own. She has partly conquered that fear, but she is still scared of going out after dark, in case he is lurking out there. Although he no longer attends the village church, neither does Vicky; she feels he violated the sanctuary of her religion. It was long after her suffering was known in the village that he stopped being a valued member of the congregation, a fact which rankles with her still because she believes others should have been able to see how bad it was for her.

'He used to wait for me outside church and insult me. One Sunday he spoke to me when I went up to the communion rail to take communion. I used to marvel at how he managed to get out of church before me – I'd make a point of sitting behind him so I could get away before he was out, but he often beat me. It was as if he had wings. The vicar occasionally found someone to walk me home.'

On one occasion Knight drove slowly behind Vicky from the church hall to her home, eventually pinning her against a wall and revving up his engine, shouting abuse at her.

'He said I was a rotten bitch and he hoped I rotted in hell, with quite a few added swear words. By the time I managed to get home I was shaking life a leaf, I was cold and I was vomiting with fear and shock.'

Vicky was at first determined not to give up attending church because she felt that would be a victory for Knight. But when she heard that he had read the lesson at a service she had not attended – she was ill – she rang the vicar and explained she would not go any more. 'I could not understand how he was still being treated like that. The vicar knew what I was going through. He said it was a mistake and since then he has been supportive. But I had made up my mind not to go;: that creature had managed to pollute even my church.'

Eventually, after three and a half years of unremitting torture, Vicky had a nervous breakdown. In the summer of 1993 she spent a month in hospital, and later that same year she went in for another three weeks.

'I could have given in earlier. I felt on the verge of collapse for a long time, but I remember thinking, "If I have a breakdown, the court will think I am the crazy one." I was frightened that he would be able to turn round and say, "She's the one who has been in a psychiatric hospital." I feel ashamed, even now, to admit that I've had a breakdown, ashamed and guilty. But that's what he brought me to.

'I fought for a long time, determined not to give him the victory of driving me out of my mind, but I reached the stage where I simply could not cope any more on my own. I have phoned the Samaritans so many times that I have lost count. I think my breakdown was largely triggered by lack of sleep, even though I was taking tablets to help me. I can remember one night going to bed completely exhausted. I took painkillers for a back problem I have and then I drank a hot chocolate, but just as I drifted off there was a loud hammering on my door. It was quarter to midnight. I looked out of the front bedroom window and saw a car roaring away, so I rang the police. I could not be sure it was his car, but then I discovered that he had put a package through the letterbox in the salon – I have had the letterbox in my own front door closed off, because so much was arriving from him. He makes no secret of who it is from. I did not get any sleep for the rest of that night.

'On another occasion two years ago it was my day off from the business and I'd been shopping in Colchester. I got home at about 6.30 p.m. and the phone was not ringing. It did not ring all evening, and I began to feel quite good. I genuinely felt he had got tired of the whole thing and had given up. At bedtime I thought, "This is wonderful," and I went to bed feeling quite different. I woke at about 1.30 a.m. feeling thirsty and went to get a drink – and that's when I saw his car parked outside. I couldn't see him in it and I was terrified. I went from being secure and happy to shaking like a leaf – I thought he might have broken in and be in the house with me. That was my imagination, but the terror was enormous. I rang the police and they told me to put every light in the house on and they would get over to me. By the time they arrived he had gone, but while they were here he rang twice. He had obviously driven home and started ringing immediately.

'One night he rang my number and after I answered it he left his phone off the hook. That was terrifying because it meant I could not ring anybody, and I was convinced he was coming to get me. I was shivering with fear.

'I can't imagine what it's like to go to bed and feel safe. I don't think I'll ever know that feeling again.

'In the end it was the police who arranged for my GP to see me, just before I went into hospital. I was suicidal. I could not cope, and there was nobody to look after me. I feel so desperately alone with this problem, despite the help of a few good friends.

'He has robbed me of my self-respect, my dignity, my confidence and my sense of humour. Because of him I have become involved with the police and I have had to go to court – I had never previously been in a court in my life. When I'm in hospital he rings up pretending to be a doctor – he says he has a Ph.D., but he's not a medical doctor – and asks how I am.'

By the time Vicky was admitted to hospital the police, with the help of BT, had assembled enough evidence against Knight to bring a court case. He was convicted on six charges, four of making improper use of phone equipment and two of using the phone for offensive messages. The case came before Sudbury Magistrates court in September 1993, by which time Vicky had been in hospital for a month. She attended the court case, with a nurse at her side, and because of her condition she was allowed to give evidence and go straight back to hospital. She was dreading the ordeal and went against medical advice by going.

'I felt that we had got that far, we had got him into court, and I did not want to give up because of my health. But it was a terrible experience. He told the press afterwards that he loved me. It is very hard to reconcile love with what he has done to me. He torments and tortures me: how can anyone call that love?'

In court, Knight denied that he had harassed her. 'Dear God, I love that woman with every fibre of my body and soul . . . I value her more than anything, including my own life,' he said. He was fined £1,080, ordered to pay £843 costs and bound over to keep the peace for three years. The court heard how the police had found a diary of his obsession at his home, but Knight claimed this was a work of fiction, a first draft for a novel he was writing. He also told the court that he had a 'full sexual relationship' with Vicky, and that he wrote to her every day as a 'lover's tryst'.

In retrospect, Vicky believes she should have involved the police earlier, and she should not have been so reluctant to report to them every small problem that Knight caused for her. She would counsel any other woman who is being harassed to keep all the letters they receive and give them either to their solicitor or to the police; at first she threw them away or returned them unopened to Knight.

'I was still working on the basis that somewhere inside him was a rational human being, who would eventually take the hint. It took me a long, long time to realize that a truly obsessional person will not take a hint, will not suddenly grow tired of the game.

'I believe that he is seriously mentally ill, but I also believe he is evil. I feel no pity for him. I loathe him and if I could think of a way of ridding this earth of him, I reckon I would do it. When he threatened to commit suicide a couple of times it was like a tiny ray of hope. I knew he wouldn't do it, but I wished with all my heart that he would. I was phoned once by a female voice, telling me that he had taken an overdose and accusing me of killing him. Luckily a good friend was here to say that I was not killing anyone. I was very disappointed to hear that he was still alive the next day.

'He must spend all day trying to think of new ways to destroy me, and I think he has succeeded. I do not see much point in my life any more. I've never even had the chance to grieve fully for my husband. I have been so depressed that I have told the police that I will die soon, and I have asked them to do me one last favour, and make sure that he does not go to my funeral.

'There is one small way in which I am glad that he picked on me. I think I was very unlucky, but I do think if he had picked on a young, inexperienced girl it might have been much worse.'

Her physical health has suffered as well as her mental health. She smokes more heavily now than she has ever done, after successfully giving it up a couple of months after Derek's death.

She has put her house on the market, after living there for more than fifteen years. The estate agent was warned not to allow Knight to present himself as a prospective buyer to be shown around, but within days of it being offered for sale he had rung up offering to buy it for the full asking price – as long as Vicky agreed to live in it.

Before her breakdown Vicky's constant companion was her black and white cat Smartie. When she went into hospital Smartie had to be found another home, with friends of friends.

'Because I was not really well for some months, he stayed with these people,' she says, looking at her collection of framed photographs of Smartie. 'They adopted him. They even changed his name. He was my cat for nine years and I loved him more than anything, but I knew that it was better for him to stay in a stable home, because my health was so precarious. Smartie is back now, yet I feel that even there, my persecutor was victorious. He invaded my life and robbed me of something precious for months when I most needed a companion.

'If anyone had told me, after Derek's death, the way my life would unfold, I would not have believed them.'

'HAPPY VALENTINE'S DAY'

LAUREN BARNES IS more feisty than most stalking victims. It's not because she's tough or hard, and she's not particularly big or physically powerful. In her own words, 'I'm no Bionic woman.'

But Lauren, who was only seventeen when she attracted her stalker, has from the start of the whole nightmare episode been determined that the man pursuing her will not change or spoil her life, even though he has been a more constant physical presence than many of the telephoning or letter-writing cases. She has alternated between fear and anger, and it is the anger that has made her accost her stalker in the street on more than one occasion.

Even a funeral wreath left outside her door, with a disfigured Barbie doll spattered with fake blood attached to it, has not shaken her determination 'not to let him win' – although she admits that was the most frightening episode of the whole affair.

Lauren's problems started in 1991, when she left her mother's and stepfather's home to move into a flat in the centre of Leicester, near to her work at

Top left: George Harrison has spent a fortune making his homes secure and, in the months following John Lennon's death, he had a seventeen-man police escort.

Top right: Rod Stewart had to fight off a female attacker who had managed to gain entry to his Los Angeles home.

Above: Phil Collins (pictured with his wife) was harrassed by a Frenchwoman he didn't even know who was convinced *he* was trying to kill *her*.

The world of tennis also attracts its obsessive followers. German player Anke Huber has been pestered for two years by a fan who constantly sends her gifts, watches her every match and trails her back to her hotel.

Guenther Parche was besotted with tennis star Steffi Graf (*above*). TV cameras captured the moment when he decided to stab her opponent, Monica Seles, and was then overpowered by security men (*left*).

Above: The author Stephen King has had a lot of experience with stalkers and fanatical letter writers. He has come to accept this as part of his life – but employs a private detective to keep tabs on them.

Right: Lisa Grayson and her parents, the young gymnast whose life has been overshadowed by the constant attentions of a stalker since 1988.

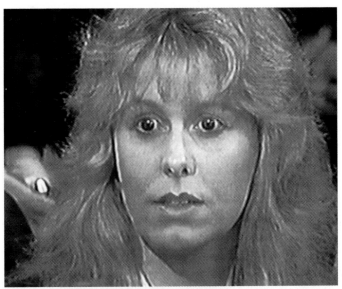

Above: Judy Barclay and her two young sons live under virtual seige conditions, barricading themselves into their home every night in fear of the continuing persecution they suffer at the hands of their stalker.

Left: Claire Elliott's life has been blighted by the threats, recriminations and manipulations of a former friend whose infatuation turned to hatred.

Above: Janey Buchan, retired Euro MP, who was relentlessly pursued by an acquaintance after the death of her husband.

Right: Vicky Caldwell is constantly bombarded with phone calls from her stalker (once as many as 200 in one night), a casual acquaintance who became so obsessed with her he even changed his surname to hers.

Left: Roy Aziz and his mother Rene Sampat, who became obsessed with fellow church-goer Ancell Marshall. Acting on Rene's orders, Roy murdered Ancell's wife Janet.

Below: Ancell Marshall suffered the double horror of discovering his wife's body and then being arrested for her murder.

Above: Gillian Vincent was sentenced to a year on probation for sending snooker star Stephen Hendry pornographic items and for leaving obscene remarks on his answering machine.

Right: Simon Reynolds was arrested five times for his threatening behaviour towards Lady Helen Windsor, with whom he was obsessed. He was sent to a mental hospital but eventually committed suicide.

Leicester Ambulance Service headquarters. She knew nobody in the new area where she was living, but after a while she became friendly with a young man who lived in the same road. He was a scaffolder who spent a lot of time away from his family home, but when he was around he would pop in occasionally for a coffee with Lauren. One day she was leaning out of the window of her attic room flat talking to him as he stood in the street below. He was joined by his brother, who shouted up to her, asking if she would like to go out for a drink. Lauren agreed: she liked the scaffolder so she assumed she would like his brother, and she wanted to make new friends in the area.

'It was only when he knocked on the door for me that night that I realized he was quite a bit older than me — about eleven years. As I was only seventeen, that's a big difference. As I saw him at the door I was immediately a bit concerned about going out with him, but I told myself that it was only for a drink and there was nothing to worry about.'

They walked to a pub and went in for a drink. As they sat chatting Lauren became more worried.

'I thought he was weird, especially his eyes. They were strange, staring. I politely mentioned it in conversation. I said something about how sad his eyes were. That's when he told me he had been ill, but that he had sorted himself out now. Warning bells were going off in my head. I thought, "My God, I've got a right weirdo here."'

Now really worried, Lauren told her companion that she had to phone a friend who was ill. She said she had promised to sit with her mate that evening if she was feeling really bad. She called her friend Vicky, explained what was happening, and asked Vicky to drive immediately to the nearby bus station and pick her up. The man with the strange eyes walked with her to the meeting point, and within minutes Vicky arrived. As she climbed into the car, the man asked Lauren if he could see her again. She did not want to hurt his feelings, so she told him that as she was moving from her flat that week she did not know where she would be living, so she couldn't make any arrangements. She breathed a sigh of relief as they drove away, having spent no more than three quarters of an hour in his company.

'I just thought it was a bad date, like happens. I never thought anything more about him, and when I moved that weekend I never expected to see him again.'

Lauren moved back to the village of Birstall, where her mum and stepdad were living and where she grew up. At first she shared a flat with her friend Vicky. It was two weeks after her move that her stalker walked into one of the local pubs where the two girls were having a drink and came across to talk to them. Lauren's heart sank.

'Where were you the other night?' he asked.

'What do you mean?' said Lauren. 'I told you I wasn't going to see you again.'

'Can't I just talk to you?' he said.

It was a question Lauren would hear many times over the next three years. She and Vicky finished their drinks and left.

It was another week before they saw him again, once again in one of the village pubs. When they spotted him they left and went to another pub, but within five minutes he appeared. At this stage he had no car, so he was regularly walking the four miles from his home in Leicester to Birstall. Lauren knew that he was in business with a partner from the village, so he had 'a sort of excuse to be there'. Over the coming weeks she and all the regulars at the village pubs became used to the sight of him, but she was able to avoid speaking to him.

'Then we had a celebration for Vicky's mum's birthday. We were all having a drink and a good time, and we decided to go on into Leicester to continue the party. Vicky had met a couple of blokes she knew, and they were going to give her and me a lift, and Vicky's mum and some of the others would follow later. We walked out of the pub with these two men and he was standing there. He started shouting at me for being with these men. He said they were involved in drugs and he didn't want me to be with them. He said he was trying to protect me. He was swearing and I was swearing back at him. We had a massive row just outside the pub. The two men disappeared – I think they thought he was my boyfriend or something, and they did not want to get involved.

'Vicky fetched her mum who came out to help me, and Vicky ran to get the car so we could all pile in and get away. I was furious. He was interfering in my life and he was also making a spectacle of me, dragging me into a public slanging match. It was horrible.'

A few days later the landlord of the pub handed Lauren a letter that her stalker had left for her – and the only consolation she drew from that was that he obviously did not know where she lived. The letter made no reference to the angry scene.

'It was a weird letter. If you hadn't known the full story, you'd have thought it was a love letter from an ex trying to get back with his girlfriend. Somehow in his twisted mind that's what he saw me as. It said things like, "I'm sorry I couldn't come over and talk to you the other evening. All I want is to talk." On and on about wanting to talk to me and wanting to protect me. I ripped it into small pieces and flushed it down the loo.'

After that, everything went quiet for three or four months, and Lauren believed that he had finally taken the hint. All through the summer of 1991 she was able to put thoughts of him behind her and get on with her life, still sharing a home with Vicky. Then, just as she was feeling really relaxed, a large bunch of flowers and a box of chocolates arrived for her at work. With them was a note in which he said he had been away for a while – he didn't say where – and he gave Lauren a mobile phone number on which to ring him. Angry, Lauren threw away the flowers and gave away the chocolates, and rang the police, explaining that she had been followed before and that the man concerned had reappeared. She was advised that it was not a criminal offence to send flowers to a woman, and there was nothing that the police could do.

Then something more worrying happened. Vicky gave Lauren a lift to work one night, when Lauren was on the night shift. As she drove back to Birstall Vicky was aware of being followed, and she deduced it was not the first time, because as she approached the road where she lived the car behind put on its indicator before she used hers. He knew in advance where she was going. Lauren felt sick when she heard: not only did he now have a car, but he knew where she lived. The following day she decided to take the initiative and rang his mobile number. She was connected to an answering service, and she left a number for him to call her back. It was her mother's number.

'Looking back it was a mad thing to do, completely wrong. But I knew the police couldn't help, and I wanted to get the whole thing sorted out. I still half believed that if I had a good talking to him, and was completely straight, he would give up.'

When he returned her call Lauren accused him of following her, and he initially denied it, even denying that he had a car. After a while he admitted it.

'I tried everything in that conversation. I tried being nice to him, I tried being horrible, I tried to confuse him, as I thought by this time that he was mentally ill. I even told him that he was ill and I told him he needed help. I explained that he was more ill than he realized. But I now know that though he may be mad, he is not thick – in fact, he's quite clever.'

His reaction to Lauren's pleas to leave her alone was chilling. He started to read out to her a list of her movements over the past few weeks. He had detailed everything, from her work shifts down to what time she went into Tesco's and how long she spent in there.

In the next few weeks she regretted giving him her mother's phone number. He started to ring regularly, and if her mother answered he would hang up. Up to this juncture, Lauren had not told her mum about him, she did not want to worry her. But her mother now had to know. At first she assumed that Lauren's problems were with a young lad who would not take no for an answer, but she soon found out that it was much more serious, especially as her phone was ringing at midnight and 1.00 a.m. When Lauren answered the phone herself on one occasion he began again to tell her that he only wanted to speak to her, to look after her.

Angry, Lauren threatened him that if he continued to pursue her she would get somebody 'to have a word with him'. 'It was a straightforward threat, although at the time I had nobody to call on. I've got no brothers or uncles, and then I did not have a boyfriend. But I thought it might work, scare him off.'

What it did was to flush from him a stream of four-letter abuse. As, by this time, his blue Sierra was frequently parked in the road and often followed Lauren to work, she rang the police again. Once again she was told that he had not committed any offence. Sitting in a parked car was legal.

'What was so unnerving was that he wasn't there every day. He'd be there for a couple of days, and then I wouldn't see him for three or four days. It was worse than him being there all the time, it gets to you more. There was always this awful feeling when you left the house: would he be there or wouldn't he? He never approached me, he was just there. It was awful. Then he'd disappear, maybe for three or four months, and then one day he would be back again.'

In April 1992, a year after meeting him, Lauren moved to a new flat in the village. For a time she felt safe because once again he did not know where she was living. But within a couple of weeks she spotted him cruising down the main street while she was waiting at a bus stop, and all the old fears – and anger – returned. Within a few days she saw him again, and this time he kerb-crawled behind her, weaving in and out around parked cars, as she headed up the village to a pub where she had just started a part-time job as a barmaid.

'It was only my second evening working there and the last thing I wanted was him walking in. When we reached the pub car park I went up to his car and shouted at him not to follow me in there. He drove his car against the entrance to the pub so I couldn't get in, but then he suddenly reversed away and I went inside. Five minutes later he walked in. I wasn't enjoying the job behind the bar, and the sight of him finished it for me. I apologized to the landlord and said I would have to leave. He followed me out. I was blazing. I marched up to him and went mad at him. He was crying and saying he just wanted to look after me, and the more he said it the more angry I got. I really ripped into him verbally, I slapped his face and then I kicked the door of his car and stormed off.

'Looking back, I was just getting rid of a lot of pent-up emotion. It had been going on for a year and I felt very alone with it, and helpless to stop it. Even though family and friends are sympathetic, they've no idea how isolated you feel. It seemed that it was no good going to the police because they couldn't help, and nobody had mentioned to me that I could get an injunction against him. In fact, it is hard to get an injunction and it costs money for legal fees, so I'm glad I didn't get involved in that.

'When I stormed away from him he did not follow me, but he saw me again later that evening when I popped out to buy some cigarettes. I was very, very scared: I thought that by upsetting him so much I might have forced him into doing something. But after that evening I did not see him for three days.'

Events escalated when he did reappear, the following Tuesday. It was about 6.00 p.m., and Lauren was walking from her flat to her mother's house for a meal. She saw the familiar blue car driving towards her and he pulled up at the kerb alongside her.

'I was thinking, "What's it going to take to stop this man? What can I do?" I felt desperate,' says Lauren, who was just eighteen at the time, and who had been given no advice by the police or anyone else as to how to handle the situation.

'I walked over to his car again and once more I told him, politely, that I did not want to see him, I did not want to talk to him, and would he please just leave me alone. He said that I may not want to talk to him, but he wanted to talk to me. I stayed calm and rational, and asked him to respect my wishes, but the more I talked to him the more we just went round and round in circles. He stubbornly refused to understand what I was saying – it was like talking to a brick wall. In the end I said I would have to get someone to sort him out if he didn't leave me alone and he replied, "You'll go down in the box with me."

'I wasn't getting anywhere so I carried on walking towards mum's. His car was facing the wrong way, so he could not follow me immediately, but he was soon alongside me again, kerb-crawling. I lost my rag and went over and kicked his car again and swore at him. For a moment it seemed to work; he stopped following me and I walked on. I didn't want to give him the satisfaction of looking back, but suddenly I heard a car right behind me. He had mounted the pavement and drove straight into me. I went flying over the bonnet and landed on the grass verge.

'Luckily, I was only bruised and there were no broken bones, so I got up. Looking back, I probably should have lain there until somebody called an ambulance. But I could walk, so I stood up. It was a light evening and there were plenty of passers-by, but nobody seemed to be doing anything. I called out, "Will somebody get the police?" and an old man said there was no phone box nearby. I was furious and I shouted back, "You are standing in front of shops, they have phones."

'There was a man who had been walking along with a small child and I turned to him and asked him if he would be a witness. Luck was on my side, and he was an off-duty policeman. I walked into a shop and the stalker followed me, but this policeman took him back outside. I looked after the policeman's little girl while he called his colleagues and detained the stalker.'

When the police asked Lauren if she wanted to prefer charges she jumped at the chance; at long last, he had broken the law and could be arrested. When police searched his car they found a knife under the front seat.

Lauren spent that night at her mother's, and in the morning learned that the police had bailed him at

2.00 a.m., on condition that he did not go near her and that he turned up at court the next day. What happened next, she says, was like something out of a film.

'He didn't turn up for court, but I did not know. I did not go to work because I was very badly bruised and sore, but I was determined to go back to my own flat. Early that evening some friends of mine came round, and after I'd told them what had happened they suggested we all go out and relax. We had to drive to another friend's house to water his plants while he was away on holiday, then we went for a drink. They brought me back home at about midnight. As I arrived I could see four policemen outside my flat.

'Do you know how much trouble you have caused?' they asked me. Apparently, when he failed to show up at court, they went looking for him. They couldn't find him and they couldn't find me either, and they were worried that I had been abducted. They called at my flat a couple of times early in the evening, and they called at my mum's house. She told them I was probably with friends, and they drove her round the village to all my mates' houses. My mum was beside herself by then.

'They wouldn't let me into the flat until they had searched it, then they told me not to stay there that night. I was angry that he had been released the night before, but I agreed to go to mum's. We got a call from the police at 5.00 a.m. to say they were going to carry out a dawn raid on his home, and that's where they found him. He appeared in court the next day and guess what? The court granted him bail. And this time the police didn't come round to check that I was all right. I was alone again.

'Worse, the next time I saw the police it was for them to caution me and tell me that he was accusing me of attacking him. He had a couple of small scratches on his nose from when I slapped him. The police took down my story and I was not charged. Giving that statement felt like walking on broken glass; I could not deny hitting him, but I wanted to make sure they knew the whole history of provocation. He had apparently said he would drop his charges if I would drop mine, but there was no way I was going to do that. This was the first chance I had to get him to court, and I'd rather have gone to prison myself than lost the opportunity. But it was a very worrying thing to happen, finding yourself being cautioned and told that anything you say may be taken down and used in evidence. It felt, again, like I was living in a film.'

A condition of his bail was that he stayed away from Lauren: he broke it. By this time she had met her boyfriend Mark, a 6-foot 4-inch tall ex-Grenadier Guardsman. As they left a Chinese take-away one night the stalker reversed his car up to them, then slammed it into a forward gear and drove off. He also rang her mother's phone number a couple of times before the court case.

'The police had advised my mum to change her number but we decided not to do that. In a way, his phone calls to her were a warning that he was around again. After he'd not been seen for weeks he would always ring that number before he started following me, so it was useful to us. I also had a recurring

dream. I dreamed an alien from a spaceship was trying to get to me, but I was surrounded by people
in uniform. That dream always seemed to happen
just before he turned up again, so I always took it
seriously.'

During the court case in September 1992 Lauren
faced the ordeal of seeing her stalker in court every
day. He stared at her. She also had to give evidence
and be cross-examined.

'I was really worried that he was going to get off.
His defence was that he was looking behind for other
cars when he ran into me, and that it was an accident.
Thank goodness the off-duty policeman had witnessed it, because he was able to say in his evidence
that he was staring at me as he drove into me. In his
own evidence he said some bizarre things. He said,
"I've got a good heart – I'll rip myself open and show
it to you," and he also said, "If I wanted to have got
her I would have had her by now."'

At the end of the trial, at Leicester Crown Court,
he was found guilty, and the following day he was
sentenced to three months, suspended for one
year. He was also ordered to pay Lauren £150
compensation.

'I was not disappointed that he did not go to jail,
because I don't believe prison would do him any
good. He'd probably just sit there brooding about me,
and he'd be bitter because he would lose everything if
he was inside. But I was disappointed that there was
no order for him to have psychiatric tests.'

The £150 was paid in instalments, but eventually
Lauren received it all.

It was Christmas before he reappeared. Lauren and

her mum had gone together into Leicester when her stepdad spotted the familiar car driving up and down the road. He rang the police, who said they could do nothing.

'Because he had already been in court for his previous behaviour, the slate had been wiped clean, and to get him into court again we had to start from scratch. We were back with the police saying things like, "Driving up and down is not a criminal offence." They were very sympathetic, but their hands were tied by the law.'

For a few evenings he patrolled outside her parents' home and in the area of her flat – Lauren believed he did not know exactly where she lived, although he knew the road. One morning the local greengrocer, up early to stock her shop, told Lauren she had seen him parked outside from 5.00 a.m. to 9.00 a.m., but again he seemed only to know which area of the road Lauren lived, not the precise address.

Just after New Year 1993 he pulled his car alongside Lauren as she walked up the road.

'I just want to wish you a happy New Year,' he said.

'You ran me over not long ago. How dare you wish me anything,' she replied.

He became angry and said, 'I'm never going to leave you or that flat alone.'

Later the same day he followed her down the road again, with his car window down shouting, 'Bitch, slag.' An elderly couple parked nearby offered Lauren a lift, because they could see she needed help.

'I got them to take me to my mum's, because I did not want to lead him back to my own flat,' she said.

'I've never seen them before or since, but I was very grateful to them. After all I've been through, though, I would not have got into the car had they not been elderly and had one of them not been a woman.'

Again the police were informed, and again the only help they could give was to advise Lauren not to live on her own in the flat, without a telephone. 'But I'm stubborn and angry, I did not want to lose my independence because of him.'

It was Valentine's Day when the wreath arrived. It was propped between her door and the flat next door – he'd narrowed her address down to one of two. Pinned to the funeral wreath was a blonde Barbie doll with a nail through its heart, covered in fake blood. The card attacked to the wreath read: 'Happy Valentine's Day, Bitch. Slag. R.I.P.'

It was the worst moment of all for Lauren. 'I fell back against the stairs. I was hyper-ventilating. It was the first time I really believed he intended to do me physical harm. Even when he drove the car into me, it had seemed like a spur of the moment thing. This was calculated and horrible.'

The police could not find his fingerprints on the wreath. 'That's what I mean when I say he is not thick; he always seemed to know how far he could push the law. When they rang him he agreed to see them the next day, but in the end they could not spare an officer to interview him. They told me they couldn't arrest him, anyway.'

Since then he has made a couple of death threats against Lauren to a third party, and he has put a magazine article about rape through her door. 'He'd highlighted certain paragraphs in it. And alongside he had written, "I can't wait to see you without your bodyguard," because he knows that Mark was a guardsman. On one occasion he followed Lauren round a frozen food shop in Leicester, and another time he stood outside her office for hours. But she hopes now that he has finally got bored with her and it is all over, an ending that may have been precipitated by the presence of Mark in her life.

Lauren has met her stalker's brother, the scaffolder, a couple of times since her ordeal started. He seemed embarrassed and reluctant to discuss what has happened.

'It's not his fault, except perhaps he could have warned me not to go for that first drink. I was just a very trusting person. You don't go around imagining things like this can happen. I hate my stalker, hate him. I know he's probably in need of help, but I don't think that's any excuse for what he has done to my life.

'I've been frightened of him and I've been very angry with him. I sleep with a knife beside my bed, but I know that if he broke in when I was alone and asleep, I wouldn't stand much chance. I'd fight, though, and if I stuck a knife in him I would gladly go to jail for it. When I'm angry I think, "Come and try it, you coward, you know where I am."

'My mum has been very upset by it all. I'm still, to her, a little girl, and she wants to protect me. I've been able to reassure her that I can look after myself. I'm a little bit taller than he is, and I'm not weak. But he's had Territorial Army training, and anyway, men are stronger than women.

'I'd still take him on. After three years you feel like

that. I won't give in, I won't move house and I won't go into hiding. Friends have suggested that I ask for a transfer in my job, or that I live in a different area, but I'm damned if I will. That would be a victory for him.

'It almost becomes a game between him and me, a mind game. I've even had a friend drive me round his home area to see where his car is. It's not a role reversal. I'm not in danger of being obsessed by him. But there were times when things were bad and I just wanted to know where he was, keep tabs on him.

'I wish I knew what the answer is. He's mentally disturbed, but I don't know if there is any treatment that would help him. He's canny. I think he's got smarter as this thing has gone on and he knows now how far he can push the law. My biggest fear is that he's doing this to somebody else, although I'm relieved he's leaving me alone.

'After he ran me over people asked me if I was affected by it, and at first I said no. But I think it takes a long time for these kinds of effects to show. I realize that I am now jumpy if I am walking with my back to traffic. If a push-bike comes up behind me quietly I nearly jump out of my skin.

'The experience hasn't put me off men, but I'm very straight with them now. If a man starts chatting to me in a pub and I hint that I'm not interested, I will then tell him in no uncertain terms that I don't want to talk to him. I don't stand for any messing. I'm much more wary about people than I was, it takes longer to get my trust. I think the whole thing has hardened me, but I don't think I am particularly tough. I don't want people to think I can cope with it all – there have been times when I have been very scared, lying in bed on my own at night, especially if he has been driving up and down outside all evening.

'But I refuse to give him the satisfaction of seeing me have a breakdown. That would mess me up for the rest of my life. I'm too young, I've got lots to do.'

'A FATAL ATTRACTION'

IT IS THE ULTIMATE horror for any stalking victim: the knife that flashes in a dark doorway, the hammer that cracks open a skull, the gun that blazes a final, twisted tribute to a murderous obsession. Most stalkers are not violent, but all are unpredictable. The irrational mania that drives them to pursue their quarry is beyond interpretation within the normal framework of social behaviour. It is the unpredictability that generates the most fear, coupled with the knowledge that, in some extreme cases, stalking leads to physical attack and even death.

The words that Rene Sampat shrieked as she was led from the dock at the Old Bailey would send shivers down the spine of any stalking victim.

'I am guilty of love, not murder,' she shouted, as she was taken away to start a life sentence for the murder of the wife of the man she claimed to love – a man whose life she had turned into a wretched hell.

The day Ancell Marshall first met Rene Sampat, when she came to him for driving lessons, was the beginning of an on-going nightmare for him. His is, arguably, the worst stalking story of all: not only was his life wrecked by her persistent pursuit of him, but he suffered two such massive traumas that it is remarkable that he has survived as well as he has.

First, he arrived home from work one day to find the body of his wife Janet, his wife of seventeen years, savagely and brutally murdered. She had fifteen stab wounds and the assault had been so ferocious that one of the two knives used had sheared in half as it was plunged into her body. Her hands were cut to ribbons as she had raised them to protect herself. She had also been strangled. She was lying on the settee, and the television was blaring loudly, probably to cover the noise of the attack.

It was the worst moment of Ancell's life. But he was devastated again when the police made him their number one suspect – and eventually arrested him for the murder of the wife he loved.

Rene Sampat, who Ancell describes as 'the woman from hell', first came into his life in 1985, when she enrolled for lessons with his driving school in Stoke Newington, north London. Twice married and twice divorced, the mother of five quickly decided that the next man in her life was going to be Ancell Marshall. Before long she was using her lessons as an excuse to try to seduce him. She touched his hand and his leg as they drove along, and let her hand fall into his lap.

'At first I did not read too much into it but she persisted. One day she made a gesture towards me and the car almost went out of control as a result,' he said.

'I still was not sure it was a sexual come-on, but I suggested she had another instructor. I was very happily married and a lay preacher in the Seventh Day

Baptist Church, where marital infidelity is a big sin. We take the Commandments very seriously.'

Ancell swapped his pupil to another instructor. She took a few more lessons, but the interest had gone out of it for her and she cancelled.

Ancell had met his wife Janet when they were both still at school, and there had never been anybody else for either of them. They were both sixteen years old when they married. Janet had two miscarriages before their first daughter Charlene was born in 1980, followed by Naomi two years later, then Stacey in 1986 and Rebecca in 1990.

'The miscarriages made us stronger, more together. We shared a very strong family life and a deep faith. Janet taught at the church Sunday School. She was a kind person who would do anything for anyone.'

All the Marshalls were very involved with the Seventh Day Baptist Church in Victoria Road, Tottenham, north London. It's a strict and demanding religious regime, which involved them spending all day Saturday at the church.

'There are about fifty in our congregation, and like the Jews we celebrate our faith on a Saturday, not a Sunday,' said Ancell. 'Saturday is when the Lord told us to celebrate him. We don't eat pork or watch TV on the Sabbath. We get to church for the first service at 9.00 a.m., and we go through the day until about 8.00 p.m. with a mixture of services, hymns and Bible readings. Perhaps we are a bit of a cult, but we have churches across the world.'

Realizing Ancell's commitment to his faith, Rene, a Muslim, abandoned her own religion and converted to Christianity to join the same church. It gave her an excuse to spend long tracts of time in the same room as Ancell, but he still did not know that she was obsessed with him.

'She would always try to get me on my own. At first I felt sorry for her, she seemed to have had it rough. She told me she was fourteen when she left home. She fell in with a guy a lot older than her and had five kids. I think she saw herself as a very sexy lady, but I was honestly not interested.'

Rene began to systematically insinuate herself into the Marshalls' life. She befriended Janet, and became a trusted babysitter for Stacey, who was then their youngest child. She found any excuse to visit them, organizing a celebration for Janet's birthday and showering their daughters with gifts. She spent £70 on a coat for Ancell. 'She was always asking where we bought things, or if we did some decorating, she would do her house just the same. It was eerie. Janet and I discussed her and we decided to get someone else to look after the kids.' Denied this access to his life, Rene took dramatic action to try to force Ancell to pay attention to her. Three times she rang him, claiming that she had been raped. As a senior member of the church community Ancell felt it was his duty to support her, so on the first occasion he went round to her home in Tottenham. When he arrived she was half-undressed and she begged him to make love to her.

'I couldn't understand how she would want another man to touch her if she had been raped, but she was kissing me on the lips and pressing herself against me. I was shocked and frightened. I could think of nothing else to tell her but that I was unable to make love, and I left after telling her to go to the police.'

On another occasion she phoned at midnight, as Janet and Ancell were in bed and drifting into sleep. She was in tears and again she said she had been raped. Ancell told her he would ring the police, but she pleaded with him not to. When he agreed to go round himself she put the phone down. Ancell immediately rang the police and they were at Rene's house when he arrived. At first they would not let him in, as Rene was half-naked and tied up.

'She told the police that a man had climbed through her window and asked her to do all sorts of things to him at knife-point,' said Ancell. Once untied, Rene ran into the kitchen in tears and tried to stab herself with a knife because, according to Ancell, 'nobody believed her story'. She calmed down after a police officer explained that he had power to take her children away.

Ancell and Janet were still seeing her at church.

'She would continue to seek my help as a counsellor. I gave her what succour I could, but there was no sexual element to it. It was straightforward religious teaching, and I was always telling her I was happily married. She spoke of another rape, and she was still giving us gifts and surprises. It was all rather unhealthy. Then I began to get telephone calls. We just dismissed them as crank calls. Most of them were nothing, just the sound of traffic passing, as though they had been made from a call-box on a busy street.'

In 1988, on holiday with a friend of the Marshalls in Tunisia, Rene claimed she was having an affair with Ancell, that she had had an abortion, and that she would marry him if anything happened to his wife.

Gradually, as Rene began to realize that her campaign to inveigle Ancell into bed was not going to work, her tactics got rougher. Poison-pen letters started to arrive at his home, accusing Janet of having an affair.

'Janet and I were a very close couple and at this stage we had three lovely daughters. We had built up a business from nothing – a driving school and a Caribbean food take-away. We had bought our own home and we were hoping for another child. Janet had stuck by me through thick and thin. When I decided to become a preacher she backed me and we dropped everything. I left a good job as an engineer and we moved to Birmingham, where I enrolled at a Bible college. We virtually lived on hand-outs because I couldn't get a student grant. It was very hard, but I was happy because I was on the road to what I hoped would be my vocation as a minister. Janet was as committed as I was – everything we did, we did together.

'So when the first poison-pen letters arrived I dismissed them instantly. They claimed that Janet was having an affair, but they were written by someone who had been in our house, knew details about our family, knew us. They could accurately describe things. We wondered who it could be. Was it a neighbour? Or someone who had been to collect their children from a party at our house? It was absurd. Whoever it was knew my movements, because the "affair" allegations were all for times when I was out, either at work or on church business. Some were quite graphic.

'One or two were stencilled, but most were hand-written, in a disguised writing. They were all post-marked in London. Some I didn't bother to open, but I'm glad I kept them all. Initially I went to the police, but they weren't particularly interested. For some reason I needed to go to two different police stations.

'At one stage I received a big box, so I called the police to open it. Inside was a dismembered doll, with its arms and legs ripped off. Rene later said she had been sent something similar.'

When Janet became pregnant with her youngest daughter, Rebecca, Rene's fury tipped her into new activity. A box of dead roses was delivered to the Marshalls, and the church they all attended was daubed with graffiti which said, 'Janet's having my baby.' At the same time one of the poison-pen letters claimed that Janet's mythical lover, a man called Erek, was really Rebecca's father.

Another letter said Janet preferred her lover to Ancell. Disjointed and badly spelled, it read, 'When you touch her body she say it feels like a snake. Your breath stink. You cannot kiss good.' Yet another claimed that Erek had made love to Janet in the family home and left a condom in the lavatory.

Although both Ancell and Janet suspected at times that Rene might be involved in the campaign against them, neither could believe that she was capable of so much hate. They had decided she was a minor nuisance, an attention-seeker who deserved their pity and concern. They had no idea of the depth of her obsession.

It was a tragic miscalculation. One of the poison-pen letters had warned them that Janet was going to die on the first birthday of baby Rebecca, in May 1991. But it was a few days earlier, on 28 April, that Ancell returned from the take-away business to find his wife murdered, while their four daughters slept upstairs. Devastated, Ancell frantically dialled 999. He believed that an intruder had broken into the house and murdered his wife when she disturbed him.

'I felt numb, cold, empty, as I picked up the phone to call for an ambulance and the police,' says Ancell, who was thirty-one years old at the time. 'Losing her killed me too. We did everything together. I still feel a huge part of me is missing.' On the night of the murder, Rene had rung him several times, begging him to go to her.

'I took a stack of calls from her. To her, it was important that both of us should be in the clear. She correctly believed that husbands are always the prime suspect.'

Rene, who had tried to provide the man she loved so fanatically with an alibi, was right. Not only did Ancell have to cope with losing his wife, but he soon realized that the police suspected him of being the murderer.

'They seemed to look no further than me. They just decided I was guilty. You see how suspects are treated in films and books, but this attraction was happening to me in real life. One officer even said I had confessed to him. They found there was a £30,000 insurance policy on her life, with me as beneficiary, and that clinched it for them.'

As the police tried to build a case against him,

Ancell found the old adage of there being no smoke without fire working against him. First his friends backed away from him, then his church colleagues, and even Janet's mother and father and the rest of her family accepted that he was her murderer. He was arrested and held in custody for two months. His case came up at the Old Bailey in February 1992, ten months after Janet's death. 'The weeks after the police arrested me are a blur. I tried to explain, but nobody would listen. My faith carried me through. It gave me inner strength, even during the bleakest moments.'

During the time Ancell was held in prison, Janet was buried. He was refused permission to be at her funeral 'for security reasons', and he is understandably bitter about that. As a deeply religious man, he feels he missed an important rite of passage, as well as an emotional chance to bid his wife farewell. He also found opinion in his local community, and in particular within the church congregation, hardening against him.

'I don't know what I would have done without my faith. I prayed long to God every day. I couldn't believe what I was going through. It was beyond words. I cannot start to describe my suffering, I was in hell. I found my wife covered in blood on the sofa, my four daughters were asleep in their bedrooms – and then I was accused of her murder. Everyone seemed to turn against me.

'I wish I could say my church helped me. But Rene, who was still a member of the congregation, convinced them I was a really bad man. To them I was evil: both an adulterer and a murderer. When I needed help they not only turned their back, but turned on me. I was on my own. The wife I loved was dead and everyone, including my in-laws who had known me for twenty years, thought I was guilty. It was a real-life nightmare I woke up to every morning. It hasn't really stopped.

'Because of the animosity I quit preaching. When I needed God most, it seemed the church was trying to stop me reaching him. Some were embarrassed, some were openly hostile. Rene had them all lined up against me. I still went to services. I needed to. But there was a chill, I was made to feel unwelcome. Ironically, the church kept faith with Rene. Once they even tried to reconcile us.'

The lies that Rene was spreading among the church congregation were the same lies she told the police, and repeated in the witness box at Ancell's trial. 'She had the tongue of the devil. It was nonsense. She said she had repeated abortions with me as the father. Yet it was ludicrous, it could have been checked with clinics, medical files. But I was in the frame.'

Even though she was helping the police build a case against Ancell, Rene was still invading his life. On one occasion he had to ring her friends to remove her from the entrance to his driving school office – he refused to speak with her himself. 'Whatever madness possessed her was now out in the open.' Ancell prayed particularly hard on the night before his trial opened.

'Appearing in the dock was not the most awful experience of my life – that was finding Janet dead. But I felt very low. My belief in God had never deserted me, though, and I got justice in the end. It was the turning point. My prayers were being answered.' The judge at Ancell's trial threw the case out for lack of evidence against him. But although Ancell had achieved justice in court, the attitude of local people towards him did not change. The attitude of the police, however, did. A second investigation was launched, and Ancell's faith in detectives was at least partly restored.

'The second inquiry team was marvellous. The boss, Detective Superintendent Gavin Robinson, said to me, "Look, Ancell, just tell me the truth." He believed me. At last someone believed me. They picked up the trail of the poison-pen letters Rene had sent me, tracing for the first time the record of me taking them to the police station – the first inquiry team couldn't find that report.

'By then, things were beginning to drop into place about Rene. She was giving hints of some involvement, daft little things which eventually added up.'

The police team gradually assembled their evidence against Rene. Although she had not physically killed Janet herself, they discovered that she had worked up her oldest son, 16-year-old Roy Aziz (he was her son from her first marriage), until he was prepared to commit murder for her. She told him she had been raped in an attack set up by Janet. Rene and Roy were arrested, and Rene found herself in the dock of the Old Bailey in October 1993, with her son by her side. This time, it was Ancell's turn to be a witness against the woman who had put him through eight years of hell.

Prosecutor Nigel Sweeney told the court: 'Although Mrs Sampat had not been present at the murder she was the person with the motive who set it up and who assisted on the night and thereafter. She was infatuated with him and tried in various ways over a number of years to win him over, without success. So she determined that Janet Marshall should be murdered and Ancell could be hers.'

Rene's own counsel, Graham Boal, said the case could realistically be described 'as a Fatal Attraction and also a Fatal Obsession. The woman was obsessed to a point that can only properly be described as mentally abnormal.'

Rene was sentenced to life imprisonment for what the judge described as 'a cruel murder', and Roy, because of his age (he was eighteen when sentenced), was ordered to be detained in youth custody. He maintained during the trial that a friend committed the murder.

For Ancell, one of the biggest shocks of the trial was seeing Roy in the dock.

'The last time I had seen him he was a boy. Now he was huge, a man. It is hard to believe that he could stab a woman fifteen times, and strangle her, at the age of sixteen. The times I had seen him before he was always cheeky to Rene. I cannot understand why he could kill on the orders of his mother. What went on between them?'

The judge at the trial also asked for an inquiry to be set up into how Ancell came to be charged with Janet's murder. After the case Detective Superintendent Robinson said: 'The sort of woman who can plan the death of a mother of four who has never done her any harm, and use her 16-year-old son to do it, is beyond words. I accept aspects of the first inquiry were wrong, and we tried to right the wrong.'

But the conviction of his wife's killers did not right

the wrongs done to Ancell Marshall. Rene Sampat was still able to hold on to a lot of local loyalty, and when he left the court Ancell had to have police protection from a crowd who jeered and threw stones at him. The 'dream home' he and Janet had struggled to buy has been sold; Ancell and his daughters found it impossible to live there. The family now live in Hackney with his mother and father, who look after the children while Ancell works. But his driving school has been badly hit by the scandal of the two trials. Janet's family still believe that Ancell was involved in her murder.

'My children no longer see their grandparents, their aunts or uncles. I think it is wrong for them to hear their father branded a murderer. At Rene's trial they could not accept that she was guilty and that Roy murdered their daughter. I received verbal abuse – real words of hate.'

He is naturally worried about the future for his daughters. 'You probably never find out until much later how much they have taken in. They lost their mother, then their father – charged with murder. One set of grandparents and their mother's relatives remain convinced their father is the murderer. I try and give them all I can. We live with my parents now and we surround them with love.'

Rene has made no attempt to contact Ancell since her sentence.

'For the first time in nine years she has left me alone. Perhaps the enormity of what she has done has got through to her for the first time. She thought such a lot of herself. To her it was inevitable that I would fall for her. Janet was the stumbling block, and with her out of the way she could have me. I suppose I was lucky, she could have murdered my children too. She is sick, she is the woman from hell. I am a Christian, but I find it very hard to forgive her. I look at the girls and I see Janet.

'I have thought a great deal about what I could have done to save Janet. Ironically, if I had had an affair with Rene my wife would probably still be alive today. I never encouraged her. I was kind, Christian, no more. I never knew the depths of obsession that festered in her heart. I don't think anyone could have known: it was abnormal.

'She was obsessed, but I believe she was something else besides: she was evil. The woman is wicked, she was taken by the devil. When I look back, I think we did the right things. I saw some sign when I stopped her driving lessons. Then, when she joined the church and started ingratiating herself with the congregation and befriending my wife like a Judas, we tried to distance ourselves. With her rape allegations, I called the police. I spurned her seduction attempts, but I had to show charity and Christian compassion in case she was in real trouble.

'It's difficult dealing with such a force of evil. By hook or by crook she was going to try to possess me. To her, killing Janet must have seemed a small price. But whatever I have suffered it is nothing to the price that Janet has paid. I often wonder why our family have suffered so much, but we're in God's hands, and there must have been some reason.'

When Rene Sampat was found guilty she screamed her vicious vindication across the Old Bailey court-room: 'I am not guilty of murder, I am guilty of love.'

For Ancell Marshall, as for so many other victims of stalkers, it is a very strange, twisted, dangerous kind of love.

He wanted her, but he knew she was beyond his grasp. And because of that, Martin Stevens set out to destroy her . . .

Stevens, a 17-year-old apprentice plasterer, was obsessed with the pretty young housewife he met on his first job after leaving school. He was infatuated by her, but he knew that she was unattainable. To Stevens, Julia Barrett represented the kind of world you only read about in books or saw on Australian soaps: a happy, well-adjusted family, an expensive, well-furnished house, two beautiful children. The jewel in the crown was Julia herself, a small, bubbly blonde who was kind to the young lad who came to help with the plastering work on her home in the picturesque village of St Leonards, Buckinghamshire.

In the diary he kept hidden under the floorboards of his family's home in nearby Chesham, Stevens wrote about how 'nice' the Barretts' home was, and fantasized about making love to 31-year-old Julia. But he knew that she would never be a willing participant. He also fantasized about robbing her of her lifestyle, taking her property – particularly her car – as if some of the magic of her charmed life would rub off on to him if he could possess her things. He stalked her, watching from nearby woods and observing her movements, writing down the times of her regular comings and goings. He even managed to break into her home once, and make off with over £500-worth of property. But it was not enough: owning Julia's things did not give him the buzz he had hoped it would. It had to be her . . .

In the school exercise book he used as a diary, Stevens wrote out three plans for his attack on Julia, and by the third one the violence and sexual content of his fantasies had escalated. This plan was dated 9 January 1989. On 7 February, Julia died. She had thirty-one separate head injuries, three skull fractures, a broken jaw, an air-gun pellet in her temple and a five-inch stab wound from a kitchen knife in her back.

Stevens's diary was childishly titled 'Uncensored Gosh!!! Martin Stevens's very very very very private book, the famous green book'. Underneath was written the rhyme, 'Roses are red, violets are blue, you touch my book, I'll kill you.' His first plan for attacking Julia read:

Walk up to front door. Ring the bell and wait for big moment when it opens. Hit her over the head and rush in. Hit her on back of neck, not too hard. Put her on bed and ransack house then pick up her car and load goods. Calmly learn quickly how to drive properly, go back to my house and unload everything then dump car.

In his second plan, he favoured breaking in while Julia took her two children, Simon, nine, and Rebecca, six, to school. He knew that when she returned she always cleared up downstairs, and he planned to wait upstairs behind a door until she came up, when he would be 'ready for the crunch' of attacking her.

Plan three was much more graphic, and was the first one in which he revealed overtly his sexual desire for Julia, and also his intention of killing her. His diary instructions read:

Go to house and wait for her to come home from taking kids. Wait by front door. Then walk calmly over to her and make up some excuses, making her stop just by the bushes, and then as I say goodbye I would hit her with the handle of a gun and pull her behind the bushes, then shoot her in the temple and carry her into the house. Then up the stairs to the bedroom and strip her naked as if she had been raped, then back up the car to the door and ransack the house. I would take her clothes and burn them then give her a love bite or something. Take most of my clothes off and get into the other side of the bed and have a little cuddle.

He stipulated that he would not have sex with her. He said he was scared, and that after carrying out his plan he would ring up a friend and meet him at a pub. 'By the time I get back home I should have been told the news about the death of Mrs Barrett and will hopefully get away with it . . . The End!!!!'

The plan was executed clumsily. Stevens used his brother's mountain bike to get from his home to the village where his victim lived, dumping the bike in nearby woods. He did fulfil his fantasy of joy-riding in her blue Fiesta, taking it back to his home town and parking it carelessly, with two wheels on the pavement. He made little or no attempt to avoid being seen. Inevitably, he was arrested the day after the murder.

Stevens was jailed for life for murdering Julia Barrett. Her husband, Graham, the managing director of a building company, was not in court to hear the sentence passed on the youth whose obsession with his wife had led to tragedy.

* * *

The story of the stalking of Ahmed Osman was even more tragic, if tragedy can ever be quantified by a body count. Two people were killed and two more were seriously injured because the stalker, a schoolteacher, was frustrated in his quest for a 16-year-old schoolboy with whom he was obsessed. As the teacher's crazed fixation grew, so did the threat of violence, yet the warning signs were ignored.

Paul Paget-Lewis was a maths teacher at Homerton House School in Hackney, east London. He was by all accounts a good teacher, and had been on the school staff for twelve years. But he was odd and other members of the staff were worried about him; once before he had become obsessed with one of his pupils. In 1987 Ahmed Osman, whose parents were Turkish Cypriots, joined the school. Ahmed was fifteen at the time. Paget-Lewis's interest in the boy did not, at first, seem excessive, but it soon became clear it was not normal. He asked Ahmed to give him lessons in Turkish during the lunch hour and, although nothing sexual ever occurred, he insisted that the classroom door was locked and the blinds drawn. He became jealous of the boy's attention, following him home and trying to interfere in his friendship with another pupil, Leslie Green. During March 1987 the school reported three worrying incidents to the police.

The following month the teacher stencilled an obscene message about Ahmed to his friend Leslie on two of the school's entrances. It said, 'Leslie, do not forget to use a condom when you screw Ahmed or he will get Aids.' Concern at the school was growing, although it was not initially established that Paget-Lewis was responsible for the daubing. When he changed his name to Osman, though, the police were again informed, and this time a fear was expressed that Paget-Lewis might attempt to abduct the boy. (Paget-Lewis had changed his name before – it is believed that his real name is Ronald Potter.)

For the next six months the Osman family lived in fear. The maths teacher smashed a window at their home, slashed car tyres, put super glue in locks and smeared dog excrement over the car and the front door of the house. On the night of 15 October, Paget-Lewis smashed all the windows of Ahmed's father's car. When his father, Ali, and his uncle went to Hackney police station they were told that it would be difficult to prove that Paget-Lewis was responsible for the damage. Prophetically, Ahmed's uncle asked, 'What has to happen? Are you waiting for this man to kill or injure one of our family, or for one of us to kill or injure him?'

Paget-Lewis had, in the meantime, been transferred to another school, but his campaign of harassment continued unchecked. He drove the wrong way up a one-way street to ram a van in which Leslie Green was a passenger, for which crime he was arrested and cautioned.

Like many mentally ill people, Paget-Lewis did not lack self-awareness, and on 15 December he gave a very clear warning of impending doom: he told education chiefs that he was planning 'some sort of Hungerford' – a reference to the killing spree of crazed gunman Michael Ryan four months earlier, when sixteen people were killed in the Berkshire town. He said that it 'would not take place at school'.

Again, the police were alerted, and two days later

they went to Paget-Lewis's home to arrest him. He was not there: he was at his post, teaching maths. They left a message for him to contact them, but he never did. Shortly afterwards he left London for three months, and the Osman family dared to hope that their troubles were over. Then in March 1988 the mother of Ahmed's friend Leslie called the police, because he had been hanging around her home for three days. The police did not return her call.

Two days later, the maths teacher burst into Ahmed's house at 11.00 p.m., ordered the boy and his father to drop to their knees, and shot them with a sawn-off shotgun. Ahmed was wounded, his father was killed. Paget-Lewis ran out of the house and drove to Bishops Stortford, in Hertfordshire, where the deputy headmaster of the school lived. He shot at and wounded the deputy head, Nick Perkins, and killed his son, 17-year-old Gareth Perkins. Paget-Lewis believed it was Nick Perkins, who had warned him about his behaviour, who had kept him and Ahmed apart.

He was caught soon afterwards, after a car chase down the M11. His words to the arresting officers were: 'Why didn't you stop me before I did it? I gave all the warning signs.'

It is a question that Ahmed and his mother would like answering. Paget-Lewis pleaded guilty to manslaughter and attempted murder, and is now held in Broadmoor. The Osman family have gone as high as they can through the courts of England and Wales in an attempt to make a claim for negligence against the police for failing to stop a crime being committed. The House of Lords refused to allow Ahmed a right of appeal against an earlier ruling that the police were immune to negligence claims. The last person to attempt to take a similar action was the mother of one of the Yorkshire Ripper's victims. But the Osman family continue to argue that there were clearer, more specific warnings about Paget-Lewis's obsession, and if any notice had been taken of them two lives could have been saved.

PART FOUR

In the Name of Love

'The Doors Are Locked, Aren't They, Mummy?'

Is it better to know, intimately, thine enemy? Is the stalker who emerges, unknown and unbidden, from the shadows more terrifying than the one who was, once, invited not just into your home but into your heart and your bed? The answer is that it does not matter; it is nothing more than an intellectual debate to argue the relative merits of the stalker you know against the stalker you do not know, or only know as a fleeting acquaintance, because the degree of fear generated cannot be placed on a graph according to the circumstances in which the obsession was launched. The sheer mind-blowing persistence and lack of reason that is the common denominator of all stalkers can come because the victim is glimpsed at a distance, or because he or she was once a willing partner.

Ex-wives, ex-husbands, ex-boyfriends, ex-girlfriends are all common stalking victims, and the only real factor which distinguishes them from those who attract the lonely outsider is that it is, initially perhaps, more difficult to recognize that their stalker's feelings are obsessional and not normal. In *Sleeping With The Enemy* all the signs are there for Julia Roberts's character to recognize: hers is no ordinary loving husband, and the print of his possessiveness is all over their relationship. In reality the man or woman who turns into a stalker may have been an inconsiderate and uninvolved partner; it is only when the relationship disintegrates that they become obsessional about what they have lost.

If their loss includes a home and children, as well as a partner, it is harder to label their behaviour as stalking, at least until it reaches a certain level of persecution. An ex-partner has an excuse to ring, to write, to turn up on the doorstep, to have access to children, to haggle about property split, even just to want to talk through their grief and desire for a reconciliation. But for some, the compulsion to cling on to the past relationship becomes an obsession, and their behaviour clearly is stalking. In America, Cheryl Tyiska, spokeswoman for the National Organization for Victim Assistance in Washington, estimates that as many as 70 per cent of all stalking cases involve ex-partners, and there is some US evidence to show that these are the cases that are most likely to lead to violence. One third of all women who are murdered are killed by an ex-partner and the majority of those, according to one piece of research, have been stalked.

One teenage girl who was seriously injured by a stalking ex-boyfriend is Paula Benson, who was only seventeen when Richard Tipping knifed her repeatedly in front of a store full of Christmas shoppers.

Paula was just fifteen when she first went out with Tipping, who was two years older than her. It was an intense teenage passion for both of them. The schoolgirl from the village of Kempsey, near Worcester, was besotted with the apprentice electrician who lived in Malvern. They spent all their free time together and even began to discuss marriage.

It gradually dawned on Paula that she was too young, and that maybe Tipping was not the man she wanted to spend the rest of her life with. But after she ended their twenty-one- month relationship, Tipping could not let go, and began to follow her. He threatened her, telling her that he would cut her face into small squares if she did not return to him. His obsession drove him to insomnia, and in his disturbed state he began to fantasize about killing her. He boasted of his plan to friends, showing them a bottle of poison and a kitchen knife with an eight-inch-long blade. When he followed Paula and saw her kissing another boy, he felt physically sick and resolved to carry out his threats.

The last remnants of his self-control dissipated one Saturday afternoon in 1991, with only twenty-two shopping days to Christmas. Paula had a part-time pocket-money job in Debenhams department store in Worcester every Saturday, working in the ground floor ladies' department. Tipping tracked her down, pulled the kitchen knife from his pocket and plunged it into her repeatedly as she screamed for help and begged him to stop. At one time she managed to break free from him, but he caught her again and the frenzied attack continued. Shoppers were slow to react to help her, because many of them thought that it was a stunt for a film. By the time they realized they were witnessing a desperate attempt on a young girl's life, Paula had collapsed in a pool of blood. Tipping was chased by staff and shoppers but managed to escape into the crowded city centre.

Paula was rushed to the nearby Worcester Royal Infirmary. She had eleven stab wounds, to her face, neck, chest and back. Both her lungs had collapsed. The closeness of the hospital and the speed with which the ambulance service were at the store probably saved her life. She had a twenty-four-hour police guard as she lay in intensive care, because Tipping was still at large.

He was caught several days later in Manchester. He pleaded guilty to attempted murder and was given a life sentence, which he is now serving in a psychiatric unit. Paula, who subsequently went to university, needed long-term counselling to help her recover from the traumatic attack, and she and her family have kept her whereabouts secret ever since. At his trial, it was revealed that Tipping still fantasized about killing her, and that the only regret he had expressed was for not having succeeded at his first attempt. Paula's parents are genuinely concerned that the conditions in which he is being held are not secure enough.

Colleen Kelly, like Paula, was an immature teenager when she first had a relationship with a man who would turn out to be one of the most dedicated and vicious stalkers of the lot. Colleen, a pretty young Australian schoolgirl, was happy enough to go out with the curly-haired boy from next door. At that age, his extra two years made him seem sophisticated, and his Honda motorcycle made him a good catch. Colleen did not realize she was the one who was being caught – and that Mark Harrison's appalling behaviour would dominate and dictate her life for more than a decade.

Like Paula, it did not take her long to grow out of the relationship. But when she tried to end it Harrison became violent, beating her up savagely. After each beating he would repent and become an attentive, perfect boyfriend for two or three months. Then a wrong look, a wrong word, an imagined slight – anything could tip him into barbarous violence. Out of sheer terror, Colleen remained by his side. When he broke her jaw and she had to spend five days in hospital, he sat by her bedside, an ever-present reminder to her that she must pretend her injuries had been caused by a surfboard slapping into her. Even though her family guessed the truth, Colleen was too scared to give him away.

She finally left him after a particularly vicious assault which lasted for an hour and half, and was caused by her being half an hour late getting home from work. She was so badly hurt that she was surprised to wake up alive the next day, and she determined to break free from him, five years after first going out with him. She changed her job and changed her address, and left strict instructions with everyone who knew them both not to pass on any information to him. Furiously Harrison roamed the streets of Sydney looking for her, breaking into her parents' home three times in one night, ransacking the place looking for Colleen. Both her parents were attacked, and from then on no member of her family or friends was spared. Harrison turned up on his motorbike at the factory where Colleen worked, revved up the engine, drove in through the doors and tried to run her down as she stood by a conveyor belt. She hid in another room, terrified, while other staff managed to arrest him. He was charged with attacking her boss, but was bound over to keep the peace and freed to resume stalking Colleen.

Then Harrison coolly enacted an incredible plan to get closer to the girl next door who would have nothing to do with him. He tunnelled under the floorboards of her parents' home, came up through the floor of a wardrobe and, when the house was empty, made his way into the bungalow attic. From above, he drilled holes into the ceiling of every room, and he bugged the telephone. For three months, Colleen and her family had no idea he was lurking above them, spying and eavesdropping on their whole lives. When they were all out at work he would use the rooms downstairs, sometimes leaving mysterious clues to his presence – a newspaper left open on a bed, a sticker attached to a mirror. When the family were in, he retreated to his lair, where he had made himself comfortable with an old mattress and a supply of tinned food.

To her horror, Colleen's mother discovered him in the wardrobe one day, but he fled back to his parents' home next door, and the Kelly family assumed he had broken in using a key. The whole truth did not emerge until one day he held Colleen's parents hostage, threatening them with a hunting knife with Colleen's name carved on to the handle. He told her father to ring Colleen and get her to come home.

Always on her guard because of Harrison, Colleen immediately realized from her father's tone that there was something wrong and she contacted the police. Harrison escaped, but was later arrested. It was only when police searched the bungalow that the family found out about the tunnel and realized he had been living in their midst. It was, for all of them, an horrific discovery. This time the court jailed him.

Colleen moved to England and her family moved to another secret address in Australia. But a prison term did not dampen Harrison's obsession, and when he was released after eight months he broke into the home of one of Colleen's friends and discovered letters with her address in London. With all the plausible deviousness of the true obsessional, he persuaded his social worker to help him get a visa to visit Britain, claiming to have relatives here. As soon as Sydney police discovered he was on his way they tried to intercept his plane at stopover points, but failed.

A day or two later Colleen Kelly, who was working as a restaurant manager and using a different name, looked out of her London window and saw a shadowy six-foot tall figure on the corner, looking up at her. It was Harrison. Colleen barricaded herself in and called the police, but by the time they arrived he had fled. He left England for France, and was then arrested when he flew back into Heathrow. He was deported back to Australia – he could not be charged with any offence in Britain because he had not broken the law.

Susan Homes did not suffer physical attacks on the same scale as Colleen or Paula, but the mental anguish her stalker inflicted on her will be with her for the rest of her life. Susan is a glamorous former air hostess who owns an exclusive boutique in Wimbledon. In 1992 she met Mark Braithwaite at Stringfellow's nightclub in London, and there was an instant attraction of opposites. She is sophisticated; he is brash and loud. She is beautiful; he is pock-marked and ugly. She has an exciting past, as the former lover of a Saudi prince; he has a sordid past, with numerous criminal convictions for theft, bur-glary, possession of drugs, criminal damage and even, appallingly, the rape of a 71-year-old pensioner whose home he ransacked and whose jewellery he stole.

Susan knew nothing of his past when she went out with him for a few months. But she soon realized he was a womanizer and a drug-user, and after a roman-tic holiday together in Cyprus disintegrated into rows, with Braithwaite kicking her, she tried to finish the relationship. Braithwaite refused to accept she no longer wanted to see him, and began a terrifying stalking campaign. He rang her number constantly, once calling her sixty times in one day. He threatened to kill her on numerous occasions, and he threatened to kill her mother by stabbing her 'eighty or ninety times' and petrol-bombing the house, telling her she would then 'see what it is like to live without a mother'. He smashed the windows of her fashion shop and damaged her BMW car. His harassment even extended to six tennis umpires staying in Wimbledon for the world's most famous tennis tour-nament. They were renting a flat from Susan, and he persecuted them until they were driven to find other accommodation, depriving her of valuable rental income.

Braithwaite admitted to police that the phone calls were intended to cause distress and said, 'I wanted her to commit suicide.' He nearly achieved his aim: Susan became so depressed that at one stage she took an overdose.

'I was a nervous wreck,' she said. 'It seemed like a never-ending nightmare.'

The messages Braithwaite left on her answering machine were sick and abusive, branding her a whore and promising to get someone to cut her throat. British Telecom put a trace on Susan's phone, and Braithwaite was arrested when the police became concerned about the level of threats. He was found guilty of threatening to kill her and threatening to petrol-bomb a flat she owned, and sentenced to seven years in prison. It was only after his arrest that Susan heard his catalogue of previous convictions, including a sentence of five and half years for the rape of the old lady and fifteen months for wrecking the home of another girlfriend who dumped him.

Jenny Wheelwright and her parents have had to put up with obscenities screamed down the phone at them at all hours of the night, death threats, and – in Jenny's case – physical attacks on both her person and her home. Jenny lives in fear of her ex-partner Kenny, and she resignedly accepts that she will probably never be free of him.

'He's a mad driver, and I find myself wishing he would crash and kill himself. I want him dead, because that's the only way this will ever end,' she says. 'I even fantasize about murdering him, and one of the police who has had to deal with him said they'd all give evidence on my behalf if I did it.'

Jenny is a sensible, attractive young woman who met her ex-partner when she was twenty-three – and has spent more than ten years since then in fear of him.

'Looking back, I was in love with him for about two months, then I became pregnant, and that was it. The seal had been set on the rest of my life. I was tied to him, and now I don't think I will ever get free. He follows me; if I turn a corner, he's there. He rings me all the time. It took a police typist thirty hours to transcribe the tapes of the phone calls he has made to me, and that was just some of them. The girl who did the typing was so upset she asked to be replaced.

'The language he uses is foul, the things he accuses me of cannot be repeated. The law cannot help me, because I have been to court to get injunctions against him forty-three times, and he just ignores them. He has served many prison sentences – he has been sent to jail for three months, six months and nine months, and several smaller sentences of just a few weeks, and it makes no difference. He has even rung me from prison. The only reprieve I get is that while he is locked up I and the children can have more freedom. When he is loose we live like prisoners.'

Jenny works as a warden at an old people's development, and lives in a council house that is provided with the job. She moved there soon after giving birth to her older son, Dominic.

'I had not intended to have a baby, I was fitted

with a coil. When I went for a regular check-up I was told that I was already three months pregnant. At the time I had a council flat and Kenny had moved in with me. I should already have been picking up clues about the way he was going to turn out, because they were there. When I watched *Sleeping with the Enemy* I cried, because the whole film could have been my story. Kenny was just as obsessional as the husband in the film.

'After Dominic was born we moved into the house that went with the job. I had given up my other job, and Kenny rarely worked. He's a car mechanic and when I first met him he had his own workshop. But he never liked work, he didn't like getting out of bed during the day, although he was happy enough to stay out at night.

'By the time my second son Dennis was born I knew I loathed and detested him, but somehow I was trapped. You can't tell people that your partner is vile, it's your problem. He had cut me off from my friends and family; he said all my friends were "stuck up" and they disliked him so much that they would not come near our house. He also cut me off from my family – he would not allow me to have a car, although I had always had one before I met him. He never wanted me to take the children to my mum's and dad's house. My mum was one of the few grannies who was never asked to babysit, because he didn't want my family near us. My mum literally did not see him for over twelve months, because if she called around during the day he would be in bed and we never visited her. Whenever I did anything he didn't like, he thumped me.

'Life became a pattern of him staying in bed all day and going out in the evening to his friend's home, coming back at 4.00 a.m. With luck he would go straight to bed, if not he might start ranting and raving and hit me for something. I used to be glad when he went out.

'When Dominic was two he decided he was going to teach him to read. It was late in the evening and he had Dominic sitting there, shouting at him if he did not recognize a word. Dominic was stuttering with fear. I couldn't say anything because that would tip him over into violence. I used to just hope that I'd have the children in bed before he was around in the evening. He went out so much that one of the first phrases Dominic said was "Gone to Bob's", which was my answer whenever I was asked where he was – Bob was his friend.

'He swore all the time and blamed me for everything that was wrong with his life. I was a four-letter word every five seconds. A friend of mine told me later that nobody should even talk to a dog the way he talked to me – and that was in front of a third party, when he was better than he was when we were alone.

'He threw my sewing machine through the window once because he told me to stop sewing and I inadvertently touched the pedal with my foot and he thought I wasn't obeying him. He's insanely envious of any success I have. We were broke one week so we went to a sale and I sold three patchwork quilts that I had made for £230. He went mad because he couldn't sell a car engine he had done up. He was really narked – but he took the money from me. On another occasion I made a leather pouch handbag and he did nothing but criticize it, saying he could do better. He insisted on sitting there doing it, to prove his point, and of course he made a mess of it, which made him even more angry.

'He used to break things if he knew I liked them. Mum and Dad had given me a limited edition china model of a Jack Russell terrier for my twenty-first, and I am very attached to it. I had to wrap it up and hide it in my underwear drawer, because he said he was going to break it.

'Despite the fact that he never worked, he had grandiose ideas about spending money. He always wanted the biggest, most expensive toy for Dominic on his birthdays, things costing hundreds of pounds which we could not afford,. If I said we could not afford it he would order me to sell something.

'I look back and wonder why I put up with it, but it creeps up on you. You find yourself working around him and his violence, for the sake of a quiet life. All I ever wanted to do was to avoid another confrontation.'

But there was a very violent confrontation, after one of Jenny's friends told her mum and dad that Kenny was beating her. By this time her second son Dennis was nearly a year old and Dominic was two and a half. Her parents went round to her home, and Jenny was out. Her mother spoke to Kenny.

'I didn't want to provoke him so all I said was that I was worried about Jenny because she wasn't looking well,' says Jenny's mother, Mrs Angela Wheelwright. 'In fact, she was looking so ill and so thin that one of my neighbours had asked me if she was anorexic.

She had lost three stone in weight and was beginning to look like something out of Belsen. He didn't say much and we left it at that.'

When Kenny returned from his usual night out he dragged Jenny out of bed at 5.00 in the morning and began to beat her savagely. He wanted to know what she had told her parents.

'He also went mad because I had left the hot water heater on. Things like that would tip him into an incredible rage. He was worse than I had ever seen. I wet myself in sheer fright. He made me stand there while he waved his finger at me and yelled and hit me. He dragged me into the bathroom to run the water, to prove how hot it was. He said I was wasting money – it was my job that paid all the bills, but he didn't care.

'Eventually he punched me so hard that I blacked out. I came to after a few seconds, but I decided to pretend I was still unconscious because I knew that if I sat up he would hit me again. At that stage he picked up the phone, rang my parents, and screamed down it: "You'd better come and see what I've done to your fucking daughter. I've killed her." My parents rushed round and he ranted and raved at them, and started kicking and punching my dad who is much older and smaller than him. Mum pushed Dad outside and Dad ran to call the police. Dominic was sitting on the settee screaming, but luckily Dennis slept through it all.

'Suddenly Kenny calmed down. He could do that: snap out of his violence as quickly as he snapped into it. He said coolly that he would go and put the kettle on, as though nothing had happened. Then he saw the police arriving. "Oh shit, the pigs are here," was all he said.'

He was arrested and held over the weekend, the first of many times that the local police would be called to Jenny's home. She and the children moved out, and for the next couple of weeks she lived out of a suitcase with friends and family.

'Then one day I thought: he's living in my house, a house that goes with my job, and I and the children have nowhere to live. It's not right. So I got an emergency injunction to have him evicted. The court ordered him not to come within a hundred yards of me, but I have learned over the years that injunctions are not worth the paper they are written on. He can sit 101 yards away watching me and not be breaking the law. Or he can break it, be arrested, and come back to stalk me as soon as he is released.

'On one occasion I came back to the house and found he had got inside and was waiting for me. I arrived home and went upstairs to the loo, pushed open the bathroom door and there he was. I was terrified. I waved to my neighbour, in the hope that she would realize that I needed help, but she just waved back. He started yelling and verbally abusing me, and luckily the man who lives next door to me rang my parents. When my mum arrived he told her we were back together again, but I was standing behind him shaking my head. And mum could see that Dominic was as white as a sheet. We got rid of him and changed the locks.'

Jenny was relieved when Kenny went to America for eighteen months, working for a friend of theirs. While he was away he phoned her once a month, but they were reasonable calls in which he asked about the children. He offered to pay for her and the boys to fly out to Florida, and she agreed.

'I did not want to get back with him, but as he was being all right I thought it was fair that he should see the children. I also thought that a job and a new life might have made him a more reasonable person. But he was very odd, and I knew for certain when we came home that there was no way that I wanted anything more to do with him.

'But as we approached Dominic's fourth birthday, which is on the same day as his, he rang up to say he was coming home for it. I made it clear he could not live here, but his mother picked him up from the airport and dropped him and his luggage at my house. I agreed to him staying a couple of nights, but that was a terrible mistake because I could not get him out. He was there for a month.

'I finally told him he had to go, and he dragged me out of the house by my hair, he dragged me along the floor and took the skin off my back. Dominic was at playgroup, so I grabbed Dennis and ran. It was the week before Christmas, I had no clothing for myself or the children, nothing. He barricaded himself in the house and I had to go to court to get him evicted.

'As I arrived to move back in, he turned up – so I drove straight to the police station. The electricity had been cut off and the phone had been cut off, the house was disgusting. I didn't feel safe, so I went to my mum's and dad's.'

Since then, Jenny's life has been one long round of court battles against Kenny, punctuated by vicious confrontations with him. When she went Christmas shopping in an area of Birmingham a few miles from her home, he suddenly emerged from the crowd and confronted her.

'I bet you're shitting yourself,' he said before starting to beat her up. She had to plead with passers-by for help, and was rescued when some special constables appeared. On Boxing Day 1992 he followed her as she took the children, then aged six and four, for a walk with their new bikes and attacked her as she walked up a lane.

'I never, ever walk, but on this occasion because it was Christmas I agreed to let the boys ride their bikes. I saw a mini-van pull up and my heart sank. He jumped out and started beating me. My face was black and blue, both my eyes were swollen. Dominic picked up Dennis and ran to a nearby house for help. When the police arrived he denied doing it, but luckily there was a witness who saw him in his van and heard my screams.

'That was his Christmas present to his children: he beat their mother up in front of them. He never sends them a card or a present. He's turned up outside their school, where all the mums meet, and he's walked up telling everyone I'm "a fucking whore and a slag" and other choice expressions.

'He's done lots of damage to my property. He threw a breeze block through a window while one of the children was having a birthday party. There were lots of other children here, and the glass shattered across all the food so I had to throw it all away. He's damaged my car and other cars that are parked on my drive. I've worked out that it has cost me £1,200 replacing and repairing things.

'One night when I went out and Mum stayed to babysit for me he took away a manhole cover from the drive. Luckily Mum realized and put a milk crate over the hole, or I might have driven my car into it. One of the children could have been killed falling down it – he wouldn't care.

'The phone calls are constant, sometimes thirty a day. I've had my number changed and I've got an answering machine. Before I got the new number he used to just scream obscenities into the answering machine at all hours of the night. The children would hear it, because the machine records out loud. Kenny would be saying things like 'How many blokes have you fucked today?' Dominic says, 'Is that Dad?' At night he piles his skateboard and bike and the dustbin against the back gate, in case Kenny turns up. If I tell him his Dad's in prison he just says, "Yes, but he can escape."

'They both wet the bed, especially when Kenny's around. Dominic rarely mentions him, and he'll walk out of the room if anyone talks about him. Dennis is tougher, he has fewer memories – although before he was two years old I remember him screaming at Kenny to "leave my mummy alone". One day recently he was building something with a modelling set and he told me it was "to trip Daddy up if he comes round". Dominic tells him not to call him their daddy. They don't feel safe, even in their own home. A doctor who was assessing Dominic told me that although he loves school and does very well there, he is deeply worried about leaving me on my own because once I got beaten up while he was at school. He's very clingy and a bit withdrawn.

'Every night I have to lie with him until he goes to sleep, and he always asks the same question: "The doors are locked, aren't they, Mummy?"'

'They are only really happy at my parents' house, and when I was in hospital they insisted on staying there – they didn't want to be looked after in their own home.

'People ask why I don't move house, but I like the house and I like my job, and the children are settled at school. It's my work that supports us. I do ironing for people as well as being a warden, but I daren't take the children with me when I go round delivering the ironing, in case I end up in another high speed chase to the nearest police station, which has happened a few times – he once chased me at 80 m.p.h. through Solihull. So I have to get someone to look after them whenever I go out.

'We can't lead a normal life in this house. I can't sit in the garden with a cup of tea and a book like anyone else would. I can't even go shopping on my own with the boys – he follows us. I always have to make sure there's someone else with me, someone who could at least call for help. When I go to court against him – and I think I've been on average once a month in the past four years – I always take a couple of my brother's friends.

'When he is in prison we feel liberated. I can take the boys for days out, like other mothers do.'

The legal battles against him have not been easy. His refusal to accept court documents being served on him meant that Jenny's solicitors had to take her case to the High Court in London to get permission to serve him by post. Both her solicitor and an ex-policeman who was employed to serve documents have sworn affidavits in evidence against him, after being attacked by him.

When Jenny was in hospital in March 1994, when she was pregnant with another baby from a relationship with a new boyfriend, the police had to provide the hospital with a photograph of Kenny to make sure he was not allowed to turn up at her bedside. She had to have a serious operation to remove an ovarian cyst, and although she was pregnant it was necessary to perform a partial hysterectomy. Her parents were very worried about her health.

'Kenny rang us up and said, "I hope she's got cancer and dies,' reports Angela. 'He rings us almost as much as Jenny, but I ignore him: I think if I speak to him I am giving him the satisfaction of provoking me.'

Jenny's pregnancy angered him, but he does not know who the father of her baby is – Jenny refuses to live with any other man. Over the phone Kenny claimed that various friends and even police officers were the father. He told her he hoped she died in childbirth.

'He's affected my life in every way. I will never have a normal relationship with another man, because I don't trust men. And anyway, his shadow would always be across it. He would always be there. One thing he has taught me is to be independent, and I intend to stay that way. That's one of the things he can't stand: when we were living together he used to tell me I'd be in the gutter without him. But I've survived, and he hates me for it.'

Jenny is tired of people saying to her: 'How

could someone like you end up with someone like that?' 'I really don't know the answer. It just happened. It crept up on me, and now I'm living this awful nightmare. I'd never have believed it possible.

'Sometimes I'm hardened to it, other times I feel vulnerable. We live in a quiet road, and if I hear a car going past and dropping down a gear, I instinctively know that it is him. For a time I had a large guard dog, borrowed from a friend, but it was too much of a handful and I was worried about it with the boys. Now we've got a lovely dog, who barks at everyone – but she's terrified of Kenny. She ran away the last time he was here making a scene. He's kicked her, he really does not like animals. But I need her because she is a second pair of ears for me, she can sense when he's around.

'I'm not going to let him beat me, though. He always tells me I'm a determined bitch, and he's made me like that. I don't think he will ever give up. One of the judges who heard one of the cases against him told me as much: he said he did not see me ever being free of him, not unless he met someone else to be obsessional about. Now I think it's too late for that. He had another girlfriend for six weeks at one time but she finished with him, and he switched his attentions back to me.

'There isn't an answer. Prison does not stop him – we had to ring one prison governor and point out that there was an injunction in force banning him from contacting me. He was ringing my number from the pay-phone in the prison!

'He has seen psychiatrists, but nothing seems to be

done. I don't know if there is anything anyone can do. All I know is that time passes quickly, and the boys will one day be grown up and I will have less to worry about because they will be able to take care of themselves. Oh, and my other fervent hope: that he kills himself in a car crash.'

Stalking by an ex-partner is more likely to be male on female, but there *are* ex-wives and ex-girlfriends whose grief at being rejected spills over into obsession – although women are rarely as guilty of the same levels of violence or threatening behaviour as men and the following two cases contrast greatly with the previous cases mentioned in this chapter. American actor George Peppard, who died in May 1994, was forced in the summer of 1993 to take legal action against an ex-girlfriend of his who refused to accept that their relationship, which had not been a deep or long-lasting one, was over. The girl, a stunning-looking 28-year-old, showered the 64-year-old actor with presents, made numerous phone calls to him and waited outside his home, watching his comings and goings. When Peppard married his fifth wife, 34-year-old Laura Taylor, his ex-girlfriend followed them on honeymoon – and the new Mrs Peppard became genuinely concerned for their safety.

'About three or four years ago I went on several dates with her,' the veteran Hollywood star said. After they stopped going out together, he said, 'she began to annoy and harass me. She continued to call me, often repeatedly, up to eight or nine times a day. She sent me numerous cards. She parked her car in front of my home and would sit outside and watch.

I hoped that if I ignored her she would grow tired and leave me alone.'

It seemed his wishes had come true, when a year elapsed without any contact from his ex. Then news of his wedding brought her back into his life.

'My wife and I have become concerned for our safety,' said Peppard at the time. 'She acts as if I had never gotten married. She apparently followed us to the golf course. She approached me and asked me why I had gotten married and told me that when I "get past it" I should call her. She asked about "our relationship". I told her that we had no relationship and that she should leave me alone.'

The new Mrs Laura Peppard added, 'I'm in great fear of what she will do next and am worried she will injure me in some way.'

Pop promoter Rod MacSween was forced to go to the High Court in 1988 for an injunction banning Stefanie Marrian, an ex-Page Three girl, from his life. After a tempestuous affair with Stefanie ended in 1982 Rod was subjected to a barrage of letters and phone calls, and even had to cope with a ranting and raving Stefanie on his doorstep. She sent taxis to his house when he did not want them, usually in the middle of the night. She rifled through his dustbin looking for evidence of other girlfriends. Not content with ringing Rod, she also rang his friends and relatives, including his elderly mother.

'I had many other problems at the time, particularly concerning my twin sister, who was dying of cancer . . . After my sister died Stefanie phoned me and – putting on a strange voice – claimed to be possessed by my sister's spirit. At other times she would telephone, sometimes in the middle of the night, and make abusive and on occasions threatening remarks. In one call she said she hoped I would die from cancer. She said she hoped my first child would be born a cripple, and that she hated me ... In the past she has even asked me questions such as whether I was frightened of being stabbed to death or shot by her.'

Stefanie Marrian admits most of the things that her ex-lover accuses her of doing. But her own perspective on it is different from his, as we shall see in the next section.

PART FIVE

THE STALKERS' PERSPECTIVE

'I JUST WANTED TO TAKE CARE OF HER'

'I JUST WANTED to take care of her' . . . 'She needs to be with me – she just does not see it yet' . . . 'He was everything I had, and when you've got nothing else you hang on' . . . 'I just wanted to save her, this is a horrible world' . . . 'The Martians were telling me, we have to be together for the future of the world.'

These are all quotes from stalkers about why they do it. The man who says 'I just want to take care of her', referring to his ex-girlfriend and meaning it with all his heart, would feel he has little in common with the man who believes the aliens from Mars have pre-ordained his marriage to a television newsreader he has never seen in the flesh but who he believes sends messages to him in the way her head moves, or the clothes she is wearing, when she appears on the screen. Yet they are both suffering from some degree of mental derangement; their view of reality is distorted, and that leads them to behave in a way that upsets, unsettles and ultimately threatens the object of their desire. Very few of them would ever resort to violence, or even threaten it, but none the less their attentions alone are disquieting enough.

Ian, whose story is dealt with later in this chapter, stalked Anna for nearly two years. He still wants to stalk her, but with the help of a psychiatrist, a therapist and a good and caring community psychiatric nurse, he is managing to restrain himself. He recognizes his problem, and at times can see that he is being unreasonable; at other times he accepts only that the law says he must not go near her and he has agreed to stick to that — but the law, he believes, is an ass.

It is this dichotomy that has led in recent years to the suicides of two well-known British stalkers, two men whose choice of high-profile victim meant the spotlight was turned on them. They switched from being the hunter to being the prey, as the media pursued them as relentlessly as they had pursued their celebrities. It was being hammered home to them by court action, by newspaper and magazine articles, by the lack of response from their chosen ones, that what they were doing was not normal; yet it was a compulsion that they found impossible to fight. Nobody can know what went through their minds as they faced their own lonely deaths, but the confusion and unhappiness that brought them to it must at least in part have been fuelled by these mixed signals.

Ulrika Jonsson was catapulted to TV stardom when she became a TV-AM weather girl, attracting a solid core of fans who found the gloomy forecasts were brightened by her sunny smile and cheerful personality. But as she explained the details of cloud cover and rain belts, she had no idea that to one lonely bachelor what she was really talking about was love. Peter Casey, a British Rail ticket collector, watched her avidly, and put his own peculiar interpretations into the messages she was delivering about icy roads and fog on high ground. To him, the pretty blonde was communicating her love, devotion, and her agreement to marry him.

He started to make phone calls to her, leaving sexually explicit messages on her answering machine. He sent her flowers, letters and even nude photographs of himself. So completely out of touch with reality was he that he really believed she would welcome his obscene and graphic sexual fantasies. He started to turn up outside the TV-AM studios, anxious to catch a glimpse of her; and so distraught was she at the physical presence of a man who was intruding so horrifically into her life that she travelled to and from work with a bodyguard. She reported his behaviour to the police, and they visited him at his home in the Buckinghamshire village of Colnbrook to warn him off. Perhaps it was their visit, or perhaps the continued refusal of the woman he loved to even acknowledge his existence, or perhaps the mental illness he was suffering from allowed him moments when he could lucidly appraise his own behaviour – whatever it was, something finally made 41-year-old Peter Casey so miserable that just before Christmas in 1992, two years after developing his obsession with Ulrika, he lay down on a railway track and was decapitated by the 110 m.p.h. Reading to Paddington express. He died instantly.

A neighbour who had befriended him gave the inquest a glimpse of his lonely and pathetic existence.

'When we first met Peter we just thought he was a quiet, nice, pleasant man who was very helpful but perhaps a little bit sensitive,' said Kim Offord. ' He used to enjoy coming out for a drink with us but he would never give anything away about his background or his family. As time went on we came to realize he was a little odd and thought perhaps he was drinking too much. It wasn't until a lot later that we realized he had a mental problem. At first we put it down to him just being eccentric. He did have times of depression when he would go into his flat and not come out again for days. He was obsessive about cleanliness in his flat and wore Marigold gloves. If he was going to clean his car engine he wore a pair of socks on his hands so he wouldn't get dirty. If he came to my flat and I hadn't Hoovered, he told me to get cracking.

'But when we moved house he came round to see us and out of the blue he started saying he was getting messages through his TV. He said Ulrika Jonsson was sending him messages from her weather map and that she was in love with him and wanted to marry him. He used to sit and watch the whole of TV-AM from start to finish to get the full message.'

Another, less sympathetic, neighbour said (not at the inquest, but to reporters): 'He was a right weirdo – quiet and withdrawn but really hyped up sometimes.'

Recording an open verdict, the coroner described Casey as a loner who manifested symptoms of mental illness. After the inquest, Ulrika Jonsson's mother said she was 'pleased' he was dead.

'It may sound awful, but we are glad that this man

is no longer with us. You never know what people like that can do.'

Lady Helen Taylor, the beautiful daughter of the Duke and Duchess of Kent, managed to be more charitable after the death of the man who had made her life miserable for over three years. Like Casey, Simon Reynolds killed himself by lying on a railway line (his death came just a month after the inquest on Casey was widely reported). His victim's thoughts were for his family and for the driver of the train. 'It's awful, really awful. It's so sad. I feel terribly sorry for his family and I feel deeply sorry for the driver of the train. He will never forget it,' said the 29-year-old Lady Helen in June 1993, when she was told of Reynolds's death.

Reynolds, a freelance television cameraman, was in court charged with criminal damage in October 1990, after an horrific incident in which he forced his way into the art gallery in London's West End where Lady Helen worked. He had arrived carrying a sledge-hammer, which he dropped as he forced his way past other staff to make his way to the basement of the building, where his frightened victim had barricaded herself into an unlocked room, holding the door against him with her own weight. Reynolds picked up a chair and hit the reinforced glass window in the door five or six times until it shattered, showering her with broken glass. He was overpowered, but shouted at those who held him: 'Please leave us alone. I want to talk to Lady Helen about ancient and modern art.'

His rampage through the gallery followed a campaign of phone calls and visits to the premises. It had become clear very early on that his interest was in

Lady Helen, not in the works of art on display. After being freed on bail pending psychiatric reports, Reynolds said after the court case: 'I just thought she was a nice girl. I would be a fool not to say I was attracted to her. I am not blind. But that was not why I wanted to talk to her. She is a bit young for me, I would have thought.'

When he returned to court for sentencing, Reynolds was sent to a mental hospital, after magistrates heard he was suffering from a psychotic illness. But he was back in court fourteen months later, when he was bound over to keep the peace after turning up at the gallery again. In all, he was arrested five times for threatening behaviour towards Lady Helen, but charges against him were dropped twice because Lady Helen declined to give evidence against him. Despite the horrific time he had given her, friends say she was always able to sympathize with the fact that he was obviously mentally ill, and never thought that prison would help him.

Immediately before his death Reynolds, who was always well dressed, had been staying as a voluntary patient at a psychiatric hospital in his home town of Scunthorpe.

The messages that Ulrika Jonsson's stalker believed he was picking up from his television screen are classic symptoms of paranoid schizophrenia, an illness in which sufferers have, overlaid on the fractured thought processes of schizophrenia, the delusion that they are possessed of special powers and unique talents, and that they are receiving commands and orders to behave in certain ways. The commands are commonly voices in the head, but modern technology has added new dimensions to the way patients experience these. Young people often hear them through rock music (or they may use loud rock music in an effort to drown out the voices). Charles Manson believed the Beatles' track 'Helter Skelter' contained secret messages telling him to go on his killing spree, which included the murder of actress Sharon Tate. Other sufferers quite commonly pick up coded messages from other sources. For Stephen King's stalker, Steve Lightfoot, American news magazines contained key phrases which had a meaning for him that was far beyond their author's innocent intention. Television, with its ever-present companionship in even the loneliest of homes, is a natural source of displaced delusions.

Ronald Ellis believed that he could communicate telepathically through the television screen with Channel Four newsreader Zeinab Badawi. He explained to her telepathically, he claimed, that Martians had landed in his back garden in west London in a UFO, and had commanded him to marry her. She received his thoughts, he said, and agreed to the marriage, but then the aliens blocked his thoughts to her, and 'she seemed to go all in a quandary . . . I became frustrated, I sat in front of the telly thinking, does she love me? Does she want me? We have to marry for the sake of the black people of this country. Zeinab is a sole model for her black sisters . . . Mine is not a perverted lust, it is a pure love.'

Ellis's delusions included the belief that Zeinab was the reincarnation of the ancient Egyptian queen Nefertiti. 'I was also an Egyptian in a before life and we are destined to be together . . . I just want us to get together and do what we are supposed to do,' he said, admitting that he fantasized about making love to the newsreader. He also believed that he was in telepathic touch with Prime Minister John Major, and that he had been promised £25.2 million of government money when the wedding took place. The fact that Ellis already had a wife and baby did not deter him – he had stopped making love to his wife to keep himself pure for Zeinab. He was anxious that the television star should not be put off by the existence of another wife. 'I hope she doesn't mind – I don't want her to feel like a wifelet.'

Ellis's delusions are obviously bizarre in the extreme, including as they do aliens, past lives and sexual fantasies. Yet to him they presented a cogent reality. Similarly Susan Brisbourne, a former TSB bank worker, held together a 'normal' life until her delusions about Ricky Ross, the singer with Scottish rock band Deacon Blue, became so overpowering that to her they were normality. She sold her house and embarked on a five-year 'Wife Development Plan' to make herself into Mrs Ricky Ross, despite the fact that the singer was already married to Lorraine McIntosh, backing singer with the group.

She filled eight bin-liners with information about Deacon Blue and Ricky in particular, and wrote her eighty-three-page document 'as a study using Ricky as a key figure in how my career has gone so far and what the future holds'. She said, 'I am not some crazed fan. All I want to do is meet Ricky and show him my project. I almost got to meet him after a concert in Glasgow but he had a sore throat and was unable to meet me.'

She was able to acknowledge that he was married – but would only refer to his wife as 'the backing singer'. 'I am attracted to Ricky, but he is married, and I do not sleep with married men. In fact I have been celibate for some time now, although I would like to marry. I don't like the backing singer but that is purely musically because I think they would be better as an all-male band. I have never met or touched Ricky so I do not know if I would want to marry him or if he would want me.'

Having given up her bank job and spent the proceeds of the sale of her house in Birmingham in her pursuit of the band, she was living in cheap accommodation in London with no income apart from state benefits, brooding and writing about Ricky and fantasizing about a large sum of money she calculated was owed to her by the TSB. More than a third of her £80-a-week income was spent on stationery, postage and photocopying, to keep her 'project' up to date.

Another girl who spent a similarly large proportion of her income on the object of her obsession was Nicola Stewart, from West Lothian, Scotland, who became fixated on Radio Clyde disc jockey 'Tiger' Tim Stevens when she was a very young teenager. Over eight years Nicola became increasingly wrapped up in her fantasy world, which was dominated by three hours of listening to her favourite DJ every evening. She phoned his show regularly, wrote letters three times a week, and spent her unemployment benefit on boxer shorts, aftershave and chocolates for him. Her letters were sexually explicit, and on one occasion ran to a hundred pages of foolscap paper. It started as nothing more than the usual crush of a schoolgirl on a show business celebrity, but at the age of eighteen Nicola graduated from sending adoring fan letters to graphic sexual descriptions of what she planned to do with Tim on the 'one night stand' that, she said, was all she was asking for.

Gillian Vincent, whose stalking of snooker star Stephen Hendry over several years resulted in her being taken to court, was able to articulate the mental gear shift that changed her from a devoted if over-persistent fan into someone who was able to send obscene messages of hate to the star she worshipped. When the number of letters she was writing to the young snooker wizard began to get out of hand, his manager contacted Gillian, an office worker from Greater Manchester, and told her to stop or he would inform the police.

'I was devastated, heartbroken, although admittedly my pride was hurt more than my heart,' said Gillian, in a television interview. 'I felt something precious had been taken away from me . . . I was living on my own, I had no social life, I've never had a boyfriend, never had any friends. I'd retreated into a fantasy world.'

She admits that she was tipped into sending pornographic items to Hendry in the post, and phoning his office and leaving obscene remarks on the answering machine – charges for which she was sentenced to a year on probation.

'Why did I do it? When you've had something taken away from you and you have nothing in your whole life, and everyone else has people that care for them and you've got nobody, you need to get back at someone who kicks you in the face. I was feeling very vindictive and very bitter but very excited in a way because I knew I had such power. Power not with a machine gun, power just with a telephone and a pen.'

The easy translation of love into hatred is something that Sting's stalker, Elizabeth Griffin (the girl who changed her name to Roxanne Sumner in honour of her hero), would understand. After police were alerted to her obsession she switched from idolizing Sting to blaming him for all her problems.

'All I can think of is him. I can't even sleep because of him, he has taken over my life. But now if I saw him I'd want to kill him for making me like this. I've even had trouble from my family because of him, and I blame him for everything. This is like a nightmare and I just wish I could get him out of my mind.'

Stefanie Marrian, the former-Page Three girl who stalked her ex-boyfriend, pop promoter Rod Mac-Sween, admitted to most of the catalogue of chilling things that he accused her of – including claiming to be speaking with the spirit of his dead twin sister, shortly after her death. But she, too, blamed him; in her case she claimed she was pregnant by him and had an abortion because he rejected her.

'When I made some of the phone calls to him saying I was his dead sister's spirit I was on Valium after trying to kill myself. I didn't really know what I was doing. I was so crazed with grief [over the abortion] that I even cut great clumps off my hair because I knew he liked it long . . . I did send taxis round to his house, but that was only because he had thrown me out. I felt hurt and just wanted to strike back . . . I never want to see him again, he can go to hell.'

The tendency to blame the love-object for the obsession is more typically female than male, probably a direct line from the sexual stereotype of the woman as the receiver rather than the giver – the obsession is given to her by the person she is obsessed with, making her role more passive. If she can displace the blame, especially for activities like Gillian Vincent's which involved obscenities and pornographic material, she can feel more at ease with what she has done and more feminine. Male stalkers are more prepared to stand by their own fantasies, although where their actions are extreme, as Robert Bardo's certainly were when he shot and killed Rebecca Schaeffer, it is still easier to accept if the victim can be blamed for their own fate. Bardo says his feelings for Rebecca changed from love to hate when he was thrown off the set of her television sitcom.

'I thought she didn't deserve to be a star if she had that sort of attitude, and I decided to do something about it,' said Bardo, who gunned down the 21-year-old actress in cold blood.

Andrew Farquharson, who stalked actress Helena Bonham Carter, could in some of the interviews he gave to journalists present himself as nothing more than a normal young man with an infatuation for a pretty young actress – despite the fact that his behaviour in stalking her belied normality. Yet in other interviews the mask slipped and he came out with remarks that showed the degree to which he was gripped by his obsession with her. He told how he intrinsically believed they would marry one day, and that spiritually she was already his wife. In his letters to her he gave a graphic description of how he and she must go about having children together.

'I am a little disappointed that she is not a virgin,' he said, 'but I am looking forward to our wedding night so that we can be intimate and forget everything that has gone on in the past and begin our relationship together. I love her body. She has wonderful breasts ... A woman has to be taken. You must tell them your intentions, and until she is taken by a man and says that is taken, she is still available.'

Farquharson first became fixated on the star after seeing one of her films while he was a student at Aberdeen University. He moved to London to be near her, and claimed that she and he were like Romeo and Juliet because both their families were coming between them. He, too, shifted the blame for his letters becoming pornographic on to her, confusing a role she had in the American TV series *Miami Vice* with her real character. 'She was sleeping with men in *Miami Vice* – she was saying sluttish things and playing the sluttish part. I thought, she's being forthright and it's clear she's someone who enjoys talking about it and I brought it into my letters.'

For male stalkers the justification for their behaviour is often that they see themselves as protectors, believing that the woman they are pursuing needs their care, even though she repudiates it. Where their thought processes are clinically disordered, as with the schizophrenic stalkers, they often believe that their quarry is being prevented from recognizing her need by outside intervention (as with Ronald Ellis's aliens, who were blocking his telepathy with Zeinab Badawi). In other cases, their obsession blinds them to reason, and they refuse to accept that the woman is able to judge her own needs.

A fascinating insight into the mind of this type of stalker was given in an interview in the *Daily Mail* in June 1993. The same newspaper had, a month earlier, given a lot of space to the story of a young woman, Jane Ratcliffe, who had been pursued for nearly five years by her former fiancé Steve Chadwick, who had been given a seven-day prison sentence for breaking a court-undertaking not to harass her. Jane, from the East Midlands, told in detail how her life had become a nightmare, with horrific incidents like the time Steve sat on her lawn and poured petrol over himself, threatening to torch himself. On another occasion he cut the British Telecom phone line to her house and sat outside watching the building, knowing that Jane was isolated and could not call for help.

The *Mail* gave equal space to Steve's side of the story, and his overweening need to possess Jane came across in his own words: 'I don't call it an obsession; it's a caring thing. I love finding things out about her and I'm very good at it,' he said.

He talked about trying to get Jane to resume their previous relationship. 'Whenever I asked her, begged her, to come back to me her answer was always the same. "Steve, I can't." I don't know what that means. Why can't she? Whenever I asked her what I had done wrong she always repeated, "Nothing, you've done nothing wrong." But if I have done nothing wrong, I can't understand why things cannot go back to the way they were. She just doesn't understand how much I care for her. I want to look after her so much. If she ever got ill, I wouldn't hesitate to nurse her. If she didn't mean so much to me I would have given her up after a few weeks. But even after five years, I still want a lot of questions answered.'

When she was his girlfriend, Steve kept a diary log of all her working shifts, and phoned her at work so often that she was in trouble for receiving so many personal calls. When she left him, he filled the void in his life researching information about her (he had looked up the death announcements of her parents) and watching her movements. In one of his court appearances it was revealed that he even monitored what time of day she opened and closed her curtains.

Ian, a retired civil servant who lives in Suffolk, would understand Steve's need for meticulous observation of Jane's movements. Ian has several exercise books full of closely written details about the day-to-day routines of Anna, a woman who lives in the same small town to him. Ian is married, and has been for thirty-five years. His children are grown-up and the relationship with his wife is distant, although she has stood by him through his problems over Anna. He has never appeared before a court because he agreed to see a psychiatrist. If he had not, Anna would have proceeded with the injunction she intended to take out against him.

'I used to see her on the train to work – we both commuted into London. I suppose I saw her every day, only in the mornings, for about three or four years, up to my retirement when I was sixty. I noticed her every day, but not more than I noticed lots of other regular passengers, I don't think. She was just somebody I looked out for every day. We never spoke.

'When I retired I felt I needed to keep on seeing her, just to look at her. It was not really anything sexual, I just thought she looked very vulnerable. I would have felt sexually about her if I had been younger, I'm sure. I would even have wanted to marry her, I suppose. But I think my interest is much more fatherly than that, although I have been in trouble for touching her bottom in the supermarket.

'I waited at the station until she came home one day. All the time I was travelling to work with her, she was coming home just one train earlier than the one I was on. I could have run and caught it if I had known. Anyway, I followed her home and I started watching out for her. I wanted to know about her: who she lived with, what her interests were, everything. She became my hobby if you like. Some people take up golf when they retire and I took up her.

'She is almost thirty years younger than me but I don't understand why she is not married: she's in her thirties and she should be thinking about having a family now or it will be too late. I would like her to marry, but I don't want to think about who she will choose. She used to spend a lot of time with a man she played squash with, but I think that is over, although another man comes to see her sometimes. I like to think he is her brother.

'I like to imagine what she was like as a child. I'd love to have an album of photos of her at all the different stages of her life. There's nothing I would not do for her. I've even overcome my fear of dogs to stand outside her house, because the man next door to her has set his dogs on me twice. But I have found that if I stand still they go away.'

Anna and several of her neighbours have called the police about Ian standing in their road, and the police have spoken to him several times about it. About a year after his retirement he had a complete mental breakdown and spent seven weeks in hospital, and although his obsession with Anna was not revealed to the medical staff at the time, it has come out in on-going therapy since then. He has been back into hospital twice, both times for less that two weeks.

'I think Anna was the root of my breakdown. I worried about her so much. I wanted to know who was sitting in my seat on the train, in case it was some man who was harbouring lecherous thoughts about her. I went along to the station as though I was going to catch the train to work. After that I did not seem to be able to think or talk straight, I began to imagine things and the doctor took me into hospital.

'When I came out I still went round to her house. I phoned her, as well, and wrote to her. I kept a log of all her movements. I know how often she visits her parents and where they live because I've driven behind her all the way there. She has spoken to me a couple of times, telling me to go away and leave her alone, but she obviously does not realize that if I am outside her house looking after her no rapists or burglars can get in.

'I have not been round to her house for several months now. My community psychiatric nurse is the only person who understands; he comes round to give me injections, and he helps me cope, but it's not easy. I still think about her all day long, every minute. I just want to know what she's doing, that's all. My nurse tells me – he says, 'Well, it's ten o'clock, so she must be at work.' He says it's not interesting knowing what someone else is doing every minute of the day, but it is.'

PART SIX

REMEDIES, PRECAUTIONS AND THE LAW

'A Paper Shield'

'WOMEN ARE BROUGHT up to be polite, so they often ignore the instincts that warn them they are in a dangerous situation. They wonder, when is the line crossed? Is it phone calls twenty times a day? Fifty times a day? Following you in a car? Camping on your doorstep?'

Mitzi Vorachek, who said these words, is director of community education at the Houston Area Women's Centre. She is part of the extensive support network for stalking victims that now exists across America. Although she specifically singles out women as victims, her words apply across the board to all stalking casualties, men as well as women. It is one of the most difficult problems for the victim: deciding just when they have a problem.

There is a well-worn path down which the victims of stalking travel before they reach a final all-pervading feeling of hopelessness, the acknowledge-ment that there is little or nothing they can do to break out of the web of someone else's obsession.

They start out down the path with sympathy, or at least off-hand politeness, convinced that the simple message that they do not want the attentions they are receiving will get through. They assume, as everyone must who lives in an ordered society, that their behaviour, the things they say, the non-verbal signals that they give out, will be picked up, understood and acted upon by the other side.

Further down the path they realize that this does not happen with stalkers. Stalkers will not be deterred by normal conventions, they either ignore or are genuinely unable to interpret the clear signals being aimed at them. So the victims give up on sympathy, on polite rejection, on hoping that the message will get through. They become far more direct. They state their case clearly, in terms that cannot be construed ambivalently: get out of my life. When this, too, fails, they look outwards for help, convinced that a third party will be able to impress on the stalker (either by reason or, in some cases, by physical threat) the strength of the rejection. Ultimately, they believe the law will weigh in on their side. It cannot be right to have their lives dictated by an unwelcome intruder, and there is a naive but deeply-held conviction among all right-living members of society that the law is there to administer and uphold moral justice.

The final blow to the victim is the realization that obsession is a force which will not be turned by law – and that the law in Britain is not framed to stand fair and square against the onslaught of it. Yes, there are legal remedies against stalking but, no, they do not necessarily work: the number of stalkers who have been deterred by police or courts is far outweighed by those who have continued with their persecution, even in some cases from inside prison. If, as the experts believe, most stalkers are mentally ill, can the law ever be expected to restrain and contain them? Or are the victims, in the depressing prediction of one expert, 'in for life', with their only hope that their stalker will switch to persecuting somebody else?

America has led the world in pioneering specific anti-stalking laws. Every state in the country now has legislation on the statute book that makes it a criminal offence to harass and persecute another person. Whilst these laws do not stop the endemic problem of stalking, they can, and do, make it easier for victims to cope. Not only do they provide a straightforward mechanism for dealing with the offence, they also – probably more importantly – have made stalking a recognizable threat, one that victims are prewarned about. They have put the debate on stalking into the public arena. It took attacks on, and murders of, the famous to do it, but the net result is that it is not only the celebrity victims who are helped. When a stalker emerges from the shadows the quarry at least can recognize what is happening, and at best has advice and information on tap about how to deal with it.

A recurrent theme among the victims interviewed for this book is that if they had known what they were dealing with, they would have acted differently from the word go. They tried so hard, for so long, to treat their persecutor like a normal human being, like a person to whom reason was not a foreign country. They even worried about the feelings of their pursuers, bending over backwards not to hurt or humiliate them. With hindsight, they recognize the futility of this, but at the time many of them felt at least partly to blame. Guilt and fear of ridicule compounded the natural exasperation and anger they experienced. Crucially, almost all of them reported an inability to communicate the size of the problem to others.

'My mum thought at first it was just a young lad who wouldn't take no for an answer,' says Lauren Barnes.

'I did not want to give him the victory of driving me to a breakdown or people would think I was the mad one,' says Vicky Caldwell.

'I did not want to talk about it all the time for fear people would think I was obsessed, not him,' says Janey Buchan.

The existence of an anti-stalking law may not completely eliminate these emotions, but it does give the victims a reassurance that they are not imagining or exaggerating the problem; that they did not in some way, by their initial behaviour or by their responses to the stalker's behaviour, encourage or create the problems. And legislation brings with it support networks for victims; until recently there was no organization for stalking victims in the UK.

It was the state of California, where more celebrities live than in the rest of the world put together, that pioneered the American legislation against stalkers. It was in 1990 that stalking became recognized as a crime in its own right, and since then a series of amendments have tightened the definition of stalking and sealed any loopholes in the legislation. In its first year, the Californian anti-stalking law was used to prosecute ten cases; since then there has been an annually increasing number of prosecutions. In the wake of the introduction of the law, the Los Angeles Police Department set up a Threat Management Unit to deal specifically with stalking complaints, and in its first three years of operation the unit handled over 200 cases.

The law varies from state to state in America, and there have been problems with it – there have been civil rights objections to certain aspects of it, which could be used out of a stalking context to limit the general rights of citizens. There have also been debates about the seriousness of the offence, which obviously varies. Many states, including California, have introduced laws which allow stalking to be classed as either a misdemeanour or a felony, depending on how serious the threat is. The American Bar Association (the equivalent of Britain's Law Society) eventually drew up model legislation to help guide state legislators.

British victims experience a varied response when they take their problems to the police. It ranges from being greeted with smirks and giggles to being given counselling and support. The offence is not common enough for there to be much experience of handling it among the rank and file of the police, and the scale of the problem is not necessarily any more appreciated by a policeman than it is by other members of the public. As any individual officer gets to know more of the details of a case, his sympathy and support for the victim invariably grow – but that does not mean that he is better able to help.

So what are the legal options open to victims? There are two possible routes, both fraught with difficulties. The first, and in some ways most promising-looking, is to get an injunction banning the stalker from making contact or coming near the victim. In some cases, it is all that is needed to end the stalking, although these are very rare cases. The existence of an injunction means that if the stalker breaks it, the police have powers of arrest. Until there is an injunction in force, it is hard for them to do anything even against the most persistent stalker unless he threatens or attacks his victim. As many of the victims interviewed for this book have been told by the police, it is not an offence to park a car on a public highway for hours at a time, it is not an offence to walk along the road behind somebody, it is not an offence to write to them or send flowers.

But even with an injunction limiting his behaviour, the stalker has to be caught breaking it, and he may be clever enough to avoid that. He also may be driven to even more dire harassment of his victim by the existence of an injunction. The Californian equivalent, a Temporary Restraining Order, has been found to be nothing more than 'a paper shield' according to a police officer who specializes in anti-stalking work. It is impossible, both there and here, for a victim's home or other premises to be watched by the police at all times: there are simply not enough policemen.

'There's no way we can watch every woman who gets a Temporary Restraining Order, so the woman is taking an enormous risk in getting one,' says Policewoman Dana Flynn, who believes that no court order will dissuade a determined – and deranged – stalker from pursuing his quarry. The risk, she says, is that a court order like an injunction makes the stalker angrier, and precipitates attacks on victims by stalkers who were previously content to just watch and follow. Some stalkers actually enjoy having injunctions taken out against them by their victim; they crave acknowledgement of any kind, they want any sort of relationship, even an adversarial one, with their victim. An injunction forces them into court together – at least they get to see their victim, hear her speak, often they sit near her.

Even if the injunction works, and the stalker is arrested and prosecuted for breaking it, the sentences imposed offer very little relief to the victims. Stalking, unless it involves a physical attack, does not merit a long term in prison. Even persistent re-offending only results in a few months' reprieve for the victim while her persecutor is in prison, and it is difficult, with prisons groaning at the seams, to imagine it ever being otherwise. Neither prison nor psychiatric hospital offers any hope of cure; health service resources are as stretched as Home Office ones, and the most that can be given, again, is some sort of temporary curtailment of the stalking activity. Getting psychiatric help is not automatic when a stalker is sent to prison. Unless a court orders a psychiatric assessment or the prisoner's behaviour suggests it would be a good idea, it will not happen. And even if it does, the stalker may, as Dr David Nias points out, appear perfectly normal in all matters except his obsession.

There is another huge problem with dealing with stalking through injunctions. Injunctions are obtained through civil law, and this means that victims have to initiate the court procedure at their own expense.

Some victims qualify for legal aid, but the legal aid limits are stringent and low. Unless they are not working or very lowly paid (Lisa Grayson got legal aid because she was a student, and later a part-time worker), victims will have to meet their own initial costs. And even though they may win their case, and the court may order the stalker to pay the costs, he is often unable to do so because he has no financial resources.

The alternative route is for the stalker to be prosecuted under criminal law. There is some legislation, which can be used to cover certain stalking activities, but – in the words of barrister Philip Turl, an expert on anti-stalking legislation – 'It is a hotchpotch of laws covering personal harassment and domestic violence.' What he and many others, including several MPs, would like to see is some clear-cut legislation similar to that introduced across the States, with the added benefit of hindsight through examining the Americans' difficulties in framing watertight laws.

'Victims at present have limited legal means of protecting themselves,' Turl said. 'There is a need for a general law against harassment. The subject needs to be taken much more seriously, as it is in the USA.'

Turl was asked to become involved in an attempt to improve the legal standing of victims by framing a clause that would have made an addition to the Criminal Justice Act, but it was eventually rejected by the parliamentary committee considering the amendments and additions to the Act.

When he was first invited to get involved early in 1994, Turl's initial hope was to strengthen the civil law as it applies to injunctions, making it easier to get them and easier for the police to arrest stalkers who break them.

'The opinion of parliamentarians, however, was that it would be quicker and easier to make stalking a criminal offence. It might then be possible to slip a new clause into the Criminal Justice Bill which was under consideration by Parliamentary Standing Committee B,' he said. He spent a lot of time working on the wording of the clause.

'Too weighty an offence might well produce an offence which was too difficult to prove and too cumbersome to administer. So I went back to the drawing board and drafted an extension – a modest one, I thought – to the police powers under the Public Order Act, section 5. I wanted the offence to be similar to the prevention of a public nuisance under the Public Order Act. A constable could have a responsibility to warn a potential offender, then if the offender insisted on continuing with the bad conduct which he or she had been told to end, a minor criminal offence would have been committed. Such an offence could be easily, quickly and cheaply prosecuted. Any conviction gained would enable magistrates to punish or, better still, to put an offender on probation with terms added into the order designed to protect the victim. For example, if a stalker was an alcoholic who stalked his victim every pay-day after getting drunk, then a term might be included in any probation order requiring the stalker to attend for rehabilitation therapy at an Alcoholics Anonymous centre.

'Such an order would stand a reasonable chance of stopping a problem at the earliest possible moment – hopefully preventing it from developing, and preventing weeks of gathering evidence, spiralling costs, preparing documents and then waiting for the case to come up in court. In addition, any criminal conviction could be cited in later civil proceedings stemming from the same set of facts and relevant to them.

'Very many stalkers are middle-aged bachelors. They can appear in court, protesting innocence and suggesting to the magistrates that really it was the girl who was in the wrong being attracted to a chap who looked a million pounds in his posh new suit. Such a tactic can cast doubt on a valid prosecution case and can even lead to a "not guilty" verdict.

'I wanted to circumvent this and to offer immediate protection and help to needy people.'

The new clause was drafted and proposed for inclusion in the Criminal Justice and Public Order Bill. It read:

A person is guilty of an offence if he stalks another in that he repeatedly molests or pesters or follows another, so behaving within the hearing and sight of such other person that the other person is likely to be caused harassment, alarm, distress or fear for personal safety including his safety or the safety of a third person nearby.

The clause was supported by Tory MP Lady Olga Maitland, who said it should be entitled 'I'll be watching you' – aimed at the stalker. Speaking in support of the clause, she mentioned some of the famous victims, to show how unconstrained obsession could lead to a serious crime, but she also stressed that most victims of stalking were ordinary people. She said no one came to their aid in the way they did for celebrities.

'Her most memorable phrase was "They suffer alone and without the support of the law," which was my point,' said Philip Turl. 'She went on to mention the untold misery of victims of the 'cursed crime'.

However, the junior Home Office spokesman on the committee, David Maclean, said he was not convinced that the creation of a new criminal offence within the 1986 Public Order Act was the best way to deal with the problem. He accepted that stalking and nuisance calls were both criminal and appalling, but felt they did not present a threat to public order. The hurt, he said, was more personal than public.

Philip Turl disagrees. 'Surely there is sufficient "public order" element in the proposed crime: the acts done are in the public domain, the obsessive behaviour hurts the victim and in many cases is designed to cause hurt. What's more, a hurt victim might well be stung to retaliate either by his or her own actions or through the actions of friends.'

Turl's clause was defeated by fifteen votes to nine, probably because members of the committee were assuaged by Maclean's objection that the clause was not dealing with stalking as a serious enough crime, and that specific legislation may be needed. He threw in an argument that under Turl's clause, genuine, innocent fans like autograph hunters might find themselves bracketed with stalkers. To the clause's supporters that is a red herring. They also believe that a bird in the hand is worth two in the bush; Turl's clause could have been implemented quickly, whereas a promise of more specific legislation may take years to be fulfilled.

'I believe it will take longer, cost more and be more difficult to prove,' said Philip Turl, who described losing his attempt to improve the law for victims as 'a great disappointment'.

Yet despite this setback, the law was improved in 1994, almost inadvertently. As the Home Office struggled to draw up laws to crack down on racial harassment, it came up against the problem of wording the new legislation without, in effect, being racist. To get round this, the phrase 'harassment with intent to cause alarm or offence' was used in the amendment to the Criminal Justice Bill – and this newly defined offence offers a catch-all protection against stalking, as well as racially motivated attacks. It carries a potential six-month prison sentence, and fines of up to £5,000.

One area in which legal redress against stalkers is improving with leaps and bounds is with the problem of malicious telephone calls. The law provides for telephone stalkers to be prosecuted. Modern technology is making it possible to identify them, catch them, and bring them to justice. There was a massive 600 per cent increase in the number of offenders caught in 1993 compared to the previous year, with 1,200 people either cautioned or prosecuted under the 1984 Telecommunication Act. Section 43 of the Act says:

A person who a) sends, by means of a public telecommunications system, a message or other matter that is grossly offensive or of an indecent, obscene or menacing character or b) sends by those means, for the purpose of causing annoyance, inconvenience or needless anxiety to another, a message that he knows to be false or persistently makes use for that purpose of a public telecommunications system shall be guilty of an offence and liable on summary conviction of a fine not exceeding level three on the standard scale.

New technology means that up to 7,000 lines can be 'on trace', with equipment monitoring their incoming calls, at any time, and the success rate for tracing the malicious callers is 90 per cent. Yet the scientific developments are only keeping pace with the growth in the crime. There are as many as 2,000 telephone numbers a week being changed because of problem calls, and an independent survey showed that in 1992 a staggering ten million malicious calls were received by women, with men receiving half that amount. Not all of these calls are from stalkers, of course – British Telecom research shows that one in seven is obscene, one in eight is made at random and one in three is made by a woman. More than half of all malicious calls are silent, often made late at night or in the early hours, and the rest are straightforward abuse, threats or hoax calls. According to BT, an estimated 75 per cent involve a link between the caller and the victim.

British Telecom defines a malicious call as 'made by one person to another with the intention of causing annoyance, inconvenience or needless anxiety.' They do not include calls made in error, telesales or telephone research.

'Enhanced technology and improved police liaison mean that it is increasingly easy to catch offenders,' says Michael Helpher, British Telecom Group Managing Director.

Malicious Call Identification is the name of the

system used to root out offenders, and its widespread availability is due to the upgrading of BT exchanges. With police authorization, a telephone investigator (and BT now have squads of them across the country) can know within seconds of a call being made which number it was made from. When the trace is placed on the victim's line, the victim is asked to log the time and date of all malicious calls. When these are matched against a print-out of the incoming calls it is possible to start to trace the culprit. (Problems arise when company numbers are used, or when the caller has access to a phone which is not his own.)

Once traced, the malicious caller can be prosecuted in a magistrates court. But to the chagrin of victims, the maximum fine that can be imposed is the same as the fine for stealing a bicycle (in 1994 the amount was £1,000). The caller will only be sent to prison if the malicious calls are part of a wider charge, such as the breach of an injunction, and the case is heard in a Crown court.

There was, however, a very significant break-through in May 1994, when a malicious caller was prosecuted for the first time on a charge of causing grievous bodily harm (an assault). Although bank clerk Christopher Gelder had made no physical attack on his victim, a customer at the bank where he worked, the court accepted that the severe psycho-logical injuries she had suffered as a result of his anonymous calls to her were as real as any bodily injuries. Chester Crown Court heard that Mrs Christine Howells had been happy and healthy before the obscene calls from Gelder started, and that the series of fifty menacing calls in nine months, during which time Gelder revealed that he knew everything about Mrs Howells, including the names of her husband and children, had reduced her to sleeplessness, irritability, nightmares and physical sickness.

Gelder had been prepared to admit charges under the Telecommunications Act, but the Crown prosecution service determined to try a grievous bodily harm charge, as a test case.

'We felt that the lesser charges did not reflect what the victim had suffered, so we went ahead with the GBH charge and won,' said a spokesman for the Crown prosecution service. Sentence on 25-year-old Gelder was passed in July 1994, when he was sent to prison for eighteen months. The judge strongly endorsed the GBH conviction. Gelder plans to appeal against the sentence.

For British Telecom, as well as for hundreds of stalking victims all over the country, the court's attitude can only be encouraging.

The inadequacies and vagaries of the law mean that protection for the victim of stalking is patchy; some manage to get cases against their persecutors brought to court, others fail. When it comes to sentencing, some stalkers are given custodial sentences; some walk out of the courtroom to recommence harassing that same day; some get orders for psychiatric assessments while some don't (one of the advantages of the assessment is that when the stalker is released he may well be assigned a social worker who can, at least, help to control his behaviour.) Some injunctions are life-long and all-embracing, some give the stalker a lot of leeway.

'We had a case in Iowa where the perpetrator had been stalking a woman for years,' said Matthew Reed, of the US National Victim Centre, whose HQ is in New York. 'He had orders on him that he was not to come within fifty yards of her. So he stayed exactly fifty-one yards away, at the end of her drive. She could not look out without seeing him. In the end he broke the order and came within the fifty yards – and killed her.'

So if the law cannot be relied upon, what should a victim do? And how can the legal protection that is available be called upon with the greatest chance of satisfaction for the victim?

There are some basic rules for those who are being stalked which, in general, improve their chances both of minimizing the mental and emotional damage of the experience, and ensure that when they do look for legal help they are armed with the best possible evidence. Jane McAllister, who runs one of America's support groups for stalking victims, has come up with the following checklist for anyone who believes they are being pursued by a stalker:

1 Document the harassment. Take photographs, use a video camera, collect statements from witnesses.

2 Tell neighbours, family and friends as soon as you suspect a problem, and get them to help.

3 Invest in a car phone for your own protection.

4 Call the police every time the stalker phones up. Insist they log your call, even if their initial reaction is indifference.

5 Ask the police to come and check the security of your home.

The National Victim Centre agrees with all these rules, adding that it is important to save all letters and keep taped messages from an answering machine, starting with the first one. However tempted you are to give the caller or writer the benefit of the doubt, hoping that it is a one-off incident, keep the evidence. If no more calls or letters come, you can always throw it away later.

Don't try to talk to or reason with a stalker. If they are in the grips of erotomania they are already misinterpreting things said or done by the person on whom they are fixated: any confrontation, even an angry one, may be relished as that much-longed-for reaction.

There *are* occasional stories of a confrontation with a stalker working. Michael Crawford has been quoted as saying he stopped his car to talk to a woman who had followed him home through the streets of Los Angeles every night for three months after he left the theatre where he was starring in Phantom of the Opera. 'You don't know what you are going to meet in Los Angeles. It was scary, but I had to deal with it,' he said. The woman drove off and later apologized and sent a cheque to his favourite charity.

Crawford's actions would have horrified any of the American security advisers, however, who would regard the outcome of his actions as extremely lucky. Gavin de Becker advises making no response whatsoever, otherwise the stalker is being rewarded for his persistence. He also says victims should show no fear, but take avoiding action without being seen to do so, for example, if it can be afforded, by getting another telephone line as well as the one that the stalker is ringing, so that he is left permanently addressing an answering machine.

British Telecom advice includes never answering the phone with your name and number; simply say hello; never enter into conversation with a malicious caller, but put the receiver to one side and replace it later; don't use your first name or title (Miss, Mrs, Ms) in the directory, or give any other indication of gender; don't blow a whistle or an alarm down the phone as this counts as a response and can encourage the caller; never give out your address over the phone unless you know the caller. Various levels of help are available from BT, ranging through intercepting calls, barring incoming calls, changing numbers and eventually tracing calls.

Recognizing a potential stalker is almost impossible, although there are clues when the stalker is an ex-partner with whom the victim once had close contact. Signs of obsession may initially be seen as evidence of absorbing love, but it soon becomes apparent that they are excessive. Watch out for extensive quizzing about your movements; the re-dial button on the phone being pressed to see who you've called; the mileage on the car being checked; your partner turning up unexpectedly at your workplace or somewhere else ; friends and colleagues being questioned about your movements; wild accusations; pockets and wallets being searched, bank statements checked. Also be very wary of any partner who tries to isolate you from your family or existing friends.

Where the stalker is no more than an acquaintance, be on the alert as soon as you see any sign of an inappropriate interest being taken. If he or she turns up in your company more than seems normal or necessary on several occasions, allow your natural instincts to warn you. If you are asked for a date or approached in any other way by them, be very clear in your reaction: turn them down unequivocally, preferably in the company of a third party. After that straightforward rejection, refuse to have any other contact.

Often the obsessive side of a stalker's character will only be apparent to his victim. Above all, don't rely on other people's opinions if they fly counter to your own instincts. 'He had such nice manners. I knew he didn't drink or do drugs,' said Cora Graham, an American woman whose 20-year-old daughter Tiffiney was stabbed by the boyfriend she rejected, and who stalked her for months.

'I never knew I was looking at the face of a killer.'

INDEX

INDEX